Vought F-8
Crusader

Vought F-8
Crusader

Peter Mersky

Published in 1989 by Osprey Publishing Limited
59 Grosvenor Street, London W1X 9DA

Sole Distributors for the USA

Osceola, Wisconsin 54020, USA

British Library Cataloguing in Publication Data

Mersky, Peter B. *1945–*
  Vought F-8 Crusader.
  1. Chance Vought F-8 aeroplanes
  I. Title
  623.74′64
ISBN 0-85045-950-2

Editor Dennis Baldry
Designed by Gwyn Lewis
Filmset in Great Britain by Tameside Filmsetting
Limited, Ashton-under-Lyne, Lancashire and printed
by BAS Printers Limited, Over Wallop, Hampshire

BACK COVER
When You're Out of F-8s, You're Out of Fighters. A slogan which paraphrased a popular beer commercial of the time. Many experienced aviators still feel that way

FRONT COVER
A Crusader of VFP-306 vents fuel to get down to landing weight. Note its arresting hook is lowered

Contents

Introduction

The F-8 Crusader was many things to many people. To its manufacturer, one of the leading pioneer aircraft companies, Chance Vought, it was the last—and ultimately successful—chance to regain its once Olympian status as one of the main suppliers of fighter aircraft to the US Navy.

To its early pilots, the F-8 was a proud, skittish thoroughbred which, if handled properly and respectfully, endowed its rider with a euphoric feeling of godlike invincibility, offering breathtaking speed and grace in the arenas of aerial combat. But, to this same early cadre, the F-8 could be a coffin if poorly flown, especially around its main venue, the aircraft carrier. Many young naval aviators paid for their haphazard operation of the Crusader with their lives.

To those pilots who survived their initial tours in the F-8, and eventually took the Crusader into the crucible of combat in the 1960s, the F-8 was the last of the single-seat, single-engine, clear air gunfighters which could trace their ancestry back nearly 50 years to the skies over France in World War I. Yet, loaded down with underwing bomb racks, and fuselage-mounted missile racks, the F-8 also became a credible, if not wholly desirable, ground attack bomber, far beyond the initial intent of its designers.

For the generations of naval aviators too late to see combat during the 1960s, the F-8 series became the last chance for a unique entry in their flight logbooks. Serving in the US Naval and Marine Air Reserves, even longer than in the fleet squadrons, the Crusader continued its proud tradition of reliable operation, asking only to be always considered a thoroughbred.

Forgetfulness brought soaring mishap rates and cries of anguish from carrier captains tasked with providing periodic carrier qualification training for the F-8 with its outmoded bridle-launched method of catapult attachment. Young deck crews, used to working with the newer nose-tow catapult arrangement, took many hours of working the by-now ancient F-8 before they became accustomed to its bridle.

Whatever the generation or experience, those who flew or maintained the Crusader knew they were involved with a very special aircraft, one whose like would probably never be seen again. There were variations of the joke throughout the Navy, depending on the time and people. But in the early 1960s, it went: don't ever ask a pilot what type of plane he flies. If he flies fighters, he'll tell you, himself; if he doesn't, why embarrass him? That was the time of what many consider the ultimate in naval jet fighter design: the F-8 Crusader.

Acknowledgements

While writing this book has, indeed, been a labour of love, and I had my own Crusader experiences to draw on, I could not have made the account as personal without the help of many people whom I've known for years, and others whom I only met when I began writing it.

My F-8 friends, many of whose accounts appear in the narrative, include Rear Admiral Bud Flagg and Mrs Dee Flagg, Rear Admiral Rich Maughlin, Captain Tom Irwin, Captain Jay R Miller, Jr, Captain Louis R Mortimer, Captain Will P Gray, Captain Dudley Moore, Commander John Nichols, Gene Chancy, Commander Henry Livingston, Commander Barry Gabler, and Commander Wally Baker.

Other friends who contributed photos and information are: Vice Admiral Donald D Engen, Lieutenant General J I Hudson, USMC, Captain John Kuchinski, Captain William Ecker, Robert F Dorr, Norman Polmar, Lieutenant Commander David Parsons, René J Francillon, Art Schoeni, Jim Sullivan, J W 'Top' Kinnamont, Lieutenant Bruce Greer, Lieutenant Commander Ken Parr, Lieutenant Commander John Cotton, Commander John Peck, Lieutenant Commander J 'Chuck' Scott, Captain Dwight D Timm, Paul Bauer, Dr Frank H Austin, Jr, Peter R Foster, Joe Davies, Bill Huddleston and Charles Cooney.

Those friends who contributed personal experiences and other valuable assistance are Barrett Tillman, Robert Lawson, Jean Labayle-Couhat, Roy Grossnick, Jack Elliott, Ed Marolda, Wes Pryce, Jim Sites, Captain Kevin Smith, Captain Boyd Repsher, Colonel Dave Corbett, USMC, Colonel Don Davis, USMC, Commander Larry L Morris, Lieutenant Commander Donnie Cochran, Laurinda Minke, Harold M Austin, Jr, Alan Hall, Lee Alexander, John Williams, Richard A Bishop, Charles B Scott, Hugh Risseeuw, Lieutenant Commander Dana Barclay, Dave Soulsby, Ed Nielsen, Conrad Matysiak, Fred Pierce, Rear Admiral David R Morris, John Konrad, Dottie McKotchey, G F Scharfenberger, Leo Baltierra, Gordon Swanborough, Paul Jackson, Colonel Reynaldo E Sile, Philippine Air Force, and Captain Carlos L Agustin, Philippine Navy.

To each of these, thanks for your help and encouragement, and I hope the result justifies your involvement and expectations.

Prologue: A Photo Pilot Remembers, Vietnam 1967

Generally, the big threat to the photo pilot was AAA [anti-aircraft artillery] sector barrage fire over the target. SAMs were rarely fired at us and as far as I know, only one RF-8 was ever attacked by MiGs. The escort shot the MiG and the photo bird returned safely to the ship.

I remember one particular mission where the AAA was really thick over Haiphong. It was a hazy day with a high overcast so the tracers looked like red rain. I got my pictures and decided it was time to turn right. (I always turned right because most guys turned left.)

I was doing about 1.2 Mach as I had come downhill from 35,000 feet in burner for the run that was only about two minutes long. I was as scared as I have ever been in my life and really laid in a good turn. Suddenly, I couldn't see very good. My eyes scanned the G meter—I had tunnel vision really bad—and the needle was sitting on the stop, more than 10 Gs. I lost 200 knots in that 100-degree turn while in burner.

With a 6.4 G limit and only 5.1 G rolling, I had really put a hard lick on that bird. Thank goodness Vought built it so tough. I don't know why it didn't come apart and kill me. We found the port outer wing panel was basically destroyed with all the ribs inside broken into little pieces. I still believe that if I hadn't made that turn, I would have been shot down.

Most of my 117 missions over North Vietnam I always ran above 600 knots and went into burner as needed to keep the speed up. I set the camera controls on the computer prior to ingress at 650 knots/4000 feet and turned the travelling grid in the viewfinder off so I could see the ground clearly. I did most of my work with the KA-53 12-inch lens camera and a KA-68 3-inch pan. Jinking was natural as just keeping the roads and rivers in the viewfinder caused you to really move around. On straight roads, I would vary the altitude. They always shot at you, but Vinh, Vin Son, Thanh Hoa, and the larger towns were the really hot spots.

I was mighty careful in my planning and execution—as careful as an ignorant young ensign can be. It seemed to me that most of the guys that were shot down were violating some good rule about combat. Never go to the same place twice on the same sortie; never go below 3500 feet; always go as fast as your mission fuel will allow; don't fly through, or near, clouds, and never get caught over an overcast. Also, no matter what you thought about the sortie, 'they were always shooting' was a good philosophy; and jink for one gun just as you would for 1000. Anyone who didn't respect those guys on the ground was stupid and in great peril.

Captain Will Gray, VFP-63, Det 43, USS *Coral Sea*, 1967

The only model of the XF5U which actually flew was the
V-173, a reduced scale model of the Flying Pancake

Chapter 1
Chance Vought and the Last Chance

The years immediately following World War II were not kind to the company started by Chance Milton Vought in 1917. Born on 26 February 1888, and of Dutch descent—the original spelling was Vogdt and pronounced 'Vote'—Chauncy (that was his original name, as well) became interested in aviation in 1909. By 1912, he had participated in the design of several early aircraft.

While working at Cicero Field, near Chicago, Illinois, he took lessons at the Lillie Aviation School and on 14 August 1912, gained his pilot's licence, FAI number 156. Included in his class were several notables, such as Grover Loening, Starling Burgess, Glenn Martin, T G Ellyson and Eugene Ely, all of whom would have their own individual impacts on aviation, especially naval aviation.

In November 1913, as tensions increased between Mexico and the US, Vought and members of the Aero Club of America pressured Congress to buy aircraft in preparation for hostilities. Secretary of the Navy Josephus Daniels personally pledged his support and promised to notify the group of would-be reservists 'if the necessity arises to mobilize aviation reserve groups for the Navy . . .'

Vought maintained a strong interest in developing naval aviation, and in September 1914, as the war in Europe gained momentum, he coined the phrase 'eyes of the fleet' in an editorial endorsing increased appropriations for naval aviation programmes. The phrase caught on and as later events proved, it had special meaning for the company he was to build.

In 1915, the Curtiss Aeroplane and Motor Company hired Vought as a consulting engineer for seaplanes, then called 'hydroaeroplanes'. He participated in the design of huge flying boats later called 'Americas', and designated from H-2 to H-12. Later that year, Vought moved on to the Wright Company, and when, in August 1916, the Wright and Martin concerns merged, Vought became their Chief Aeronautic Engineering Executive.

However, these early successes for the 28-year-old pioneer only fanned the fire burning within. On 1 June 1917, he formed the Lewis & Vought Company with Birdseye B Lewis. Lewis was, himself, an interesting character. An early aviator and sportsman, he had been an aerial scout for the Mexican bandit chieftain Pancho Villa in 1916 during the border war between Mexico and the United States. Lewis eventually left the new Lewis & Vought concern to continue his soldier-of-fortune pursuits, but was killed shortly after going to France as part of General Pershing's American Expeditionary Force staff.

Undaunted by the departure and death of his partner, Vought kept the company going. In 1917, he produced the US Navy's first production aircraft, the VE-7, which remained in production until 1922, serving the Navy, Marines and Army in a variety of roles, from fighter, to trainer, to observation aircraft. By 1922, the company was renamed the Vought Corporation with Chance as the president and chief engineer.

The VE-7 became a major success for the new company, giving Vought claim to many first-time operations in naval aviation, including the first take-off from the US Navy's first aircraft carrier, the USS *Langley* (CV-1), in October 1922. Other trendsetting designs followed, like the O2U Corsair series. (It should be noted that this biplane was the *first* Vought product to bear the name Corsair. Thus, the F4U Corsair of World War II, was, in fact, the *second* Corsair, and the later A-7 series of the 1960s should be the Corsair III, not II. An unofficial explanation of this apparent duplication is that the early O2U's name was a Vought nickname, and not one officially sanctioned by the Navy. Thus, the F4U is the first *official* Corsair.) Variations of the sturdy Vought radial-engined naval biplane formula saw the UO-1

Vought's first attempt at a jet fighter was the F6U Pirate, the first US Navy jet with an afterburner. An unsuccessful design, it nevertheless gave Vought useful experience when designing the F-8

An example of 'slick' humour with a message by famous aviation artist Ted Wilbur, this cartoon strip addresses safety-related issues with the F7U Cutlass, one of the most radical Navy fighters ever produced. Wilbur was a lieutenant, j.g., and a naval aviator. He retired as a captain and is well known in aviation art

and SU-2 observation types of the 1920s and 1930s, followed by the O3U development. (Vought died prematurely in 1930, in his early forties. At one point he had been under consideration for Secretary of the Navy.)

Vought's last biplane was the SBU, succeeded by the company's first monoplane, the SB2U Vindicator. The SB2U made its first flight in 1936 and the Navy bought 169 of the large single-engine dive bombers. For all its promise, the Vindicator had a dismal wartime record when it eventually saw combat. The French took several on charge in time to be used during their desperate struggle in 1940, and the US Marines used the type during the otherwise highly successful Battle of Midway in June 1942. Flying with VMSB-241, the SB2Us were systematically annihilated by Japanese fighters and anti-aircraft fire, the squadron losing three commanding officers in 48 hours of continuous combat.

With war clouds gathering over Europe for the second time in three decades, and the prospect of a confrontation between America and Japan in the

Pacific, the US military slowly began beefing up its frontline units, while giving attention to producing new designs. Vought had two useful aircraft to offer: the OS2U floatplane, the Kingfisher, and the F4U Corsair, a highly advanced carrier fighter which offered speed and great lifting power thanks to a 2000 horsepower radial. It was the first production fighter to top 400 mph.

The OS2U eventually gave yeoman service throughout the Pacific, performing aerial spotting, and search and rescue duties with great success. (The Fleet Air Arm also received 100 Kingfisher Is—OS2U-3s—and operated the type in a variety of roles.) Of course, the F4U became what many considered the most successful naval carrier-borne fighter of the war, after a protracted development and earlier refusal for carrier operations. (While the US Marine Corps first took the Corsair into combat in 1942, from land bases, along with one Navy squadron, the big, gull-winged fighter was not cleared for American carriers. It remained for the British to first try the Corsair—with clipped wings to

accommodate the restricted space in their smaller ships. Eventually, the F4U found a home in both Navy and Marine squadrons aboard American carriers as they fought their way across the Pacific.)

The Corsair continued its success long after World War II, serving with the Navy, the Naval Air Reserve, and alongside more modern aircraft during the three-year war in Korea. Indeed, so successful was the F4U series that it remained in production until 1953 when the last of 12,582 Corsairs ended the line.

The new field of jet aviation sent all major manufacturers scrambling to design planes which used this new form of propulsion. Vought was no exception, and, in fact, had been dabbling in a few bizarre designs even before the advent of jets. One such aircraft was the XF5U, nicknamed the 'Flying Pancake'.

It was, in reality, a flying disk, powered by two reciprocating engines. Although the actual XF5U never flew, a smaller example, the V-173, was delivered to Langley Field, Virginia in September 1941. The V-173 flew for the first time in November 1942, with Vought's chief test pilot, Boone T Guyton. Although the first flight lasted only 13 minutes, the V-173 eventually flew a total of 131 hours.

The experience gained with this flying model of the XF5U was useful. Work began on the construction of the full-scale fighter, using two Pratt & Whitney R-2000 Twin Wasp radials. With a proposed armament of six .50 calibre machine guns, the radical fighter's top speed was estimated to be 482 mph at 30,000 feet, an impressive figure considering its mundane, though powerful, engines.

The XF5U-1 prototype was eventually completed by June 1945, with initial flight testing to be conducted at the Air Force testing facilities at Muroc Dry Lake, now Edwards Air Force Base, California. However, problems with the huge propellers, as well as financial considerations, held the testing programme up until 1947 when taxiing trials began. But the whole XF5U programme was cancelled in 1948 when the Navy effectively said that fighters with

piston engines were *passé*; the turbojet was the wave of the future.

Vought salvaged as much material from the XF5U prototype as it could before sending the aircraft to the smelters. The V-173 was donated to the Smithsonian Institution. Strike One!

Vought had another interesting aircraft on the drawing board. Developed as a contemporary of many of the first US jet fighters, the XF6U-1 Pirate was powered by a single 2300-pound thrust Westinghouse J34 turbojet. A unique feature of the design was the first afterburner installed on a US jet. The afterburner raised the total thrust to 4000 pounds, enabling the Pirate to reach speeds in excess of 540 mph.

The XF6U came from a Navy contract of December 1944. It was constructed with Metallite, a Vought-patented material of high-strength alloy, bonded to a balsa wood core, endowing the structure with light weight and great strength. The XF5U had also been built with Metallite.

The Pirate's first flight took place on 2 October 1946, with test pilot Edward Owen at the controls. After 24 minutes, Owen landed. The plane's engine accessory drive had failed. Testing continued, but the XF6U began experiencing a rash of problems including systems failures and problems with high-speed controllability. Test pilot reactions were less than enthusiastic, and Vought's first jet design found the going tough.

The Navy, too, was unimpressed, and, although a test development squadron, VX-3, at Patuxent River, Maryland, took over 20 Pirates into service, the type never entered the fleet. Thirty production F6Us composed the entire run before the line shut down, and the remaining Pirates were grounded in 1951. Strike Two!

Even as Vought struggled with two unusual

ABOVE
After the world-beating success of the F4U prop fighter, Vought had difficulty coming up with a successor. The massive F7U Cutlass was not the answer, but it enjoyed a longer service period than other postwar Vought design before the F-8. Here, an F7U takes tension prior to the cat stroke. The plane's pronounced taildown stance is noteworthy, and is due to the lengthy nose gear strut which is extended to its maximum length for a catapult launch

RIGHT
A Cutlass from VF-124 roars down the bow catapult of a carrier in the late 50s. In keeping with practice during the early jet period, the pilot has his canopy open to facilitate exiting the cockpit should the plane go into the water right after the launch. Early ejection seats had no zero-zero capability, and were not trusted by early jet aviators

aircraft, it produced a third, in answer to the Navy's call in 1945 for an advanced fighter which could reach 40,000 feet and a speed of 600 mph. Six companies met the April 1946 deadline with a total of 12 designs. Vought's proposal beat the designs submitted by McDonnell, North American, Curtiss Wright, Douglas, and Martin, and was designated the XF7U-1. The initial contract called for three flying prototypes. One of four designs submitted for the competition, the V-346A featured a swept-wing, tail-less aircraft powered by two J34 engines. It was a radical format to say the least.

The first of the XF7U-1 prototypes was first flown in September 1948, and all three aircraft, built at Vought's Stratford plant in Connecticut, were soon flying. However, although the new aircraft, now named Cutlass in keeping with Vought's predilection for piratical names, impressed the Navy with its potential, all three prototypes were lost in a series of mishaps which occurred from March 1949 to July 1950. It was clear that the design needed a great deal of refinement, and the plane itself required a steady hand.

Carrier trials for the new fighter began in June 1950, and problems with the pilot's view forward immediately surfaced. They were never truly rectified. While the Cutlass received more than its fair share of publicity—its radical shape and short service with the Blue Angels flight demonstration team kept it in the public eye—it was clear that it needed a lot of work.

The F7U-2 was proposed but cancelled in favour of the F7U-3. The F7U-3 eventually saw squadron service, and 307 Cutlasses of all models were produced from then until 1955. But the Cutlass' fleet service was short. Only 13 carrier squadrons and three test and development squadrons operated the type from mid-1954 to mid-1957. Not Strike Three, but a foul tip!

Problems with the Cutlass, and with a guided missile design, the Regulus I/II, placed Vought in a must-win situation the next time round. In truth, the Regulus, a jet-powered missile with a nuclear warhead launched from a surfaced submarine, lost out to inter-service politics rather than its own shortcomings. The strategic delivery mission was taken away from the Navy and given specifically to the Air Force. The effect was the same, however. Vought needed a winner if it was to survive.

By the early 1950s, the jet aircraft was firmly established, and existing designs—including the Air Force's impressive Century series, i.e., F-100, F-101, F-102, and F-104—were knocking on the door of supersonic flight as an everyday occurrence. Naval aircraft seldom attained superior performance over landbased contemporaries, due, in part, to equipment and weight constraints. For example, shipboard aircraft need stronger landing gear, wing-folding mechanisms, and additional radio and survival gear, all of which add hundreds of extra pounds and reduce performance.

However, the Navy issued a call for an advanced carrier fighter in September 1952. The Bureau of Aeronautics (BuAer) request was issued to eight companies: McDonnell, North American, Douglas, Convair, Lockheed, Grumman, Chance Vought and Republic. Only Douglas, Grumman and Vought had any real experience with carrier aircraft; Convair and Republic had absolutely none. The Navy asked for a fighter capable of Mach 1.2 at 30,000 feet, and Mach 0.9 at sea level; a 25,000 feet per minute rate of climb, but only a 100 knot landing speed. Armament was to include machine guns or cannon, as well as missiles, coupled with high manoeuvrability. Not to mention the usual shipboard amenities such as folding wings, ease of handling on the flight deck, and the regular catapult and arresting gear.

While several of the competing companies had one or more successful designs either in testing stages or already in operational use, Vought's dismal postwar record had tarnished its image as a leading designer of naval aircraft. This, its fourth fighter design of the late 1940s, had to win the competition.

The experience was there, to be sure. Vought tapped John Russell Clark to lead the design team. Russ Clark had been in the forefront of Vought's earlier attempts, including the F6U and F7U, as had other team members like Lyman G Josephs, Bill Schoolfield, Connie Lau, Fred Dickerman and Whit McCormack.

The men set to work and within five months came up with a number of proposals. The Navy selected Vought Model V-383 as the winner of the competition in May 1953, and ordered several mockups and wind tunnel test models. It also awarded the XF8U-1 designation to the new design. In addition to the V-383 fighter proposal, a photo reconnaissance platform, V-392, was also of interest, and would later develop as the F8U-1P, or RF-8A.

The Vought team had made several gambles, with a few sure shots. While the XF8U's general layout was fairly straightforward—the earlier tail-less designs being thrown out—it did include several *interesting* variations. Perhaps the most unusual area was the wing. Besides being a high-mounted design, something of an anachronism at the time, it was hinged and could be raised 7 degrees. This variable incidence wing became the F8U's hallmark and, to the end of its days, always caused consternation from youngsters seeing it taxi in, and brought smiles from older veterans who remembered it.

While perhaps amusing, the movable wing had a deadly serious purpose. Forward visibility, especially during the carrier approach, had never been one of Vought's trademarks. Indeed, the F4U's long nose had been one of the main reasons for its initial refusal for US carrier operations. And the big F7U's 20 degree angle of attack on take-off and landing made many aviators very uncomfortable.

Carrier approaches are flown by units of angle of attack. Naval aviators have trained this way since their earliest days. Clark's design team endeavoured to retain the necessary angle of attack by keeping the wing at the required angle, *but* allowing the fuselage and the cockpit to be lowered for better pilot visibility. In addition to the improved view forward, the plane's landing gear could remain at a reasonable weight-saving length, and not require the stalky and ultimately weaker assemblies of the F7U, or even Douglas' later A4D Skyhawk.

Additional consideration was also given to the wing's control surfaces. Besides the variable incidence capability, the ailerons and entire leading edge surfaces were interconnected and automatically lowered to 25 degrees, increasing the camber, thus, the lift, while allowing a reduction of approach and take-off speeds. The aerodynamic braking quality of the raised wing was another bonus.

Captain Tom Irwin describes how the early Crusader pilots operated the unique wing:

There were two controls in the cockpit, one was the positioning handle, and the other, a locking handle. After the locking handle was moved to the unlocked or aft position, the positioning handle was moved aft after first depressing a thumb switch on the end. An emergency pneumatic means of activation was available in case of a hydraulic failure.

The extension of the full-span leading edge was also made to the landing position, as well as lowering the narrow inboard flap segments and ailerons. The speed brake also retracted, if extended, and an automatic retrim of the Unit Horizontal Tail (UHT) occurred. This was the normal landing configuration. When the wing was lowered, all surfaces returned to the normal in-flight position with the leading edge going to the position selected for the cruise droop on the throttle handle.

Lowering the wing after take-off was always an interesting experience for new F-8 drivers. Aerodynamically, the fuselage was actually being raised, since the wing was doing the flying. Consequently, the pilot had to 'fly' the fuselage up into the wing while the auto retrim was taking place. Procedures called for a higher speed to begin transition than most pilots were comfortable with. If too little back pressure was used, the aircraft would settle; too much, and it would climb or porpoise. The right way was a perfectly level and steady transition to the end of the runway.

Formation transitions were always interesting, especially in instrument conditions. Standardized signals were used to alert the wingman and to indicate execution. If the wingman failed to anticipate a configuration change, or missed the execute signal, vertical separation and a red face resulted.

Landing with the wing in the down position was possible ashore, but very risky aboard the ship, although it was done successfully on several occasions. The approach speed had to be increased by about 30 knots, even if the landing droop was available, to avoid touching down tailpipe first.

Special attention was also given to the new fighter's construction, using lightweight metals like titanium and the Vought-developed Metallite which had first been used in the XF5U.

ABOVE
The first Crusader prototype is prepared by its Vought ground crew for its first flight on 25 March 1955, at Edwards Air Force Base, California, only 21 months after the initial design work had begun

RIGHT
Vought's chief test pilot, John Konrad, shows five fingers after he made the 500th test flight in 899, the One X, the first Crusader prototype

BELOW
With John Konrad at the controls, 138899 begins its take-off roll on 25 March 1955. Note the long nose boom, common on prototypes, which carried the pitot tube (Art Schoeni)

Newly applied aerodynamics were included, mainly the recently developed area ruled fuselage, the so-called 'Coke bottle'. This design 'pinched' the waist of the aircraft's fuselage, producing a reduction in drag, thereby increasing speeds eventually attained by the XF8U, and all other jet fighters to follow.

A unique feature was the ram-air turbine, colloquially known as 'the RAT' by every F-8 pilot to come. Installed on a hinged panel in the right side of the forward fuselage, the RAT provided emergency hydraulic and electrical power, and during the F-8's long career, the RAT saved many aircraft.

Armament consisted of four 20 mm Mk 12 Colt cannons, two on each side of the forward fuselage, with 144 rounds per gun. There was also provision for 'cheek' rails, immediately aft of the cockpit, to carry one Sidewinder air-to-air missile each. Later development enabled an additional Sidewinder per rail, giving a total of four. However, in combat in Vietnam, four missiles were only carried occasionally due to weight and fuel considerations.

The story of the Sidewinder, the first practical air-to-air missile, is an interesting tale, outside the scope of this book. However, early testing in September 1953 involved test firings from a Grumman F9F-8 Cougar. The early model Sidewinder destroyed a Hellcat drone.

The XF8U also included a huge internal supply of fuel, over 1300 gallons in wing and fuselage tanks. With a maximum endurance of three hours, the F-8 series seldom, if ever, carried additional external fuel tanks. Indeed, the RF-8 reconnaissance aircraft's range enabled it to carry out far-ranging missions in SE Asia, and, barring extended heavy manoeuvring to evade enemy defences, the RF-8 would return to its carrier with a comfortable amount of reserve fuel. In-flight refuelling capability, a Navy requirement from September 1955, was later included in production models, the retractable probe enclosed beneath a blister on the left side, aft of the cockpit.

With all these pluses, the XF8U-1 looked just like the winner Chance Vought needed. Sufficiently impressed, the Navy gave the go-ahead to build two prototypes in June 1953.

Twenty-one months later, in February 1955, the first XF8U-1, BuNo 138899, was ready. In March, the Air Force flew the fuselage and tail to Edwards Air Force Base, with the 25th selected as the date for the first flight. The prototype's wings, travelling by truck, did not arrive until 16 March. However, two days later, test pilot John W Konrad began taxi tests. The tests were completed on 22 March, three days before the scheduled flight.

A native of San Diego, California, John Konrad flew for the US Army Air Force as a test and

Brand new, the cockpit of XF8U-1, BuNo 138899, in March 1955 (via Jim Sullivan)

development pilot in B-17 bombers, and later for projects involving radar development. Following the war, he participated in the 1948 Berlin Airlift, served as a fighter pilot, a staff pilot for the United Nations in Lebanon, and then returned in 1949 to Edwards for more testing time. He eventually flew more than 100 different aircraft. Konrad left the service in 1953 to join Chance Vought as a test pilot.

Konrad arrived in the early morning of 25 March to make his preflight checks of 899. He strapped in, started the J57 engine and taxied to the runway. After additional systems and control checks, he pushed the throttle forward, accelerated down the runway, and lifted the nose as the indicator passed 128 knots.

Two Air Force chase planes, an F-100 and a TF-86F, followed the Navy's newest fighter as Konrad took her off from the dry lake bed. After preliminary flight checks, Konrad punched in the afterburner, and climbed. As he reached 35,000 feet, he accelerated past Mach 1.0, the first time a Navy fighter had gone faster than sound in level flight.

Crusader No 2 on the Convair ramp at Carswell Air Force Base, Fort Worth, Texas. Note the B-36 bomber overhead. Vought used the Convair plant there for early operations because the runways at NAS Dallas were too short. The second prototype was scrapped after 460 test flights (Art Schoeni)

After 52 minutes, Konrad brought the XF8U back. The experienced test pilot had been greatly impressed with the new aircraft. By the time the second prototype, number 138900, made its first flight on 12 June, again with John Konrad at the controls, it had been officially dubbed the Crusader.

The XF8U-1, number 899, made 508 flights during its five years of testing, passing the hundredth flight only six months after the first one. It used 17 different Pratt & Whitney J57 engines in the process.

Eventually, the 'One X', as it came to be called, was donated to the Smithsonian Institution in Washington, DC. Test pilot Bob Rostine flew 899 from Dallas to Naval Air Station (NAS) Patuxent in early October 1960. From there, John Konrad flew it to Washington's National Airport on 25 October, where, after shutting down, he presented the aircraft logbooks to Vought and Navy officials. Vice Chief of Naval Operations Admiral J S Russell then presented the aircraft to Dr Remington Kellogg, acting Secretary for the Smithsonian.

Unfortunately, the One X languished at the Smithsonian's Silver Hill storage facility in suburban Maryland, gathering 27 years of dust and greasy soot in the corner of a darkened Quonset hut, nearly forgotten, until the end of the entire Crusader line's career drew near. The second XF8U-1, 900, after 460 flights, was scrapped.

Chapter 2
Initial Fleet Introduction and Record Runs

The first production F8U-1, BuNo 140444, left the Dallas plant on 20 September 1955. In January 1956, the Marine Corps accepted its first production F8U, by which time three Crusaders a month were being produced. The first fleet pilots had also begun training at Patuxent.

The first 13 Crusader pilots came from VF-32 at Cecil Field, near Jacksonville, Florida, and VF(AW)-3, an all-weather fighter squadron based at NAS Moffett Field, south of San Francisco, California.

The initial carrier qualifications for the F8U were scheduled for April 1956. Commander Duke Windsor, a Patuxent test pilot, conducted practice landings at Patuxent in late March with the fourth pre-production F8U, BuNo 140446. The plane was then loaded aboard the carrier USS *Forrestal* (CVA-59) at Norfolk, Virginia.

As Russ Clark and a group of company executives watched, Windsor made six touch-and-go landings on the *Forrestal* on 4 April. After these, he and the new fighter made the Crusader's first catapult launch. During the next two days, Windsor made 12 landings and launches. The fifth catapult shot nearly resulted in the destruction of the plane when, during the cat stroke, the Crusader suddenly skidded down the deck at an awkward angle.

Reacting immediately, Windsor retarded the throttle to idle and stood on the brakes. The aircraft stopped only four feet from the carrier's bow. Since no apparent damage was done, the launches continued. A second qualification period on 18 April saw 12 more launches and 11 landings.

Speed Records

As the development and introduction of the F8U proceeded, the Crusader captured a number of performance records, and, in the process, several prestigious aeronautical trophies.

To show off its new fighter, the Navy decided to better Air Force speed records. Duke Windsor was told to push the Crusader past the magical 1000 mph mark. Named Project One Grand, the attempt would be made in California's Mojave Desert. With the most F8U time of any Navy test pilot, and having got a Crusader unofficially up to 1100 mph, Windsor anticipated no problems.

The Air Force threw the Navy a curve, however, when a new F-100C Super Sabre achieved 822 mph, Mach 1.25, on 20 August 1955. Undaunted, the Navy scheduled its attempt a year later, by which time, the British held the level speed record with the Fairey Delta II, an experimental aircraft which achieved 1132 mph.

Actually, the Navy did not want Windsor to take the F8U to its top speed because it did not want to disclose the full capabilities of the new aircraft. Windsor was told to simply top the 1000-mph mark.

Early on the morning of 21 August 1956, Windsor took off from MCAS Mojave, in F8U-1 BuNo 141345, the twelfth production fighter, climbed to 40,000 feet and, in two speed runs, hit an average speed of 1015 mph, a little slower than the British mark, but nearly 200 mph faster than the US Air Force's record.

This achievement won the Thompson Trophy for the Navy and Vought. Chief of Naval Operations Admiral Arleigh A Burke, with Commander Duke Windsor, received the trophy at ceremonies in Oklahoma City in early September. It was just the beginning of the Crusader's year of records.

VX-3's Ship to Ship Dash

A trip to the new *Forrestal*-class carrier *Saratoga*

US President Dwight Eisenhower (sports jacket) greets Captain Robert Dose (third from left) and Lieutenant Commander Paul Miller (second from right) after the two VX-3 aviators landed aboard the Bon Homme Richard *following a transcontinental flight on 6 June 1957. The flight took $3\frac{1}{2}$ hours, with one aerial refuelling* (Art Schoeni)

(CVA-60) by President Dwight Eisenhower afforded the Navy its next opportunity to show off the Crusader. Captain Robert G Dose, commanding officer of VX-3, based at Atlantic City, New Jersey, led his squadron operations officer, Lieutenant Commander Paul Miller on a cross-country dash.

Launching from the *Bon Homme Richard* (CVA-31) steaming off the California coast on 6 June 1957, Dose and Miller flew toward Dallas. Above the F8U's home, the two F8U-1s refuelled from two waiting AJ-2 tankers. Disengaging from the tankers, the Crusaders blasted back up to their cruising altitude of 45,000 feet, and their cruising speed of .96 Mach.

Finally, as they approached the East Coast of the US, the two pilots descended toward the *Saratoga*, 50 miles off Jacksonville. With the VX-3 Landing Signals Officer, Lieutenant Commander Ken Sharp, monitoring their approach to the big ship, Dose and Miller made a fast flyby at 600 knots, barely 75 feet above the water. Skidding around in tight turns, the two Crusaders then lined up, desperately trying to slow down to approach speeds, and eventually trapped—made an arrested landing—aboard the *Saratoga* in front of their admiring commander-in-chief. It was an impressive display, and the elapsed time from launch to trap was three hours and 28 minutes, an unofficial record.

John Glenn's Project Bullet

Another transcontinental dash, this time involving the photo reconnaissance variant F8U-1P, took place

the following July. Then-Marine Major John H Glenn, with the sponsorship of the Navy's Air Test Center, Patuxent, Maryland, planned a west-to-east transcontinental dash, named Project Bullet. The flight would be made at supersonic speed and would also photograph the entire US.

Glenn would fly the third -1P, BuNo 144608, escorted by Navy Lieutenant Commander Charles Demmler in an F8U-1 fighter. Supported by Navy squadrons providing AJ-1 Savages as aerial refuellers—VAH-6 and VAH-11—and equipment support—VFP-61 prepared the cameras in Glenn's plane—the two Crusaders took off from Los Angeles at 6 a.m. on 16 July.

Demmler was forced to abort the flight when his plane's in-flight refuelling probe was damaged during the first refuelling. Glenn pressed on alone and three hours and 23 minutes later touched down at New York's Floyd Bennett Field. The average speed was 725.55 mph (Mach 1.1). Of course, Glenn went on to greater accomplishments as the first American to orbit the earth in February 1962, and as a Senator from his home state of Ohio.

His faithful Crusader continued flying, and was eventually remanufactured as an RF-8G. Its luck ran out, however, in December 1972 when it struck the flight deck of the carrier *Oriskany* (CV-34), and its young pilot ejected. John Glenn's Project Bullet aircraft rests at the bottom of the South China Sea off Vietnam.

The F8U's impressive performances earned Vought and the Navy the Collier Trophy which cited the 'concept, design, and development of the first carrier-based fighter capable of speeds exceeding 1000 mph'.

RIGHT
Major John Glenn in the cockpit of his F8U-1P

BELOW RIGHT
A close up of John Glenn during the Project Bullet flight in July 1957. His aircraft is an F8U-1P, photo version of the F8U Crusader. Note the two windows in the lower fuselage and the ventral fairing directly below the cockpit, housing aerial cameras. Note, too, the different 'gunsight' above the pilot's instrument panel. This was, in reality, a viewfinder for the pilot that looked out of a small window directly beneath the nose in front of the air intake, along the aircraft's flight path

While the early Crusaders garnered public recognition, the F8U-1 was entering the fleet. VX-3 received the initial production F8U-1s in December 1956, but the first fleet squadron to re-equip was VF-32 at NAS Cecil Field, in March 1957, followed by West Coast squadrons VF-154 and VF(AW)-3, then VF-211, VF-142 and VF-143.

The first US Marine Corps squadrons took their first Crusaders in December 1957, VMF-122, followed by VMFs 312, 333, and 334.

February 1958 saw the first Crusader deployment, in the USS *Hancock* (CVA-19) with VF-194 in the Pacific, and VF-32 in the *Saratoga* for the first Atlantic deployment.

Lebanon, 1958

Events in the Lebanon brought direct US intervention in the summer of 1958 when President Eisenhower ordered an amphibious landing by the Marines. While largely unopposed, the Marine amphibious landing in Lebanon in July 1958 was the only such large-scale operation in a peacetime setting. The US was not really prepared to support a major landing. Much of the required airpower was stationed in the States; the nearest carrier task force, with the new *Saratoga*, was 1700 miles away at Cannes, France.

However, on 15 July, just after 3 p.m., and preceded by a flyover of more than 50 aircraft from the carrier *Essex* (CVS-9), the Marines landed four miles south of Beirut, and half a mile from the Beirut International Airport. A second landing followed the next morning.

The bemused Marines rushed ashore meeting no opposition except the clusters of sightseers and Lebenese vendors. (It was a scene to be duplicated seven years later and half a world away in South Vietnam.) Overhead, aircraft from the *Essex* flew patrol. They were un-needed. For the first time in two months, Beirut passed the night in relative calm. VF-32 flew its aircraft—new F8U-2s—from the carrier *Saratoga* during the crisis, patrolling the eastern Mediterranean beaches while their compatriots made amphibious landings, the first time the Crusader entered a hostile area.

By noon on 18 July, additional Marines had arrived from the US, ferried by transport aircraft. Aircraft dropped leaflets in Arabic, carrying greetings from President Eisenhower, and a promise to leave Lebanon when peace and stability returned, hopefully with the coming national elections. The *Forrestal*, with VMF-333 and its F8U-2s aboard, relieved its sister carrier in September in the eastern Mediterranean.

Design of a Photo Reconnaissance Platform

As the fighter enjoyed a highly successful introduction, development of a dedicated photo reconnaissance platform also began, using the thirty-second F8U-1, BuNo 141363.

The forward fuselage was altered, with the four 20 mm cannons and related fire controls deleted. To accomodate the series of cameras and film canisters, the fuselage was flattened on the belly and in the in-flight refuelling probe completely enclosed, thereby changing the characteristic 'bump' on the Crusader's port side. In addition, the horizontal tail was reduced to increase the aircraft's speed, which would be its only defence.

The original suite of cameras included three trimetrogen cameras which provided horizon-to-horizon coverage at Station 2, actually the aft-most bay. Eventually, the definitive camera arrangement was as follows. Two cameras which could give vertical and oblique views were located in Stations 3 and 4, while Station 1, located below and forward of the cockpit, mounted a forward-looking oblique camera which photographed the aircraft's flight path. Station 1 could also operate a 16 mm movie camera.

Though the cameras in Stations 3 and 4 could give several degrees of obliquity, the most used were 5, 15 and 30. The cameras were manufactured by Chicago Aerial and were designated KA-66 (Station 2), KA-51, 53 or 62 (Stations 3 and 4) and KA-45 or 51 (Station 1). Lens focal lengths varied from 3 inches in the KA-66 pan camera to 6 and 12 inches in the oblique and vertical cameras.

The vertical cameras in Stations 3 and 4 were also used for air-to-air photography, beloved of squadron public affairs officers and enthusiasts. Nothing matched a well-lit 5 × 5 inch aerial negative and resulting prints taken by an experienced F8U-1P pilot.

Aerial photography with the F8U-1P became a

ABOVE
A view of an RF-8G cockpit. The handle of the control column is typical, with many different buttons and wheels to control systems and surfaces. The pilot's viewfinder is the large circular panel directly atop the main panel (Author)

RIGHT
A rare photo of Demmler and Glenn at the beginning of Project Bullet. Rendezvousing with an AJ Savage tanker from VAH-11, the two Crusaders lined up to top up their tanks before proceeding across the country. As shown here, Demmler made the first hook-up, but damaged his probe and had to abort the flight. His aircraft is a fighter, as evidenced by the cannon ports below the cockpit

fine art and skill could only be acquired with experience. During photo sessions, the Crusader pilot had to direct the aircraft he was shooting to get the proper lineup in formation shots, and the best lighting. It took skill and, at times, command directness, to obtain the right shot. Normally, all the photo pilot had to help him compose his view was a moveable reticle, a brass ring mounted on a pantograph arm on the sides of his canopy.

Besides the air-to-air, and vertical and oblique air-to-ground photography, the F8U-1P carried one other oblique camera in a bay directly beneath the nose, Station 1, looking forward along the flight path. This so-called 'forward fire' provided ingress routes to targets for bombers, and its coverage was extremely valuable during the Vietnam War. The 16 mm movie camera previously mentioned was rarely used.

The mid-fuselage Station 2's panoramic camera, or simply, pan, originally housed the KA-66 which gave a 70 mm 3-inch-wide strip, useful only for locating the aircraft's position and certain landmarks. However, the later change to the KA-68 with a larger 5-inch strip, allowed the pan camera to become a more useful sensor.

The F8U-1P's first flight came on 17 December 1956, and during the relatively short two-year period of production, the photo Crusaders went through several internal refinements and minor modifications, including strengthening of the wings and electronic avionic changes. The RF-8G incorporated ventral rear-fuselage strakes for increased high-altitude stability and joined the fleet in October 1965.

In September 1962, the entire US military aircraft designation system was changed to reflect a more unified, simpler format. According to one story, the reason for the change was then-Secretary of Defense Robert McNamara's embarrassment at not understanding the system of indicating aircraft manufacturers by designated letter, i.e., U for Chance Vought. Thus the F8U was redesignated F-8, with the F8U-1P photo variant becoming the RF-8A. The Crusader series will be referred to in the post-1962 system from this point.

The RF-8A Joins the Fleet

The first Navy squadron to deploy with F8U-1Ps (RF-8As) was VFP-61, which began life right after World War II as one of two fleet reconnaissance units, giving service throughout the Korean War as VC-61, flying a variety of jets such as the F9F-2P

Panther and earlier prop-driven photo-fighters, like the F4U-5P Corsair. Redesignated VFP in July 1956, it received its first Crusaders in September 1957. VFP-61's Detachment Alfa in the USS *Midway* (CVA-41) deployed with its new aircraft later that year.

Along the way, VFP-61 and VFP-62 acquired the big A3D Skywarrior and were retitled VAP-61 and VAP-62. Light photographic duties were assumed by VCP-62 and 63 who gave up their A3Ds for RF-8As.

The 1962 Cuban Crisis

The photo Crusader's first operational test came in the late autumn of 1962, and involved both Navy and Marine RF-8As. USAF U-2 reconnaissance flights had brought back initial indications, but not incontestable proof, that the Soviets had introduced intermediate-range ballistic missiles (IRBMs) into their client state, the island of communist Cuba. On 13 October, in conjunction with continued USAF flights, VFP-62 and Marine squadron VMCJ-2, were detailed to stand by at the Naval Air Station, Cecil Field, near Jacksonville. The Air Force's highly touted low-level capability of its RF-101 Voodoos was largely inoperative until 29 October, when the RF-101s flew their first missions, *after* the big week of 23-28 October. The Voodoos' camera systems were in disrepair. However, zealous USAF public affairs officials garnered lots of national attention, much to the consternation of the Navy and Marines. The RF-8As were needed for low-level, high-speed reconnaissance to confirm the earlier U-2 photos which only showed earth moving and unconfirmed

construction activity. Cuban agents gave information about possible missile bases, and the US government wanted a closer look. A high-flying U-2 might take only 1–2 frames a minute, but an RF-8 travelling at 600 knots, at 5000 feet, took several frames a second. The coverage was thus much greater and more detailed. While VFP-62 scrambled to get detachments to carriers, in case the big ships went on a war footing, the land-based 'home squadron' prepared for operations over Cuba.

Four Marine pilots were assigned to VFP-62 to provide additional resources and fly the Navy squadron's RF-8s. The flights began on 23 October 1962, under the codename 'Blue Moon'. Six aircraft flew against three targets, two RF-8s apiece. Two aircraft always flew per sortie. Fourteen flights were made on October 27, the greatest number during the entire operation.

The RF-8As made two flights daily from NAS Key West with low-level, high-speed dashes over the heavily defended island, then landing at NAS Jacksonville where the Crusaders' film was downloaded and rushed for processing and interpretation to the Fleet Air Photo Lab (FAPL) owned by VFP-62. After downloading the film, the Crusaders then returned to Cecil Field, a short distance from Jacksonville, for maintenance. Then they returned to Key West for the next mission. In a six-week period, the RF-8s brought back over 160,000 negatives.

The Missile Crisis was in full swing, as the US instituted a naval blockade, challenging the Soviets' continued movement to and from Cuba. Never has the world seemed so close to nuclear war. Finally, after a week of diplomatic furore, the Russians agreed to dismantle the missile installations and remove them from Cuba.

While the delicate negotiations continued, so did the Blue Moon flights. After landing at Jacksonville after each mission, each Crusader received another 'dead chicken' marking below its cockpit to denote another mission. (The marking referred to a comical sequence involving Cuban Premier Castro, who, on an early visit to New York City in 1960, demanded that a live chicken be killed and cooked for him on the spot to prevent someone trying to assassinate him by poisoning his food.) In addition to the 'chicken' markings, every Crusader had the phrase 'Smile, you're on Candid Camera' painted on the lower fuselage surface immediately in front of the Station 1 camera blister.

The chronology of RF-8A sorties for Blue Moon was as follows:

October	23—	3 sorties
October	25—	10
October	27—	14
October	29—	2
November	1—	2
November	2—	2
November	3—	2
November	5—	6
November	6—	2
November	7—	4
November	8—	4
November	9—	6
November	10—	4
November	11—	4
November	12—	4
November	13—	6
November	15—	2

No Navy flights were made from 15 November, until the last one on 5 June 1963.

The 12 regular squadron pilots and four Marines received Distinguished Flying Crosses, while VFP-62 received the first peacetime Navy Unit Commendation, personally presented by President John F Kennedy, on 26 November 1962.

An interesting sidelight involved Marine RF-8s of a small VMCJ-2 detachment based at the large US Navy base at Guantánamo on Cuba. VMCJ-2 had, for two years prior to the crisis, been flying electronic surveillance flights with specially equipped Douglas F3D Skyknights, large twin-engine, straight-winged jets, which, in their later careers, became important gatherers of ELINT, electronic intelligence.

The Marine F3Ds would take off from nearby Caribbean fields—such as those on Jamaica or the Bahamas—in the early predawn hours, fly well off the Cuban coast, enticing Cuban radar to show itself. The Cubans usually obliged, and the Marines always brought back a lot of intelligence which took several weeks to analyze. The Skyknights had direct radio links to the US Joint Chiefs of Staff, although missions were flown in a complete radio blackout.

With the onset of the Cuban Crisis, however, and in addition to the seconded pilots and ground crews to the larger VFP-62 effort, a two-plane detachment flew to Guantánamo, staging from Roosevelt Roads, Puerto Rico. USAF F-104s were sent out to escort the incoming RF-8s but couldn't find them, so Marine F-8s of VMF-122 rendezvoused with the RF-8s and escorted them to Cuba. A C-130 moved the 42 men and maintenance and photo gear. Harold M Austin, Jr, a young Crusader driver, was the squadron logistics officer, and he was somewhat miffed at having to stay behind to make sure the det got off and arrived in Cuba. However, he eventually joined the det which had been administratively detached from the squadron and reassigned to Marine Aircraft Group (MAG) 31 at Key West and Jacksonville, Gitmo.

Although the main reconnaissance operation was flown by the combined VFP-62/VMCJ-2 group, the Gitmo Marines did occasionally fly missions, especially several night photo runs. Unfortunately, the man in charge was a non-aviator colonel who did not fully understand air operations. Following the shootdown of a U-2 on 27 October, Captain Austin was tasked with providing high-altitude, pin-point photography of the missile site which hit the high flying Air Force plane. The Joint Chiefs of Staff suggested the RF-8 fly at 35,000 feet, which put it right in the missile's envelope, and would not provide very good photography. Austin told the ground-pounder colonel that a high-speed, low-level run would give much better coverage, and would also take him out of the missile's envelope.

The colonel replied that Austin should not worry; there would be four fighters offshore monitoring the photo plane's progress. Of course, there would have been little the escort could have done against a missile except to call out where it hit the reconnaissance Crusader, and where, and if, Austin had ejected. Austin's objections fell on deaf ears, and he flew the mission, 'very scared'.

Fighting the Bear

As American carriers became a regular presence in European waters, the Russians began overflying the ships to gather information, as well as to remind the Americans continually of Soviet interest. In a deadly serious game, carriers maintained airborne patrols which could be directed to intercept any approaching intruders. The boredom of these patrols could be relieved when an interception was made. Then, morale soared. VF-162 in the *Oriskany* had a few 'Bear Patrols', during its 1963 cruise. The Bear was the NATO codename for the huge four-engine turboprop bomber, the TU-95, which was a regular visitor to the carriers.

In late August, a Bear flew over the *Oriskany* at 1500 feet. However, the seas were so rough, fighters had not been launched, and the frustrated pilots composed a song. A group of four F-8 pilots sang their song with obvious relish. The tune was a popular calypso melody, 'Mary Ann'.

Chorus:

All day, all night, wait for bears.
One high, one low, they come in pairs.
When it rain and the clouds hide sun,
Pitching decks and CIC add to the fun.

Verse:

C-I-C, oh, C-I-C, oh won't you vector me.
I'm a whale up in the sky, you know I cannot see.
If your wings went up and down, of troubles you'd be free.
Don't worry 'bout the intercepts, just call on ready three.

Tinker toys and little boys, what will they think of next?
Air to air is not your game, completely out of text.
You've tried your rockets and your bombs, with those you do all right.
But when you switch to infra-red, our hearts you fill with fright.

A ground crewman directs an RF-8A of VFP-62 to its parking spot on the ramp at NAS Jacksonville following a mission over Cuba in 1962

CARDIV staff and air ops, too, we're in an awful
plight.
No info comes from Big AI. We'll surely miss the fight.
CARDIV screams, the captain yells, the air boss is in
fear,
Pass some word, right or wrong, tell the pilots, 'Play by
ear!'

Hell with black, and red and blue, and green and indigo,
Launch unbriefed pink and chartreuse, too, the 'go'
plans are below.
There it is, I see it there, displayed upon the PLAT.
While they launch the other nerds, upon our butts we
sat.

The flight deck crew was unimpressed, an escort there
was none.
The nearest thing there was to that was 'good ole
HU-1'.
When Russian bears go flying by, your heart will skip a
beat.
Don't hesitate, pick up the phone, and call on
'SUPERHEAT'.

CIC was the Combat Information Center, basically
an intelligence area aboard a carrier. A 'whale' was a
refernce to the big A-3 Skywarrior, while 'Tinker toy'
was a nickname for the little A-4 Skyhawk, both
bombers. PLAT refers to the television circuit which
displays landings aboard carriers, and thus, in this
case, probably had a good view of the Russian
bomber's overflight. And, of course, the 'HU-1' was
the ship's Huey helicopter. VF-162's radio call sign
was 'Superheat'.

Flying the Crusader and Initial Problems

While the F-8 was enjoying a highly successful
service introduction, several new Crusader pilots
experienced varying degrees of problems handling
the new fighter, especially during the close-in phase
the carrier approach, always the most difficult
portion of flying a naval aircraft.

The problem was especially notable during
operations around the smaller *Essex* class carriers,
known as 27-Charlies because of several modifications, including the newly developed angled deck,
these 27,000-ton ships had much smaller decks than
the newer *Forrestal* class then joining the fleet.

The Crusader's relatively high approach speed of
147 knots made judging the approach difficult for
neophytes. A lapse of concentration could end up in a
ramp strike where the plane hit the round-down, the
extreme aft portion of the carrier's flight deck. The
aircraft could then either break up, and slide across
the deck, or explode in a blinding ball of flame. In any
event, the pilot was extremely lucky to get out alive.

Consistent airspeed was the key to a good
approach, and eventually a device called the

Approach Power Compensator appeared, though not
until August 1964, although the device had been in
testing stages as early as 1960, with production
approved in 1962. Called either the APC, or autothrottle, this system consisted of a computer,
accelerometer, a servo amplifier and actuator, and the
pilot's control panel, all interfaced with the existing
angle of attack detector. The APC panel was on the
left console immediately beside the pilot's left leg and
consisted of a row of toggle switches.

The APC was engaged only with the Crusader's
wing in the 'up' position, and would automatically
disengage upon landing. The system detected
deviations in normal acceleration and angle of attack
which would result in a less than optimum approach
airspeed. During a normal approach, the APC could
maintain airspeed with a range of plus or minus 4
knots, in light to moderate turbulence.

The October 1963 issue of *Approach, the Naval
Aviation Safety Review*, ran one of the first stories on
the upcoming device.

'It must be emphasized', the magazine admonished its readers, 'the autothrottle will not *land* the
airplane for you. The autothrottle *is an assist* for you
as a pilot during the carrier approach. Should you fail
to keep the 'meatball' (approach lights) centred, and
the airplane lined up on the centreline, nothing in the
autothrottle system will do it for you. In fact, if you
accept a low approach and fail to correct, we
guarantee that the autothrottle will insure that you hit
the ramp on speed'. Having established the consequences of totally relying on the APC, the article
continued with an in-depth description of the device
and its operation:

LSOs [Landing Signal Officers] will soon learn to
recognize the characteristics of autothrottle approaches.
Specifically, the LSO will learn to look for familiar sounds
and sight which indicate normal operation of the system . . .
the familiar exhaust smoke of the F-8 [will] cease abruptly
as the airplane intercepts the glide slope and rolls out of the
approach turn. Even more important, the LSO will expect
to see a large puff of smoke when the pilot rotates the nose of
the airplane to keep from descending below the glide path,
as the airplane slows down following initial glide path
interception . . .
Many critics are justly concerned about what happens
when the system fails and the affected pilot hasn't made a
manual throttle approach for the past 60 carrier landings.

*Commander William Ecker, CO of VFP-62, and a combat
veteran of WW2 when he flew Corsairs with VBF-10,
dismounts from his RF-8A after a mission over Cuba. The
date of the photo is sometime after the squadron received
the first peacetime Navy Unit Commendation on 26
November from President John F Kennedy. Note the
ribbon painted on the Crusader's nose. The forward fire
camera bay is already open, immediately in front of the
nose gear, as is the number 3 bay door behind the plane
captain assisting his skipper*

... we believe that although the technique used in flying an autothrottle approach is different from that used in a manual approach, the pilot will not completely lose his touch for proper power control since he has been monitoring throttle movements during all his previous automatic approaches ...

When VF-124, the training squadron for Crusader pilots, began using the APC, their performance was closely observed. The replacement pilots flew manual approaches until they exhibited satisfactory performance. Then, in subsequent carrier landing practice, called FCLPs (Fleet Carrier Landing Practice), on a field outline of a carrier deck, they flew with the APC.

Each of the 25 pilots made four arrested landings using manual approaches. These were followed by day and night APC approaches. The success rate was over 33 per cent higher using the APC. The more experienced pilots initially maintained they could do better by themselves, but were eventually brought around to endorsing the APC which gave them a consistency they never had.

The October 1965 issue of *Approach* again offered guidance:

The environment in which the Crusader has been operating has changed. Increased night operation from 27C class aircraft carriers has appreciably increased the hazard of Crusader carrier operations. Despite this increased hazard, the Crusader carrier landing accident rate has improved.

The overall effect of the APC appears to be that the aviators released to the fleet are more proficient in carrier work. This has been accomplished by improved FCLP performance without an increase in FCLP sorties. . . .

The big question is: Will the APC reduce accidents? Yes, if used properly . . . smooth attitude control is an absolute must . . . Note to APC users: Be smooth with that nose—the APC, when used properly, will reduce your accident rate and improve your boarding rate.

By 1967, when the Crusader had been in the fleet for ten years, and was in combat in Vietnam, the APC was an accepted part of the aircraft's operation. However, with the great amount of operational

experience now available, veteran Crusader pilots had a few thoughts:

Something that makes any LSO quiver is the instance when a guy drops his nose farther out in the groove. Not only does the APC reduce power, but valuable lift is given away. This is the paradox of the F-8; a slight nose attitude increase will not result in any appreciable change in flight path for a second or two, but a slight nose decrease will result in an immediate increase in sink rate. Given a constant power condition, the nose drop will not accelerate the aircraft as much as a nose pull up of the same degree will decelerate it. . . .

The point is that attitude versus power in the F-8 is a twilight zone during the last few seconds prior to touchdown. If you pull the nose up, you will usually touch down a little more cocked up in the same place as you would have if you'd left the nose alone. That's why a 'no lower', which is an APC pass call for an increase in attitude when it is given in the middle of an approach, is an appropriate call to stop a sink rate. There is time for the increased attitude to generate additional lift and for the APC to add the desired power . . . '

While the APC is definitely a good deal, it is still only a

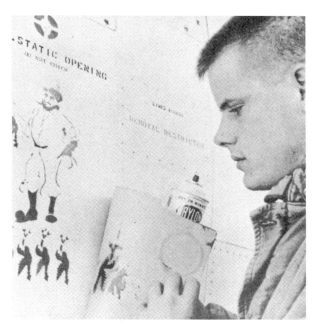

ABOVE
Another dead chicken means another successful mission over Cuba in 1962. Each RF-8A received a caricature of Cuban Premier Fidel Castro—note the baseball uniform as the game was a national passion—and a dead chicken marking for each mission. Castro's fear of being poisoned during a state visit, and his demand for a freshly killed chicken, prompted the marking

LEFT
Still in full flight gear after a mission, Commander William Ecker leans over the light table to run through mission film with photo interpreters and other interested officers at the Jacksonville Photo Lab. Note Ecker's ammunition belt characteristically worn across the chest

device and it can't think as fast as you can . . . hence, when you find 37 knots of wind or more over the deck, the hole behind the 27C is such that if you respond to the sink rate with APC (increase the attitude), the APC is just too slow . . . you should plan to break APC prior to reaching the burble . . . usually 400–600 feet behind the ramp . . .

Throughout its long career, the Crusader was an aeroplane which demanded to be flown constantly, even under the most benign conditions, but especially during the potentially dangerous landing phase. Carrier approaches separate average pilots from great pilots, and no aircraft demonstrated this more clearly than the Crusader.

Developing a Pressure Suit

The F-8 participated in a series of tests concerned with developing a full pressure suit. The requirement evolved as it was realized that flying above 50,000 feet, or even regularly above 35,000, a better device than the normal oxygen mask and pressurized cabin was needed. Completing a mission at those altitudes would be difficult. Some sort of full pressure suit was needed.

The Air Force had developed a partial-pressure suit to counter the lower pressure around the body at those higher altitudes and thus keep the blood from bubbling. The partial pressure suit applied counter-pressure with 'capstans', little ribs along the arms and legs, and an inflatable chest portion. The pilot also wore a special helmet which gave him 100 per cent oxygen under pressure. The USAF adopted the suit for aircraft like the U-2 and SR-71 reconnaissance aircraft.

The Navy was very anxious to have a full pressure suit, and came up with the idea of an 'omni-environmental' suit which would give high altitude protection as well as exposure protection in very cold water, should the pilot have to eject.

Lieutenant Commander Frank H Austin, Jr, was a dual-designated Navy flight surgeon who participated in the tests of the pressure suit in the late 1950s. Austin was a doctor who had also qualified as a naval aviator, a practice still kept alive today. These unique naval officers are well qualified to cater to the highly specialized needs of military aviators:

The helmet seal had to be pretty tight around the pilot's face because there was air from the engine pumped in, like G suit air. This air would keep the pilot cool, but, in hot weather, we had to have a special air-conditioned truck in which we suited up and which transported us to the planes. Or we carried a little portable case with ice, and a fan which blew the cool air into the suit.

Although we got away from the mask-mounted regulator, which was difficult for pilots to operate, we ended up with a very heavy suit and backpack, and a complex connector to the plane, which also had to capable of quick disconnect in case of ejection.

We got into the suit through a chest entrance. A zipper

went across, and you got into the suit with a great deal of help. Our enlisted medical corpsmen were trained to help us get into the suit and heavy helmet.

The boots, which were attached to the suit itself were thermal boots and gave pretty good protection in cold weather. We started flying the suit around Patuxent (Pax), and then we got a project to take it aboard a carrier. Four of us started doing CQs around Pax. The fleet pilots who were now test pilots at Pax gave a big thumbs-down to the suit as not being suitable for fleet testing. The Naval Air Development Center (NADC) was testing a lighter-weight version of the suit, and we got some of these delivered. That was the Mk II. We had a later rig, integrated harness—used with or without the suit—and a lighter helmet, and the oxygen is in the seat pan, instead of a cumbersome backpack. This is the one we took aboard ship.

We first tested the Goodrich suit, which had a neoprene bladder inside for integrity, and nylon seals and gloves. We had to seal the boots and helmet. There was another suit called the Arrowhead suit which was in competition, but the Navy wanted the suit it sponsored, and the Goodrich suit was chosen for further development and evaluation. One thing we did was to try to validate the Mk II light-weight suit for fleet operations. We penalized the partial pressure suit by saying that since it didn't have cold weather protection, we'd have to wear it integrated with an exposure suit—the poopy suit—and of course, it would have been a tremendous problem putting on all these bulky suits.

We tested the suits for clearance to reach the ejection handle, and we had a clear visor on the helmet, with a sun visor which would be used as required. Then, we went aboard the *Forrestal* in November 1958 with these two different suits. One of the things of interest was the silver-coated suit which would reflect heat, such as nuclear explosions. It didn't go too far in development. The carrier operations went well, and we certified the Mk II suit as suitable for the fleet.

I left Pax around 1960, and went to Cecil to fly with VF-174, the east coast RAG for F-8s. We'd go on training hops to familiarize people with the suit and do zoom climbs. We'd reach Mach 1.2 at 35,000 feet, and pull the F-8 up sharply and keep going up until we ran out of airspeed and just fall away. Often, the engines would overtemp and we'd get pressure stalls. We'd have to shut down which caused lots of anxiety as we'd lose communications until we got a relight. It was good training, though. It's possible that we got as high as 65–70,000 feet in the F-8. At that altitude, the altimeters were not reliable, so I can't be sure.

I had an engine overtemp during a zoom climb over Tampa Bay, shut down, and of course, lost communications. My wingman lost sight of me and everyone figured I'd gone into the ocean. When I returned, I had to

A little publicized operation was the Marine Corps photo det of VMCJ-2 actually sent to Guantánamo, on the island of Cuba, during the Crisis. The enlisted troops assemble for a photo along with the two pilots who flew many missions over missile sites. In khaki flight suits, kneeling, Captain Harold Austin, second from left, and Captain Gary Hienz, third from left. VMCJ-2's nickname 'The Playboys' is evidenced by the Playboy Rabbit which the unit eventually carried throughout Vietnam

confess my engine had overtemped. I wasn't too popular with the maintenance officer.

The suit was introduced into the fleet, and these RAG pilots were trained in its use. I moved out of the project and after 1961, didn't do any more flying in the pressure suit. To the best of my recollection, the suits were seldom used, if ever, because they were very hard to maintain. When they deteriorated, they had to be replaced, which was an expensive proposition. The tradeoffs were limited, and eventually, the requirement for the suit went away. These planes did very little flying above 50,000 feet, anyway. Today, modern aerial combat is at lower altitudes, and SAMs would get you at higher altitudes now.

Surviving an ejection at high altitude was a moot point, as well. I went out to the Parachute Testing Facility at El Centro, California. I did a couple of jumps with these pressure suits, and it was very uncomfortable; even though we tied the neck and helmet connector ring down around the neck with the pulley apparatus, I still got a pretty bruised chin, and I wasn't too happy about the prospect of bailing out with that arrangement. I do know there was at least one ejection, made by Richard Jester, from a Crusader in the 1960s with the suit, and it seemed to be okay.

The 'Holy Grail' for suit manufacturers of producing a suit which is easily donned, is light-weight, protects at high altitudes, and in cold weather, and makes the pilot look 'like a Blue Angel at the O-Club' is still a dream. We tried the Mk II suit in various other aircraft of the time, including the A3J Vigilante which was under development, and the F4D Skyray which had a very small cockpit and limited

President John F Kennedy (second from left) awards VFP-62 the first peacetime Navy Unit Commendation on 26 November 1962. Commander William Ecker, CO of the squadron, shakes the President's hand

endurance at 50,000 feet. Most of the pilots who work at high altitudes—such as the USAF's U-2 and SR-71 pilots—wear a partial pressure suit because they have limited concern about exposure, and it serves their purpose very well.

One point in those days, the F-8 was the hottest plane around, and Crusader pilots thought their outfit wasn't complete without a specially-fitted pressure suit. Of course, once they'd flown in it, they realized it wasn't such a good thing. We would go up on hot days and become very dehydrated. We'd faint if we pulled any G's. Once, I lost three pounds on one flight in the Jacksonville area in the summer.

In ACM [Air Combat Manoeuvres], I'd have to raise the helmet visor and valsalva to clear my ears, not a very efficient method in combat. We also complained about the problem of trying to look over our shoulder wearing the big helmet. The engineers were rather cavalier about this, and said, 'Well, modern aircraft use radar, and you hit with missiles, and you don't need to look back'. This was a bunch of bull, of course. This was the same era the armament people—since the F-8's didn't have tight patterns with their guns—were thinking we were going to do everything with missiles. They were taking the guns out, much to the chagrin of the real fighter pilots.

The return to air-to-air combat in Vietnam showed that anyone in a pressure suit was a dead duck because he couldn't move around and see. As a matter of fact, we suspected there were a lot of people who became so aggravated, they took off their helmets to see better during ACM engagements.

The gloves were quite a problem, and I had some near tragedies flying with the suit. A couple of times, I just about lost the airplane, flying with the big heavy pressure suit. Once, when the tires blew, I thought I might have applied too much brake pressure, but I wasn't sure because of the heavy boots; I couldn't feel anything. The tires blew frequently, anyway.

Chapter 3
The Crusader Models

The initial production F8U-1 Crusaders (later F-8A) were the last dedicated, clear-weather, gun-armed air superiority fighters to serve with the US Navy. As missions became increasingly complex, so did the aircraft to fly them. The 315 F-8As carried four 20 mm cannon, with 144 rounds per gun, right below the cockpit, two on a side, and two AIM-9 Sidewinder air-to-air missiles on fuselage cheek rails, one per rail. Besides the guns and missiles, the first Crusaders carried an unusual rocket pack in the speed brake, which swung down directly below the fuselage. (The large brake became the bane of any inattentive Crusader pilot, no matter how much time he had. Any aviator could forget to raise the brake prior to touchdown, and land on the metal slab, much to his embarrassment and the probable anger of his commanding officer and maintenance troops.)

The rocket pack carried 16 Mighty Mouse 2.75-inch folding fin rockets (FFARs) in 8 tubes, and was supposed to give the Crusader a small measure of ground attack capability. However, as the F-8 began to carry bombs and more advanced radar, the rockets were dispensed with for weight considerations, as well as their questionable effectiveness.

The F-8A experienced problems with its guns which gave too wide a dispersion of bullets. Even acknowledged gunnery experts among the Crusader cadre achieved limited results during training runs. The Colt Mk 12 cannon had a rate of fire of 660 rounds per minute, approximately 13 seconds of sustained fire, and with the eventual addition of electronic countermeasures gear in the nose, the F-8 series did not have a lot of expansion space for increased ammunition. It was a problem never satisfactorily solved.

In combat with Vietnam, several pilots were frustrated by ammunition jams during high-G manoeuvres, and since ground strafing became an important part of the Crusader's repertoire in

Vietnam, there was much concern. The limited amount of ammunition did not give much strafing time for the F-8.

A partial solution came from VF-124, the Miramar-based training squadron. The squadron rewired the gun circuitry, providing two switches in the cockpit. The pilot could select which pair of guns he wanted to fire, thus conserving his ammunition. Vought endorsed the change in the fleet, although Navy maintenance facilities did not like the unofficial modification. In time, the mod was officially sanctioned.

Missile wiring and switchology also caused occasional problems. A-4 pilots on Vietnam alpha strikes were concerned about their Crusader escorts' Sidewinders. The Scooters dreaded the call 'Fox away!' from the F-8s above them. The cry meant there was an AIM-9 loose—inadvertently fired—among the bombers. Going feet dry, headed inland toward the target, the F-8 pilots turned on their 'Master Arm' switches, and stray voltage could fire a Sidewinder. Charles B 'Chuck' Scott had such an experience while going through the F-8 training syllabus at VF-124 in 1968:

We were going out on our first missile shoot with Sidewinders against a BQM-34 drone. We all took the arming heading at the approach end of the runway and the pins were pulled, and the proper checks made. We launched as a flight of four on Runway 24 Right at Miramar, and I raised the gear. There was an arrangement which prevented firing with the gear down.

Suddenly, my Sidewinder fired and lofted out over the high rent district in La Jolla. Fortunately, the missile made it to the Pacific and fell into the ocean. I took a lot of heat because, as a new guy, everyone figured I had my switches armed, causing inadvert missile launch.

The maintenance people weren't too anxious to find any miswiring or stray voltage. About one month later, the same aircraft went on another missile shoot and the same problem occurred. Needless to say, I was vindicated and

A good view of a pilot conducting a preflight of his Crusader. While it is difficult to determine the exact model F-8, the Y-type missile rack makes it at least a Charlie. The XF on the tail indicates the plane belongs to VX-4. The two cannon ports directly below the refuelling probe bulge are plugged, and there is only one Sidewinder on the rack which could carry two AIM-9s

TOP RIGHT
A head-on view of an F8U-1, showing the characteristic variable incidence wing in the 'up' position

CENTRE RIGHT
The Marines operated a large number of early Crusaders. Here, an F-8A of VMF-122 sits on the ramp at NAS Willow Grove, outside Philadelphia, Pennsylvania, in 1962. VMF-122 was the Marine Corps training squadron for east coast Leatherneck F-8 drivers, and the first Marine squadron to get F-8s. It later transitioned to F-4s (Russell-Smith, via Jim Sullivan)

BOTTOM RIGHT
A number of F-8As were made into drone-controllers. Here, a DF-8A of VC-8 gets a going-over by squadron mechanics. The plane's fuselage is a deep blue, and its wings and tail would be a bright yellow. The blade antenna immediately behind the raised cockpit canopy is part of the electronics needed to control target drones

LEFT
In less than six months, this would be the most dangerous area in the world, at least for a month. An F-8A of VC-10 flies over NAS Guantánamo, the American enclave on the communist island nation of Cuba in March 1962. The utility squadron provided target towing and flying time to those aviators based at the field, as well as for visiting fleet units

TOP
The F8U-1E used an upgraded radar and after 1962 was designated the F-8B. This F8U-1E of VMF-312 appears to be on the runway at MCAS Cherry Point, North Carolina

ABOVE
The early Crusaders carried very colourful markings. This VF-84 F-8C is getting ready to launch from the Independence in 1962. VF-84 eventually settled on a black pirate flag and skull tail markings, and carried them on their F-4s, and their current F-14s

the problem with that airplane was investigated and rectified.

The F8U-1E (F-8B) carried AN/APS-67 radar, replacing the F-8A's earlier APG-30 fire control apparatus. The new installation gave very limited all-weather capability. The F8U-1E made its first flight in September 1958, and kept the A's armament, including the ventral rocket pack, although most squadrons flew with the pack sealed. F-8B production totalled 130.

The first true fleet Crusader fighter was the

Charlie, which flew in August 1957 as the F8U-2. It was powered by a new engine, the Pratt & Whitney J57-P-16, which gave 13,000 pounds of thrust in basic engine, and 17,500 in afterburner, 1000 pounds more than the earlier power plants. F-8 performance increased, as did the afterburner's temperature. To help cool the aft section of the aircraft, two air scoops were mounted on the F-8C's tail cone.

Another characteristic feature of the Crusader line also appeared on the Charlie, the fuselage ventral strakes which were supposed to increase directional stability at high altitudes.

As the F8U-2, the Charlie, as previously noted, made what could have been the first combat cruise in 1958 off the coast of Lebanon, serving in VF-32 in *Saratoga* and Marine squadron VMF-333 in the *Forrestal*.

The F-8C also gained two additional Sidewinders which could be carried with a newly developed 'Y' rack. However, the four-missile armament was only occasionally carried in combat. The pilots felt that the weight penalty and reduction in fuel load was not worth the extra missiles.

A development of the F8U-2 was the -2N, eventually redesignated F-8D. Many pilots considered the Delta, with its powerful J57-P-20 engine, delivering 18,000 pounds of thrust in afterburner, to be the fastest Crusader, but although it equipped several fleet squadrons by 1965, and saw heavy action (albeit with only two Navy squadrons, VF-111 and VF-154) in the initial phases of direct American involvement in Vietnam, it was quickly superseded by the definitive Echo.

Originally intended to be a nightfighter, the F-8D featured improved radar and avionics, as well as the addition of the approach power compensator.

LEFT
An early F-8E, viewed nearly head-on, during deck trials, with a full weapons load of Zunis and 2000-pound bombs. The horizontal stabs are fully deflected in preparation for flight, although there are wheel chocks in place and the catapult bridle is not yet attached (Art Schoeni)

BELOW
VF-13 was one of the leading east coast Crusader squadrons, but as the Vietnam War took most of the F-8s to Westpac the Atlantic F-8 community faded away. VF-13 was decommissioned, along with its wingmate, VF-62, in 1969. This F-8E was seen at Miramar in February 1966 (Clay Jansson via Jim Sullivan)

ABOVE
*This F-8H of VF-111 is
landing at NAS Atsugi,
Japan in July 1970. It may
be coming in for
maintenance which cannot
be accomplished in the
limited facilities of its
carrier, the converted ASW
carrier* Shangri-La *(Hideki
Nagakubo)*

A VF-53 F-8J over the
Bonnie Dick *during the old
ship's last cruise in 1970, a
fairly uneventful
deployment*

43

TOP
During Crusader College's last days, an F-8J takes off from Miramar. The Juliet featured a new 4000-hour wing, as well as Boundary Layer Country (BLC)

ABOVE
In August 1974, this brightly marked F-8K of VC-10 had problems with its nose gear and landed at NAS Guantánamo, Cuba, after the runway had been foamed

RIGHT
Dr Frank Austin models the improved Mark II pressure suit before a test flight in 1957. The suit was of lighter weight than the earlier Mark I, and was eventually cleared for fleet use, although its upkeep and still-bulky connectors soon relegated it to the disposal locker (Via Frank Austin)

It kept the four-cannon armament, as well as the four-Sidewinder capability, but finally did away with the speed brake-mounted rocket pack. The first of the 152 Deltas flew in February 1960.

With the introduction of the F8U-2NE (later F-8E), the Crusader had developed from a lithe gun-toting dogfighter to a broad-shouldered, powerful, jack-of-all-trades, in one moment a fleet defence fighter and bomber escort, next, a screaming divebomber, destroyer of river barges, trains, and flak sites. The Echo also made the greatest number of Crusader MiG kills in Vietnam (11).

The F-8E was essentially an improvement of the Delta, improved radar and engine, as well as additional avionics to fire the Bullpup air-to-ground missile, in the event rarely used. The Echo also included two underwing pylons, and for a long time, was the only fighter capable of carrying a Mk 84 2000-pound bomb. First flight for the F-8E was in June 1961, and 286 were produced.

ABOVE LEFT
Good views of the carrier approach from the forward fire station one camera of an RF-8G. These photos were taken by VFP-206 during the squadron's last carrier quals aboard the America *in October 1986. The white outlines denote the landing area of the angled deck, a British innovation of the early 1950s which drastically changed carrier aviation*

ABOVE
How it's done. An RF-8G of VFP-62 demonstrates the finer points of taking air-to-air photography. The subject is a formation of A-6 Intruders, and the photobird, after positioning the bombers, rolls over and below to get different views of the formation, his cameras clicking away

RIGHT
A photomate prepares to install a camera in this RF-8G of VFP-63 at NAS Miramar in 1969. PHs were the camera mechanics, and without their knowledge and dedication, the intensive photo reconnaissance effort during Vietnam would not have been possible

The Remanufacturing Programme

In reality, the F-8E was the last model of the original F-8, and the RF-8A was, actually, the only photo reconnaissance variant; thus, there were only six basic versions of the Crusader. With the growing intensity of the Vietnam War in the mid-1960s, the Navy decided to keep many of its ageing smaller 27C class carriers like the *Hancock*, *Oriskany*, *Intrepid*, *Ticonderoga*, and *Shangri-La*, in operation. Normal operational attrition, as well as heavy combat, had begun to deplete the number of available Crusaders.

The Vought Aeronautics Division of the now-renamed Ling-Temco-Vought (LTV) company, was thus tasked to refurbish existing airframes, reconditioning them and, in many cases, re-equipping them with later avionics suites. The letters G through M were allotted for these remanufactured F-8s, with the letter 'I' omitted.

The most significant modification to all the models was the installation of a wing with a service life of 4000 hours, as well as a longer nose landing gear strut. Two inches longer than the original struts, the new nosegear could absorb 10 per cent more energy. All the modified aircraft would receive stronger main gear, too.

Another major addition was Boundary Layer Control (BLC)—in the F-8J—which first appeared in French F-8s. BLC provides additional lift during take-off and landing by routing engine bleed air over the upper surface of the flaps and ailerons, permitting the aircraft to be flown more slowly, thereby improving the plane's performance around the

carrier. An extensive change, the BLC required internal ducting, a reduction in angle of incidence of the wing, and a larger UHT (unit horizontal tail) to give adequate longitudinal control at the lower landing speeds.

Actually begun in 1965, the first remanufacture concerned the RF-8A. The early photo birds—144 of which were built—were given updated avionics, navigational equipment, new cameras, and the ventral fuselage strakes. Seventy-three RF-8As were eventually modified to become RF-8Gs. The first group of 53 was refurbished from 1965–67, and the second batch of 20 in 1968–70. The RF-8G was ultimately the longest-lived US version of the Crusader, and gave sterling service throughout its long career.

Eighty-nine F-8Ds in all were remanufactured as F-8Hs, beginning in July 1967. The Hotels included underwing pylons and the Bullpup fire-control systems, identifiable by the hump over the wing. A sub-H variant was the F-8P, 35 of which were sold to the Philippines in 1977.

The last major fleet version of the fighter 8 was the Juliet, the F-8J, a remanufactured Echo. Juliet production totalled 136. It was the F-8J that saw the introduction of BLC into US Crusaders, the French having incorporated the system into their new Echos in the mid-60s. Juliets were the main fighter Crusaders on station during the last 18 hectic months of Vietnam, although no Juliet scored a confirmed MiG kill.

The F-8K and L were remanufactured Charlies and Bravos, respectively, and were largely flown by Marine squadrons, although a few Navy utility squadrons operated these later models. The Kilo and Lima featured underwing pylons and new cockpit lighting. Eighty-seven F-8Cs and 61 F-8Bs were remanufactured.

The F-8M was a stillborn proposal to remanufacture low-time F-8As, few of which could be found by that time.

It should be noted that the US Navy adopted similar remanufacturing programmes for two of its other major performers, the A-4 and F-4. While the A-4 programme only saw limited success—most of its remanufactured aircraft ending up in reserve squadrons—the F-4 Phantom achieved a virtual second life, remanufactured F-4Bs (as F-4Ns) and F-4Js (F-4Ss) served in Navy and Marine squadrons through the mid-1980s. Who says the Russians are the only ones who get their money's worth?

In 1967, a small number of F-8As were converted for drone controller duties, with the designation DF-8A. Utility squadrons such as VC-7 and VC-8, operated these unique aircraft which were usually painted in bright colours, and retained their 20 mm cannon armament.

A related control plane designation was the QF-8A, occasionally called DQF-8A. Two of these controller Crusaders were operated by the Naval Missile Test Center at Point Magu, California, and were used to track the Regulus II, a submarine-launched guided missile. Both the DF-8A and QF-8A had knobs and switches in the cockpit which enabled the Crusader pilot to fly the Regulus.

In 1957, Vought installed a rocket engine in the tail of two F8U-1s, numbers 16 and 23. Built by Reaction Motors in New Jersey, the XLF-40 provided 8000

ABOVE LEFT
An RF-8G of VFP-62 moves down the track, its horizontal stabilizers fully deflected, its wing raised, and its flaps down

LEFT
Although the long, one-piece clamshell canopy changed the upper fuselage, it did not alter the basic shape of the two-seater Crusader's family lines. In this clean white and blue-trim paint scheme, the well-travelled 'T' still looks good

ABOVE
The two-seat F8U-1T during carrier trials. The one-of-a-kind F-8 is probably making a touch-and-go to allow the pilots to get the 'feel' of the deck (Art Schoeni)

pounds extra thrust to the 10,000 pounds (15,000 pounds in afterburner) of the normal J57 jet engine. The XLF-40 was fuelled by a highly volatile mixture of hydrogen peroxide and jet fuel (JP). Unfortunately, the rocket engine blew up during an early test, killing two company mechanics, and Reaction Motors pulled out of the project. Vought continued the project using a Rocketdyne XLF-54 engine which gave 6000 pounds thrust.

Although the project never reached flight status, dummy engines were installed above the F8U-1s' tail cones, beneath the rudder. The purpose behind the rocket-assisted Crusader was to provide the F8U with extra power to reach any high-flying Soviet bombers which might appear above 60,000 feet.

Perhaps the most drastic, certainly the longest-lived modification of the basic Crusader fighters was the two-seat trainer, only one of which was built. Originally designated F8U-1T, and later TF-8A, and designed to provide new F-8 pilots with a suitable trainer to make their transition to the Navy's

first supersonic fighter easier, the -1T, dubbed the 'Twosader', was the seventy-seventh production F8U-1. The fighter was lengthened by two feet, a second seat was installed, with a full set of flight controls, and two cannons and ammunition were deleted to make room for the second cockpit. The trainer was the only F-8 to carry a parabrake, located in the tail cone.

The first flight came in February 1962, and Vought then used the two-seater as a demonstrator during a European tour. The British were interested, and would have powered their Twosaders with their own Rolls-Royce Speys, offering 2000 pounds more thrust than the J57-P-20 installed in the -1T. However, the British decided to buy the F-4, and Vought gave the trainer to the Navy's Test Pilot School at Patuxent River. After several years at the Maryland test site, the TF-8A went to the National Air and Space Administration (NASA) at Langley, Virginia, then to Edwards Air Force Base, California.

When Vought got a contract in 1977 to provide refurbished F-8Hs to the Philippines, the trainer was regained from NASA to provide transition training for the Philippine Air Force pilots. However, the T's long career came to an end on 28 July 1978, when Vought pilot Ken Fox and Philippine Lieutenant Pascualito Ramos had engine trouble and had to eject, leaving their aircraft near Dallas. The TF-8A crashed in a farmer's field, ending its 16-year career.

With just one pilot aboard, the F8U-1T taxies in, dragging its parabrake. This 1962 photo shows the lengthened one-piece cockpit canopy and the raised position of the second rear seat

Chapter 4
War in South-east Asia: The First Combat

By the time US participation in the growing conflict in SE Asia took a more active role in the late summer of 1964, the Crusader was firmly established in the Atlantic and Pacific Fleet, in both the fighter and reconnaissance roles. F-8 squadrons and detachments served worldwide. Yet, with the exception of the 1962 Cuban Missile Crisis, and a few isolated, hard to document, encounters with Cuban and other Communist aircraft, the F-8 had not seen combat. Vietnam would change that.

There was talk of a mission over Communist China in the early 1960s where an RF-8A escorted by a fighter—maybe from the carrier *Ticonderoga*'s air wing—penetrated Chinese air space only to be shot down by anti-aircraft fire. The rumour is hard to confirm but is, nonetheless, tantalizing.

The events surrounding the war in Vietnam have been well documented in the last five years, and a retelling here is not necessary. Suffice it to say that as the largely civil war in Vietnam, which had been partitioned in 1954, grew in intensity, the US found its interests lay in supporting the South Vietnamese government, not only with specific supplies and material, but training and a large task force presence off the Vietnamese coastline in the South China Sea.

Prior to the climactic Gulf of Tonkin Incident of early August 1964, US carriers had steamed north and south in support of various land-based operations. The main operation involved aerial reconnaissance using specially-configured RA-3B Skywarriors and RF-8As of VFP-63 detachments. Laos, which had been under direct Communist attack, was of special interest.

In an effort to demonstrate American concern, Air Force and Navy reconnaissance aircraft began flying low level photo runs over the Plain of Jars and along the Laotian panhandle. The *Kitty Hawk* (CVA-63) had three RF-8As and two RA-3Bs.

Early on the morning of 21 May, two of the photo-Crusaders launched for a road reconnaissance. One of the RF-8s was hit by ground fire and began to burn fiercely. Its pilot, Lieutenant Charles F Klusmann, managed to return to his carrier.

The 27C class carrier *Bon Homme Richard* brought three more RF-8As, along with two RA-3Bs. In addition, four Marine RF-8As from VMCJ-1 were also included in beefing up reconnaissance assets. Navy and Air Force aircraft made more than 130 flights in three weeks, from 21 May to 9 June, over Laos.

On 6 June, Lieutenant Klusmann's aircraft was again hit by anti-aircraft fire, but this time, the damage was too severe for a safe return, and Klusman ejected from his Crusader, becoming the first individual to make a combat ejection from a F-8, which, in turn, was the first Crusader lost to enemy action. It was, sadly, to be only the first of many.

Klusmann was captured by Laotian Communist forces and endured three months of torture before he could escape, and eventually make his way to friendly forces. He was awarded the Distinguished Flying Cross, and his experience alerted US commanders to the dangers awaiting American flight crews who parachuted into Communist captivity. How a US aviator should, or could, conduct himself under extreme mental and physical torture became an important, though largely unsolvable, problem throughout the long war in Vietnam. Klusmann's experience barely hinted at the horrible times in store for his fellow aviators.

On 6 June, the same day that Klusmann was shot down, Washington ordered another recon mission to include two RF-8s and eight fighter escorts which would be armed and authorized to deal with the increasing danger of flak and ground fire. The following day, a single RF-8A from *Constellation*'s photo det, with four F-8Ds from *Kitty Hawk*'s VF-111, overflew the Plain of Jars. Ground fire was

heavy, and the F-8Ds delivered their ordnance.

A second mission into central Laos that day included one RF-8A and three escorts. Unfortunately, Commander Doyle W Linn's fighter was hit by heavy flak, and he ejected. A massive rescue effort was immediately launched, with aircraft from the carrier task force, and a standby det from Da Nang, with an A-3 serving as a communications relay. It was not until the following day, 8 June, that a H-34 helicopter was able to scoop Linn from the heavily wooded area he had landed in, and fly him to Thailand. (Commander Linn was killed in 1965 during a strike in North Vietnam.)

The loss of two Crusaders in two days triggered demands from Washington for the reasons for the losses, and the conduct of the missions. This close—

sometimes stifling—management of a local combat operation, would highlight a basic conflict within American military circles throughout the war. One question raised was why had the fighter escort Crusaders carried Sidewinder air-to-air missiles when the defending forces were expected to be on the ground. The Navy replied the prospect of meeting aerial opposition could not be ignored. The answer did not satisfy the managers in the Capitol who had really wanted a big show of strength against Communist flak positions.

The Gulf of Tonkin Incident, August 1964

While America considered how to respond to the increasing Communist activity in South Vietnam, the South Vietnamese themselves had been busy with small commando raids on enemy bases along the Chinese coast and on offshore islands. The US had also instituted a standing destroyer patrol, code-named De Soto, which, from 1962, collected bits of electronic intelligence. The patrol was extended to include the North Vietnamese coast, even though both Communist countries were known to be quite unhappy about this offshore surveillance.

Preparations for the August 1964 De Soto Patrol included the *Ticonderoga* (CVA-14), one of the smaller 27C carriers. *Tico*'s aircraft would be on immediate call to protect one of the De Soto destroyers, the *Maddox*, if the ship called for help.

As it transpired, the *Maddox* was attacked early on the morning of 2 August after it had passed close to the North Vietnamese island of Hon Me. Communist PT boats came out from their nearby base and began to make runs on the American destroyer. Although nothing came of these early runs, another sortie by the PT boats in the afternoon resulted in a torpedo attack on the *Maddox*.

Ticonderoga sent four F-8Es from VF-51 and VF-53, already airborne, to the scene of the attack.

The F-8s were armed with Zunis and cannon. They went after the North Vietnamese boats who fired back, hitting one of the Crusaders, its pilot, Lieutenant, j.g. Dick Hastings, making an emergency landing at Da Nang. While the VF-51 F-8s, led by Commander James Stockdale, squadron skipper, and Lieutenant Hastings, attacked two PTs, the two VF-53 Crusaders (Commander Robair Mohrhardt and Lieutenant Commander Charles Southwick) hit a single PT with Zunis then cannon fire. The PT stopped and began to burn; it eventually sank. (Lieutenant Commander Southwick eventually shot down a MiG-17 in 1967 while flying F-4s with VF-114, but soon afterwards was shot down and became a POW.)

A second North Vietnamese attack, this time at night, two days later against the *Maddox* and *Turner Joy* brought increased American indignation, and more direct action from *Ticonderoga* aircraft. Whether this second attack actually took place has been the subject of discussion, but there is more weight on the side which says it did.

On 5 August, aircraft from the *Constellation* and *Ticonderoga* launched a strike—codenamed Pierce Arrow—against PT boat bases. Along with A-4 and A-1 bombers, F-8 escorts and two RF-8As made up the first strike group from *Tico*. A second group from *Connie* launched 45 minutes later.

While the attack proceeded toward its targets, President Lyndon B Johnson went on American television to address the American people. Many people in the military felt the President's speech alerted the North Vietnamese long before it was necessary, and their defences were waiting for the US

aircraft. Although no Crusaders were shot down, two bombers were destroyed. Lieutenant, j.g. Everett Alvarez, Jr, of VA-144, ejected from his A-4C after taking a hit, and became the first POW since Lieutenant Klusmann's capture. He remained in captivity until 1973. Lieutenant, j.g. Richard Sather, an A-1 pilot from VA-145, was shot down and killed during the attack, thus becoming the first naval aviator to die in the Vietnam conflict.

A gigantic buildup in air, sea, and land forces began as America flooded SE Asia with overt support. Navy ships continued their patrols, and on 18 September, a destroyer signalled she was being taken under attack. The carrier *Bon Homme Richard* launched two F-8Cs. Lieutenant, j.g. Dudley Moore was a junior pilot with VF-194 in the *Bon Homme Richard*:

Lieutenant Robert J Woodrow and I were assigned Condition CAP one night shortly after the *Bonnie Dick* arrived on Dixie Station. I was strapped in with four Sidewinders on my F-8C, BuNo 146920, back in the pack. Woody was on the port cat.

After a couple of hours of boredom, lights came on everywhere and people started running around knocking off chains and hooking up starter hoses. I cranked up as Woody launched. I followed him on a heading of 300 degrees. We were also given a departure frequency.

The TACAN failed right off—they always did. Great! Now what? I finally got the radio working near the relay destroyer. They said continue heading 300 degrees; a destroyer was in trouble. I called Woody but we were too far apart for join-up. Turning off the external lights, I set cruise at 20,000 feet over some cloud layers and droned on. The radio was intermittent.

Switching over to another frequency, I heard nothing

WAR IN SOUTH-EAST ASIA

but chaos. Lots of shooting, a big 5-incher going full blast. Taking stock of the situation, I had a full load of gas, about 300 miles from the ship, and no idea where I was. I called the destroyer, but got no answer, just a lot of shooting.

I figured I couldn't do much good with Sidewinders and couldn't see much down on the deck. Nothing visible on the ocean, just some clouds. If I spent any time running around on the deck, I probably couldn't make it back to the ship.

I just kept going. Eventually, through the breaks in the clouds, I saw city lights. Great, I thought, I'm in China! I quickly turned around.

On the way back, I ran into a bunch of F-4s, lights flashing, heading up to the big flail. Lots of luck, I thought.

I tanked on an A-4 and after a couple wild stabs at the deck, I managed to trap. Below decks, everyone was bugging down to intelligence. They wanted to know what happened. Bob Woodrow made one pass from altitude, got shot at by the destroyer, and left.

To this day, I don't know if anything went on. What was supposed to be a 30-day cruise turned into a three-month extension. Looked like we had ourselves a war—sort of.

One note: The mission, 2.2. hours, was never logged since it officially never happened. Apparently, the individual manning the destroyer's radar did not push the right button, and all the targets it was tracking were moving at the same speed as the destroyer. The ship was shooting at nothing.

Without proper illumination, the two Crusaders could not see their targets, although Lieutenant Woodrow reported seeing two wakes close to one of the destroyers. The American ships reported sinking one PT, but an exhaustive search the next morning revealed nothing, no debris or oil.

Eventually the crisis atmosphere of the August and September incidents subsided, and the South China Sea was quiet for a time. However, the attitude of the US had greatly changed, and preparations began for a wider war.

In December, a programme of armed reconnaissance and strike missions—codenamed Barrel Roll—began against specific communist facilities along various road networks. The first Barrel Roll mission was flown on 17 December, by four A-1 Skyraiders and four F-4s, followed by two RF-8As, all from Air Wing 9 in the USS *Ranger* (CVA-61). Initially, the Barrel Roll missions yielded little, but the programme continued into 1965, and eventually began uncovering the extent of the massive communist supply operation along the incredible network of trails and roads called the Ho Chi Minh Trail.

The Crusader's role during this early period of Vietnam combat was, in large part, one of reconnaissance. Fighter 8s performed escort duties, and occasionally delivered Zunis against selected ground targets, but it was the RF-8As of the various VFP-63 detachments, along with Marine RF-8s of VMCJ-1, which performed the greatest service.

VMCJ-1 had been alerted several times earlier in the year to be ready to deploy to SE Asia at eight hours' notice. After the Gulf of Tonkin Incident, the squadron sent two RF-8As and 15 men to the *Constellation* by way of Japan and the Philippines. When the *Connie* left the war zone, its Marine reconnaissance det transferred to the *Bon Homme Richard*. During a photo mission, Captain L J Draayer, overflew an enemy gun emplacement. One of the Navy pilots who had been escorting him had been shot down, and Captain Draayer overflew the crash site to see if the Navy pilot was all right.

LEFT
VF-111 was one of only two Crusader squadrons to fly the Delta in combat, in the early years of the war. The Sundowners also made use of one of the most ancient of aircraft markings, the tiger mouth. In 1965, an F-8D prepares to move up to the catapult on the Midway for a mission against Viet Cong targets in South Vietnam's Delta. The stream enveloping the deck crewmen is from the previous launch

ABOVE
The veteran carrier Oriskany early in the war. The 27C carrier displays her A-1s, A-4s, and F-8s

Although the Navy pilot eventually was recovered, Captain Draayer received a 'royal dressing down' for endangering his photos.

A second detachment relieved the *Connie/Bonnie Dick* det on 29 September. The newcomers received their indoctrination to shipboard life from their Navy hosts in VF-194.

The four plane captains in the second det had no experience on the Crusader, having only worked on the squadron's ancient EF-10Bs, the ELINT-version of the Korean War-vintage Douglas F3D Skyknight. However, the youngsters were quickly cross-trained on the RF-8As.

The Marines found life aboard the World War II era carriers less than ideal. A lack of air conditioning, and water restriction made the close atmosphere a test of endurance for everyone. However, the three VMCJ-1 dets provided a measure of relief for the hard-pressed Navy photo dets. And, even when there were not enough Marine aviators, the Navy 'borrowed' their Leatherneck cousins' aircraft.

Richard A Bishop was one of the plane captains in the second det aboard the *Bon Homme Richard*. A few of his memories of the 1964 experience follow:

I think we all experienced a certain amount of apprehension that was compounded by the fact that we did not have the luxury of time to become oriented. One night we were drinking beer in a bar in Olongapo, and, less than 24 hours later, we were actively involved in combat operations. We stumbled through our first couple of launches and recoveries by watching and talking to the Navy plane captains.

It did not take us long to find out that combat operations on the flight deck of a carrier can be hot, tiring, dirty, long and dangerous. On a typical day, we would launch and recover aircraft four or five times. It was very seldom that

ABOVE
As the deck crewman signals a successful trap, this F-8E of VMF(AW)-212 returns from a combat mission during the Oriskany's *1965 cruise. This would be the last time a Marine squadron sailed in a Navy carrier in combat until 1972*

Scenes aboard the Oriskany *in 1965:*

TOP RIGHT
'Ordies'—red-shirted ordnancemen—prepare bombs for F-8Es of VMF(AW)-212 during Oriskany's *1965 cruise*

CENTRE RIGHT
As the pilot waits, two crewmen make last-minute adjustments on his F-8's Zuni pods. This pilot of this VMF(AW)-212 Echo could be the air wing commander, James Stockdale, who was shot down and imprisoned in September 1965

BOTTOM RIGHT
An ordnanceman loads the cannons of this F-8E during the 1965 Vietnam cruise of the Oriskany. *20 mm fire was an effective strafing weapon, especially against lightly constructed barges and junks*

the flight deck crew was ever able to sleep past 0500. By the time we recovered the last flight, serviced the aircraft, spotted them for the next morning's launch, it was 2200. This went on seven days a week.

During flight operations, we were required to have two plane captains on each aircraft, at all times. We had to preflight the aircraft, service any systems requiring attention, secure the aircraft with two tie-down chains per landing gear during the day—three at night—and ride the brakes during spotting, or positioning, the plane. Since someone had to be with the aircraft all the time, we had to eat and perform our personal chores in shifts.

The only time we really had any free time was when our aircraft were out on a mission, maybe 1½ to 2 hours. Some of the guys would find a shop or office where they could just sit and drink coffee. A lot of time was spent talking with a friend and watching the water go by. Every once in a while, one of the destroyers escorting us would stop in the water and let their crews swim off the side of the ship, lowering nets to close off a small section in case there were sharks around.

I think launching the aircraft—at least for the first few times—scared me more than any other operation aboard the carrier. With all the aircraft turning up, you couldn't hear anything. If you saw someone walk directly in front of an intake, or about to walk into the exhaust blast of an aircraft, you were helpless to yell a warning. All you could do was watch. This became especially true as we got more tired and became lax in safety precautions.

I would like to think I may have saved a sailor's life while we were launching aircraft one afternoon. The aircraft to the left of my plane pulled out and made a left turn onto the catapult. I saw what was about to happen, and knew I was going to be hit by the full exhaust blast. I ducked down under my plane's nose and straddled one of the tie-down chains. With my back to the turning aircraft, I grabbed the chain between my legs and held on for dear life. I looked up and noticed a sailor standing on the flight deck in front of my aircraft. He had not seen the turning plane and caught the full blast and was thrown toward the side of the ship. As he flew by, I managed to reach out and grab his shirt while still holding the chain with my other hand.

Recovery could also get a little hairy. Once the aircraft landed, the pilots would fold the wings and taxi up to the bow. The planes would be chocked, chained, and the engines shut down. Once the recovery was completed, we would immediately start refuelling, refilling oxygen bottles, and hanging bombs and rockets for the next launch, all at the same time, something you never did during peacetime. One spark or drop of fuel in combination with liquid oxygen could have blown us all away.

Bishop's det transferred to the *Ticonderoga* on 9 October, with VF-53 as their hosts. They went to the *Constellation* on 29 October, now attached to Carrier Air Group 14, and were eventually relieved by a new VMCJ-1 det on 10 November.

As the buildup of American forces in SE Asia began in earnest following the Gulf of Tonkin Incident, F-8s served on every carrier in the South China Sea, at least in the reconnaissance role, and, in the case of the smaller 27C class and *Midway* class (*Midway*, *Coral Sea*, and *Franklin D Roosevelt*) carriers, in the fighter role, as well. While the larger ships included F-4B Phantom squadrons as their primary fighter complement, the smaller decks made full use of the F-8's bomb-toting capabilities.

While the military situation in Vietnam had quieted down following the sporadic strikes of late summer, a Communist attack on American and South Vietnamese facilities in February 1965, brought increased US response. A programme of regular bombing raids—codenamed Rolling Thunder—began in February. The carriers *Coral Sea*, *Hancock*, and *Ranger*, contributed their aircraft

61

ABOVE LEFT
Probably one of the more celebrated Vietnam F-8 drivers was then-Commander James Stockdale. The first to attain 1000 hours in the Crusader, Stockdale led F-8s in the first actions in the Gulf of Tonkin Incident of August 1964. Promoted to CAG, Stockdale was shot down in an A-4 during a strike in September 1965, taken prisoner, and endured over 7 years of torture and incarceration. He received the Medal of Honor, and eventually retired as a vice admiral

BELOW LEFT
Lieutenant Colonel Charles H Ludden was the senior aviator in CVW-16 when Commander James Stockdale was shot down. By prior agreement between Stockdale and the captain of the Oriskany, *Ludden assumed the leadership of the air wing, the first Marine to command a carrier air wing since World War II*

ABOVE
'Ordies' and the brown-shirted plane captains, prepare an F-8 for a mission over North Vietnam in 1968. The cramped space on a 27C carrier's flight deck is indicated by the fact that the Crusader's nose gear is jammed against the catapult track. The crewman near the fighter's Sidewinder missiles—four are mounted—carries tie-down chains. His right foot is over a pad-eye which takes one end of the stout chain, while the other end is attached to the aircraft

to attacks on North Vietnamese bases. The Rolling Thunder missions were originally given numbers, but as the war wound on, the numbers were forgotten.

Lieutenant j.g. Tom Irwin, a young F-8C pilot with VF-24 flew De Soto Patrols in December and January, and participated in the 17 February 1965 strike into North Vietnam, followed four days later by another raid on the Chan Hoa barracks near Dong Hoi airfield. He recalled the early days of the war:

By the middle of March 1965, daily strikes had become routine. At this time the strikes were handled as ship-wide strikes, with one big one for the day. They had all the support elements—tankers, weather, recce, AEW, CAP—and, on occasion, flak suppression with Zunis.

The CAP were armed with 400 rounds of 20 mm and two Sidewinders, sometimes four later on. One problem for the F-8Es in VF-211 was that if they returned with all four Sidewinders, their maximum landing weight dictated a max fuel load of 1200 pounds, usually at or below Bingo. So we sometimes ended up with the F-8Es flying lead, using their better air intercept radar, while we in the Charlies were the actual CAP. The Charlies, without hardpoint wings, could come aboard with the four 'winders and 2500 pounds of fuel due to their lighter basic weight.

The early strikes were fairly simple. The main group rendezvoused over the ship at various altitudes and when everyone was aboard, off we went to the target at altitudes up to 24,000 feet.

On one occasion, the A-1s had been launched early and were en route to the coast-in point for at least an hour before the jets launched. Due to stronger than forecast headwinds, they were still about 10 to 15 minutes from the target when the jets arrived overhead. We just continued orbiting the target at 20,000 until the Spads arrived and rolled in. There were no high altitude air defences at this point, except a few large calibre guns which could only be used as flak barrage and were ineffective against high flying jets. The next year SAMs were introduced, and MiGs started coming out. The tactics changed and we came in at medium altitude, 3000–4500 feet, and went as fast as the slowest element of the strike group.

As the SAM sites began to multiply, they became a big threat to the F-8s as the early ECM [Electronic countermeasures] equipment went first to the A-4s. I remember a jury-rigged set in 1966 which consisted of a D-cell battery-powered receiver with an antenna attached to the canopy with suction cups. You couldn't turn it on to test it until you were airborne because the ship's radar would burn it up on deck. The antenna came down around you like a spider web during the catapult stroke.

Most pilots felt they could avoid a SAM if they got a warning from an offshore ECM aircraft and they saw the missile. These warnings were in some kind of grid code from the ECM aircraft, usually EA-3s.

The *Hancock*'s two F-8 fighter squadrons, VF-24 and VF-211, flew two different models of the Crusader. VF-24 flew the F-8C, and used it strictly in the traditional escort and CAP roles. VF-211 also used their fighters as escorts, and in fact, became the first US fighter squadron to encounter North Vietnamese MiGs, on 3 April 1965, when MiG-17s intercepted a bombing raid on the Thanh Hoa Bridge. One VF-211 F-8E was damaged. However, the Checkmates of VF-211 who had obtained their Echoes in February 1964, used their fighters against ground targets, too.

In May, two F-8Es from VF-211 escorted an RF-8A on a photo mission over Thanh Hoa, soon to become a legend among all the American air crews in Vietnam. Lieutenant Rich Maughlin watched as the VFP-63 photobird began its run at a very low altitude, perhaps to take forward fire pictures to show progress in bridge reconstruction following Air Force attacks. Both services kept up cyclic raids on the bridge.

Following the photo run, the RF-8A pilot reported taking hits from 12.7 flak which had taken off his outer wing panel. The two fighters fired their Zunis at the gun emplacement on the north embankment. At this time, Crusaders carried a mixture of Zunis and Sidewinders on their fuselage 'cheek' mounts, leaving the wings clean. Maughlin and his wingman, Dale Deweese, escorted the damaged RF-8A clear. Maughlin could see the gunners, with the director in their centre, pointing to the American planes rocketing over their position at 500 knots, *below* 10 feet.

As the three Crusaders flew over the gun position, Maughlin felt his plane shudder from a 37 mm hit. The shell had struck the vertical tail, leaving a three-foot hole, barely missing vital hydraulic lines.

He joined the RF-8A and they inspected the damage to their aircraft. The return to the ship was uneventful, and the three planes recovered. However, the damage to Maughlin's F-8E was so severe that his fighter's tail I-beam was bent *outside* the tail. The plane had to be catapulted off to the Philippines because the *Hancock*'s facilities could not repair such major damage.

The Black Knights of VF-154, in the *Coral Sea*'s Air Wing 15, were one of only two squadrons flying the F-8D from carriers in Vietnam, the other being VF-111. VF-154 was also one of the first Navy Crusader squadrons, having taken their first F-8As (F8U-1s) in early 1957. The squadron had participated in deployments to the troubled Formosa Strait in 1958 when a short war between communist China and the Taiwanese government threatened peace in the area. VF-154's F-8s flew from the *Hancock*, ready to take on the Communists should the efforts of the Taiwanese Air Force prove futile. However, direct US assistance was not needed.

During *Coral Sea*'s 1965 Vietnam cruise, VF-154 lost five Crusaders to enemy action, three in four days. VF-211 had not lost any aircraft to the intense ground fire, and offered to help VF-154. It was the Checkmates' assessment that the Black Knights were using peacetime delivery tactics—80 per cent power, speedbrakes out, at 250 knots indicated air speed. VF-211 told VF-154 to make their runs as fast as possible. However, the Black Knights replied this recommendation was not proper. It was to be

An RF-8G of VFP-206 overflies Lake Tahoe in California's High Sierras in 1985 (VFP-206)

BuNo 140446, a Crusader prototype, aboard the Forrestal
for carrier quals in 1956

*An F-8C of VF-32 in the late 1950s. This aircraft carries
a full load of four Sidewinders and has its arresting hook
down indicating it is preparing to recover aboard its
carrier, the* Saratoga (Dwight Timm)

TOP
This F-8E of VF-162 carries two Sidewinders during an early Vietnam cruise as part of Air Wing 16 in the Oriskany (Bud Flagg)

ABOVE
Red-shirted 'ordies' finish preparing a Sidewinder-armed F-8E of VF-162 for a mission during the Oriskany's *1965 combat cruise. This Echo will carry four Sidewinders, indicating the upcoming mission is either CAP or strike escort. The Hunters had one of the more striking marking schemes of the Vietnam period, with yellow-and-black stars and stripes applied on the tail, wings, and lower forward fuselage* (Bud Flagg)

ABOVE RIGHT
An F-8J of VF-194 prepares for a launch from the
Oriskany *during the veteran carrier's last cruise in 1975.
The jet blast deflector (JBD) is coming up, and the deck
crew is huddled between the two bow cats to remain clear of
the launch area* (Chuck Scott)

BELOW RIGHT
A VFP-306 RF-8G moves up to the bow catapults of the
Ranger *during the reserve TACAIR Test in November
1976. An F-4B Phantom is approaching the deck* (Author)

The crowded hangar bay of the 27C class carrier Bon Homme Richard *during its 1968 cruise. Maintenance crews worked in the dimly lit space immediately below the flight deck* (John Kuchinski)

A flight of F-8Hs of VF-201, one of the Naval Air Reserve squadrons from NAS Dallas, Texas, in 1973. Except on specific weapons training missions, reserve fighters rarely fly with external stores, and since the F-8 seldom flew with external fuel tanks, relying on its in-flight refuelling capabilities, it is not surprising to see these Hotels 'clean'. The reserves transitioned to F-4Bs in 1974–5 (Bud Flagg)

The TF-8A two-seater at the Naval Air Test Center, NAS Patûxent, Maryland in August 1973. The red mesh screen over the air intake protects against ingesting FOD during engine run-ups. Note the black tail of a visiting EA-6A of VMCJ-2 (Author)

A red-nosed F-8E of VMF-235 at Da Nang in 1967. The Crusader is loaded with 5-inch Zunis, iron bombs, and 20 mm cannon. This aircraft has obviously seen much combat, evidenced by its blackened gun ports and dirty lower fuselage

Two VFP-206 Crusaders fly through Arizona's Monument Valley, en route to NAS Fallon in July 1985 (John Peck)

VF-154's only cruise with the F-8. The squadron returned home after a record 331-day deployment, and transitioned to F-4Bs in November.

Bonnie Dick had also participated in the heavy combat of 1965, moving up and down the Vietnamese coast from Dixie Station to Yankee Station and back again as requirements dictated. As indicated earlier, the carrier's VFP-63/VMCJ-1 photo Crusaders were kept very busy. The first combat operations began on 26 May and continued until 2 July.

Two weeks later, the carrier was back on the line at Dixie Station with two new F-8E squadrons. VF-191 and VF-194 used their F-8Es in escort and ground attack roles, even though, to their frustration, parts for their planes and ground equipment were in short supply in depots in the Philippines. Even the ship's LSO platform suffered from lack of parts. Both fighter squadrons lost several aircraft during this cruise. VF-191 lost three F-8s to anti-aircraft fire, and one to a surface-to-air missile (SAM). VF-194 lost three to flak, and one in an operational mishap.

In 1965, the *Oriskany* (CVA-34) made an event-filled combat cruise from May to November. She included three different Crusader squadrons in her Air Wing 16. VFP-63's Det G and VF-162 were the two Navy squadrons, flying the RF-8A and F-8E respectively. VMF(AW)-212 was a Marine squadron, also flying the F-8E, having converted from A-4s in 1963. *Oriskany*'s original second fighter squadron, VF-161, flew F-3 Demons, which were being rapidly replaced in the fleet by Phantoms. Thus, to keep a common aircraft in the wing, for mission and maintenance considerations, the Lancers were brought aboard in January 1965.

Having a Marine squadron was a unique situation for a Navy aircraft carrier. While Marine units had operated from carriers before—indeed, since the beginnings of US carrier aviation in the 1920s, and had even had their own small carriers in the Pacific near the end of World War II—the Navy had never regularly included Marines in the regular air wing complement. Thus, the questions of keeping the Marine pilots carrier qualified, as well as the very purpose of Marine aviation, were always before Navy and Marine planners.

However, the Lancers of VMF(AW)-212, led by Lieutenant Colonel Charles H Ludden, became an integral part of *Oriskany*'s air wing. In a unique turn of events, when Commander James B Stockdale, commander of the wing, was shot down on 9 September, during a strike, the most senior naval aviator in the wing was Lieutenant Colonel Ludden. By prior agreement between Commander Stockdale and Captain Bart Connolly, commanding officer of the *Oriskany*, Ludden, who was well liked and respected by his peers, would take over CVW-16 in the event of Stockdale's being shot down. Thus, Air Wing 16 had a Marine as its leader until 4 October, when Commander R E Spruit assumed command.

VF-162: The Hunters at War

Tuesday, 25 May 1965

Well, at long last, I can consider myself to be a combat pilot, as I made my first strike today. I didn't see anyone shooting at me, but I did blow up a house . . .

Lieutenant W F Flagg's letter to his wife told of his first mission in Vietnam, three weeks after *Oriskany*'s aircraft had fired their first shots in the 'O-Boat's' first combat cruise since the Korean War. He was a member of VF-162, and was the Hunters' Quality Assurance (QA) officer in the squadron's maintenance department. He had remained in Japan in November 1963 when the carrier went to the South China Sea to cover any possibilities after the assassination of South Vietnamese President Diem.

Flagg had also made the 72,000th landing on the *Oriskany*, much to the consternation of his commanding officer who had had the slot assured until he bolstered, missing all four arresting cables, and had to take his Crusader around for another try. Flagg, a young lieutenant, j.g., had not appreciated the protocol of the moment, and successfully trapped—made an arrested landing—leaving his skipper angrily circling above.

The CO did not speak to Flagg for several days and did not come to the traditional cake ceremony. He told Flagg,

'Damn it! You're supposed to do everything I do. If I bolter, *you* bolter!'

Later, while Lieutenant Flagg was QA officer, he found getting parts for the F-8s was a problem. However, the more the squadron flew its aircraft, the more the Crusaders remained operational. He decided this 'up' status was due to the hydraulic seals. Typically, F-8s always leaked hydraulic fluid, but the leaks became more pronounced if the individual aircraft did not fly regularly. The seals would dry out and become brittle. Thus, when the plane did fly, the seals would crack and the fluid would run out.

During the initial stages of the 1965 combat deployment, VF-162 pushed its fighter role because, quite naturally, all the squadron pilots wanted a chance at a MiG. Their Marine counterparts in VMF(AW)-212 assumed the role of the bombers, much to the amusement of the A-1 Skyraider pilots of VA-152. The A-1H drivers claimed they dropped more bombs on the catapult than the F-8s did on their targets. Eventually, the Hunters assumed more bombing duties:

After the Tonkin Gulf Incident, we found the F-8 had a new role since we were the first F-8Es with the so-called hard-point wings. We ended up carrying MERS and TERS, dropping bombs and shooting rockets. Up to now, everything had been done with the fuselage stations. We spent a lot of time at Fallon in the summer of 64, learning how to drop bombs. For us fighter pilots, that was an experience in itself. I won't say we got proficient at

Lieutenant Bud Flagg took this self portrait during a 1965 mission. Occasionally, the intelligence department issued 35 mm cameras to pilots in case they stumbled across something interesting, like a ship or target. After a long, boring CAP flight, Flagg decided to run off the roll of film and took many shots of himself as the young fighter pilot. There was little intelligence value in his effort, however, and the department never asked him for help again. His well-used helmet is all black with yellow stars (Bud Flagg)

dropping bombs, but we dropped our fair share that summer.

In 1965, the air wing was brought together. VF-161 was transitioning from F-3s, so we were joined by VMF-212 from Kaneohe, Hawaii, for the last two weeks in April. It was nice to have a Marine squadron aboard. Needless to say, as all Marine squadrons, they were very colourful. Initially, when they joined us, they had their share of excitement, but they completed the ORE and settled down to become one of the finest F-8 squadrons I ever had the pleasure of working with.

However, although the F-8s had no bomb sight, they were found to be excellent flak suppressors, as well as ground support aircraft, and the F-8 worked in these important roles throughout the war:

We first hit Yankee Station in late May 1965. The action was really strong, although we only spent two days on Yankee Station, and then went south to work in-country for two months. We later called it 'Vacationland' because seldom did anyone shoot back at you. It was neat down there. We worked with a FAC. On occasion we were called on for flak suppression because we had our four 20 mm cannon.

But, one of my first engagements was with an Army company which had been pinned down by the Viet Cong. We came in over those guys—they had panels out—and I led the fighter sweep with all guns blazing. The report came back that we'd driven the communists off with our firepower, and the Army was greatful. That was one of the few occasions I thought we'd done something other than shoot up the jungle.

Once, I led a division of four planes. An FAC gave us extensive information, especially about an area particularly VC-infested. He particularly wanted one village known to

be a supply depot. And after all his pin-point accurate co-ordinates, we rolled in and made one pass, a dummy run, to confirm it. He said, 'That's it!' So we made a second run and unloaded everything we had, and got numerous secondary explosions and pulled off. The FAC said we'd got the wrong village! I couldn't understand it. Then he said that was the other village he wanted, too. It was also VC-controlled, so it didn't matter.

There were the previously noted problems with the cannon. The pilots selected either the upper or lower pair of guns so that even if one set jammed, another pair was available. The jamming problem was due largely to the effect of high Gs on the ammunition belts. In high-G turns, the force would cause the linkage to curl and bind, creating the possibility of a missed, or jammed, round. The electronics associated with the guns worked well enough, however, at least for the Hunters of VF-162.

The big Zuni rockets also had problems at the moment of ignition. They would shoot particles back toward the Crusader's tail and could cause damage.

The multiple ejector racks (MERs), which enabled aircraft to carry several bombs on one attachment point, were difficult to obtain in 1965. The F-8 was one of only two aircraft able to carry a 2000-pound bomb. The A-4 seldom carried the huge weapon. However, the Crusaders were loaded with the big bomb in an effort to put a large amount of ordnance on a target.

Dropping 4000 pounds of bombs simultaneously caused problems at the moment of release. The F-8 became unbalanced for a second or so, which created severe control problems, as well as overstressing the aircraft. Finally, a release mechanism was devised which allowed a one-two drop of the bombs.

On 7 October, VMF(AW)-212 participated in an attack against the Vu Chua railway bridge, between Hanoi and the Communist China border. Eight Marine F-8Es, each loaded with two 2000-pound bombs, made runs through intense anti-aircraft fire at the north end of the bridge, leaving the bridge and tracks twisted and mangled.

VF-162 did its share of ground attack missions, using Zunis and 20 mm ammunition. In June, Lieutenant Flagg fired all eight Zunis at a junk which was supplying munitions to the communists. But all of the rockets missed, much to the young pilot's embarrassment. He destroyed the junk with can-nonfire.

Another mission in July was more productive. During a TARCAP (target combat aircraft patrol) south of Vinh, in southern North Vietnam, Flagg and his wingman spotted a glint of sunlight which turned out to be one of the numerous small North Vietnamese trains. At the sound of the approaching American jets, the crew abandoned their train. The F-8s strafed the helpless target, walking their bullets up and down the length of the train. A flight of A-4s demanded that the F-8s depart and let them—the *real* bombers—expend their ordnance. Flagg told them

Commander Dick Bellinger (left) congratulates Lieutenant Bud Flagg after awarding him the Navy Commendation Medal for a 1965 combat mission. Bellinger was an extremely colourful pilot and squadron commander, like the Marines' Pappy Boyington, and eventually scored the Navy's first kill over a MiG-21 in Vietnam

they could have what was left of the train when he and his wingman were through. The HEI—high explosive incendiary—20 mm literally exploded the light box cars. The A-4s then layed down 500-pound bombs, straddling the helpless little engine, blowing it completely off the tracks onto its side.

The *Oriskany*'s combat cruise lasted through to November, 256 days, with 210 days at sea. Air Wing 16's aircraft attacked North Vietnamese targets constantly, flying through intense flak. VF-162 lost one plane to flak, while VMF(AW)-212 lost two to flak, and two to non-combat mishaps. One Marine pilot was killed. VFP-63's photo detachment lost two aircraft and two pilots.

While all the losses were keenly felt, the most troubling was that of the air wing commander, Jim Stockdale. As CAG, he had led a strike on 9 September, in an A-4, although he was a true F-8 pilot; he was the first man to reach 1000 hours in the Crusader. Stockdale was interned under the harshest conditions by the North Vietnamese, and eventually received the Medal of Honor for his leadership during the time he was a prisoner.

Back in the States, the wives of the pilots formed their own support groups to deal with the stress of knowing their husbands were in combat, and especially when the dreaded news arrived that a pilot had been shot down and was killed or missing.

The leader of the group, quite naturally, was Commander Stockdale's wife. She admonished the air wing wives to be prepared for hard times.

'Some of you will be affected', she told them. Of course, it was only a little later when her own husband

was listed as missing and began his own hellish period of internment and torture.

Finally, the cruise ended. Lieutenant Flagg wrote to his wife:

Wednesday, 10 November 1965

A quiet afternoon, and here I am. We are still plagued by bad weather, so flying hasn't been too good. The word is out that we are going south for a couple of days, or at least until the weather improves. Everyone is real happy about this as it will be like a vacation—no missiles, no one shooting at you . . .

Only 16 combat days left, and this is something everyone is really counting, more so than the days until we get home. I think I am counting both, though, as I am looking forward so much to being home with you.

God knows what a terrible, terrifying thing this cruise has been. I just pray I won't have to make another one.

Wednesday, 18 November 1965

How happy I am that this day has come to an end. And I know a lot of other people are, too. It was truly a tragic day for Air Wing 16, as it was the greatest single-day losses we've ever had: six aircraft and two pilots, none from 162.

How I pray these next nine days will fly by with ever-increasing speed. This whole stinking mess makes me sick to my stomach.

There are so many restrictions on us that we don't really fight a war like we've been trained to, or should. The ignorance that is shown by the individuals that are running this war is unbelievable. Time and again we strike the same area, and each time the North Vietnamese are better prepared . . .

Tuesday, 26 November 1965

I flew my last combat sorties this morning, and in a couple

of hours, the ship will be heading home, via Cubi Point. It's hard to believe that it is all over, but I thank God it is . . .

I compiled a total of 90 combat sorties, with 188.8 hours over Vietnam. Five Air Medals, one Vietnamese medal, one Navy Commendation Medal . . . Air Wing 16 has proven to be second to none. We accomplished a lot and established many new records . . .

While his enthusiasm for the air wing and squadron is understandable, so is Flagg's resentment toward the micromanaging which characterized the entire war. Frustratingly restrictive rules of engagement (ROE), target requirements, and inter-service arguments hampered every pilot who flew, and the problem was never solved, and in a very large sense, contributed to the ultimate victory by the Communists in 1975. During a mission in 1965, two VF-162 Crusader pilots discovered how frustrating an encounter with a sister service could be at this early stage of the war:

Once, two of us launched for a weather recce in the north-west corner of Vietnam to see if a planned alpha strike could launch. When I went to the briefing, I said we'd probably need a tanker because the distance was so great, coupled with the fact they wanted a report 45 minutes after our launch, which meant max speed to get there. Everyone agreed there'd be no problem getting a tanker to us.

We proceeded to the area, checked out the weather— low, dense fog, which totally obliterated the target in a valley—and we called back to cancel the strike. We started heading back, calling for the tanker. Well, they said the tanker was delayed, but we knew our fuel was critical.

The Air Force Base at Udorn, Thailand, had been briefed as an emergency field which we could use—if we had to. So, we headed for Udorn, maybe 100 miles to the south. After landing at Udorn—there were camouflage nets and F-105s all over the place—we were met by five jeeps. An Air Force captain came up to my F-8 and told me not to shut down. We couldn't stay there. In fact, we weren't even allowed to be there since we'd been up over North Vietnam. No aircraft which had been operating over the North could fly into Udorn. What a mess.

I asked him what the 105s were doing there and he told me it was none of my business. So, I told him we didn't have enough gas to get back. He said okay, told me to shut down, and they'd gas us. Since my wingman had lost his radio, he'd have to go back with me.

We shut down, stayed in the aircraft, and they refuelled us. We started up, were cleared for an immediate take-off, and returned to the ship. Half-way to the ship, the Fudd (E-1) called us to say the tanker was airborne. I told him we didn't need it now.

After we trapped, a sailor met me before I unstrapped and told me I was to report to the bridge immediately. I tried to figure what I'd done now. We got up to the bridge to find that the Air Force had apparently sent a flash message which beat us back. They were totally disgruntled about our side trip to Udorn, after flying over North Vietnam. It was off-limits. We'd evidently been denying for months that we were operating out of Thailand into Vietnam. Actually, the F-105s there told me we were.

The captain of the ship was upset; the admiral was upset; my own CO was upset. I was told I should never have gone to Udorn. The only guy who stuck up for me was the XO, Dick Bellinger.

He said, 'Flagg was briefed it was an emergency field. The tanker didn't launch, and he needed gas. What was he supposed to do?' Then, everyone stopped picking on me. I'd done exactly as briefed. A month later, the US came out and fully acknowledged that we were operating out of Thailand, with the F-105s.

Chapter 5
Fighting the Big War, 1966-67

Enemy Defences

The Guns

As the war grew in intensity in 1966, especially with increased American attacks on Communist war-making industry, like POL (petroleum, oil and lubricants) facilities, so did the North Vietnamese defences, and they took a terrible toll of all American aircraft.

Initially, the aircrews' main concern was the small arms fire. Every enemy troop could be expected to have some form of rifle or small machine gun, and below 1200 feet, these weapons could—and did—bring a plane down. By 1965, highly capable anti-aircraft cannon, 23 mm, 37 mm, 57 mm, and the huge 100 mm—usually found in the larger, more industrialized areas like Hanoi and Haiphong—could be fired with a high degree of accuracy. In fact, neither the missiles nor MiGs ever created the fear which US crews developed for the intense flak nests encountered over the North. Forty-two Navy F-8s and 20 RF-8s, and 12 Marine F-8s were lost to flak and small arms fire over Vietnam.

Then-Lieutenant, j.g. Jay Miller was an RF-8G pilot with VFP-63's *Coral Sea* det in 1967. With 96 photo missions over the North, Miller was a highly experienced reconnaissance pilot. But his respect for communist flak never waned. Here, he describes a large strike on 28 September 1967, typical of the alpha strikes of the period, and his role as a photo pilot:

In September 1967, when we were going two or three times a day—the *Coral Sea*, the O-boat (*Oriskany*), maybe the Handjob (*Hancock*)—were flying multi alpha strikes. There'd be one at 0900 from our boat, one at 1000, 1400, 1700, all on those bridges in downtown Haiphong. The light was still there at that time of the year. Three Alpha strikes a day.

Jim Vescelius, our OINC, got shot down on the third

wave of that stuff. Someone saw his parachute, but nobody knows what happened afterwards. There was a secret message of an interrogation of some merchant seaman on a ship in Haiphong. Supposedly, he said an aviator had been captured at that time—he was the only one shot down in the Haiphong area in that time period—and they had executed him that day. We don't know the truth. Knowing Jim, resistance was possible.

Of course, he could have been hit in the plane, or something could have hit the plane which ejected the seat and the pilot. That could have happened. For example, Gordie Page was flying along fat, dumb and happy, and the next thing he knew, he was in his parachute. He took a big round in the cockpit area somewhere which caused his seat to eject. He got a good chute and was captured.

On this mission I went in by Cam Pha, because things were quiet up that way. I went over into the karst, toward China, and got set up. They wanted immediate BDA—bomb damage assessment. They didn't want us to interfere with the recovery. Even if we were the last airplane, they did not want to hold a ready deck for the photos. So we timed it so we could get max interval from bombs to photo, about 20 minutes.

I went in at a leisurely pace, back to the north-west of Haiphong and observed the situation. There were missiles, guns and airplanes. It was like a flying circus. People were calling missiles everywhere, the ECM gear was going off, you know, the warbles. And that was probably the sad part of the whole thing from my perspective. It was like being in the front row of a very exciting show. I was absolutely safe because I could pick and choose where I had to be. I was not close enough so that anyone would notice me and my wingman—the escort—and I could just observe.

Some days, we could stand off over the water and watch the strike go in. We could see the missile trails going every which way. If you did your planning and you didn't end up waiting over a 100 mm gun—something stupid because you knew where they were—you could go back and orbit at 350 knots and just watch the flak suppressors go in, watch the big CBU bombs go off—those little golfball things in them that sprinkled around. They took out 500 yards of local territory.

It was an acid-stomach, couldn't-eat-breakfast day,

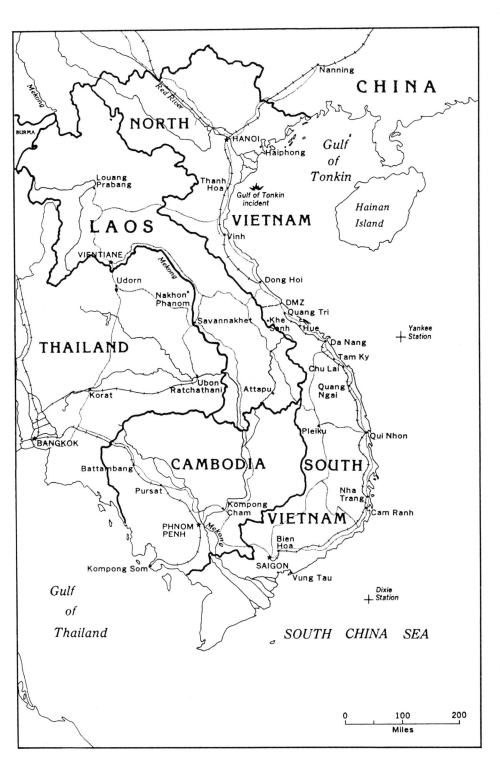

Map 1
Vietnam, 1968
Stephen D Oltmann,
Cartographer
Courtesy Nautical &
Aviation Publishing, Co,
Baltimore, Maryland

because you knew if you screwed up the pictures, CAG was going to be very perturbed, as well as the skipper of the ship and the admiral. So, I went over the mission. I had a 1/50,000 chart of downtown Haiphong. I knew exactly which canal I wanted to be set up on. The rivers over there looked like canals in Venice with concrete edges and buildings right up to the water, rather than actual rivers. And I had to get pictures of the bridges and the railyards outside the town which the strike was also going to hit. I set it up so I could shoot obliques out the right side of the plane

to get the railyard and not change heading significantly, and then fly right over the bridge and get verticals.

If I flew right over the railyards, I'd take pictures of billows of smoke, so I wanted to shoot obliquely into the base of the smoke, and they'd be able to see what the bombs had done.

So, we began the run. It had been quiet for about 15 minutes, but as soon as we started getting close, they started firing. I had the feeling that if I just opened the canopy, that I could have walked across Haiphong to the edge of this

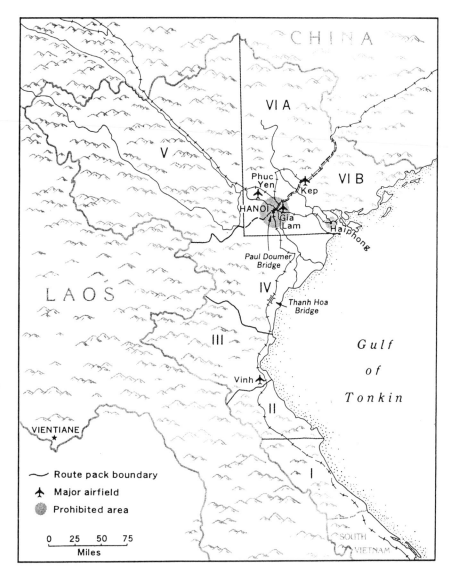

Map 2
Route Packs and Major Bridges in North Vietnam, 1968
Stephen D Oltmann, Cartographer
Courtesy Nautical & Aviation
Publishing Co, Baltimore,
Maryland

BELOW
Two light photo detachments are represented in this 1965 photo aboard the Coral Sea. *VMCJ-1, a Marine squadron, helped VFP-63's det, supplying aircraft and personnel to fly the large number of missions required during this early stage of the war*

crap. Now that's a perfect example of why you wanted to use the burner over Haiphong.

Anyway, I could see all this stuff coming up at me and as I went into burner, the nose began to tuck, and the plane climbed, just barely over all this. I got the pictures, and they turned out pretty good. My escort told the CAG that I'd stuck in there and gotten the pictures.

There were a lot of medals that day. Lots of DFCs. CAG Linder, Commander James B Linder, Commander, Air Wing 15, got the Navy Cross for that mission.

Lieutenant Miller got one of those Distinguished Flying Crosses for his part in the day's action.

North and South Vietnam were sectioned into specific areas called route packages. Route Pack VI encompassed the strategic *and* dangerous territory of north-east North Vietnam and the major cities of Hanoi and Haiphong. Route Pack VI was further divided. VI-A to the west, became the responsibility of the Air Force, while VI-B went to the Navy. While all six areas could be hazardous, a mission into Pack Six left little doubt as to the dangers.

Dudley Moore in VF-194 also saw a good deal of flak on one mission:

Bob Springer and I launched with a load of Zunis into the southern part of Pack Six for targets of opportunity. About 80 miles into the jungle, I finally saw a bridge across a canyon. It resembled something from a Tarzan movie, just ropes and boards. What the hell, I thought, rolling in.

The entire jungle erupted in 23 mm fire. The stuff was so close, I could hear the slugs popping by the canopy. Pulling out fast, I told Bob to abort; it was not worth getting shot down over this. Wrong again!

On the way out, I rolled into a 45 degree dive to salvo my rockets into the jungle. One of them exploded in front of my intake. I grabbed the throttle, slamming it into the crank, ignite detent, and jammed it straight into the burner detent. The engine began winding up when the burner fired, with some interesting engine instrument readings. With the jungle coming up fast, I didn't care.

Pulling out, I joined on Bob for a damage check. He couldn't see anything and we headed home. A few minutes later, however, he called about a rough engine. Checking him over, I decided what appeared to be a grease smudge was really a bullet hole.

'Looks like you took one in the intake', I told him. 'You've got the lead. Set power at 90 per cent. I'll call the ship'. About 90 miles from the carrier, his engine really started to come apart. The *Tico* gave us a ready deck. We rolled into the groove, dirtied up, and Bob kept adding throttle as he crossed the ramp and grabbed a wire. The engine seized as he rolled out.

On the hangar deck, we tore the F-8 apart. Pieces of cannon shell were everywhere, including a thumb-sized piece in his ejection seat pack. Another 500 feet lower and . . .

Like Bob said, 'We almost lost two F-8s for nothing'.

The fighter F-8s were extremely active against anti-aircraft sites, and frequently flew flak suppression runs ahead of the main strike force. On 18 August 1967, Lieutenant Commander John W McDonald of VF-162 in the *Oriskany*, led two F-8Es in a small strike against an ammunition storage area in Vinh.

McDonald's first run against an 85 mm flak site silenced the gun. He had to make a second run to protect the approaching strike force, and using his remaining bombs, then his 20 mm cannon, Lieutenant Commander McDonald took out three more flak sites. Even with his ordnance expended, he continued making dummy runs against the remaining sites in a successful effort to draw fire away from the strike aircraft. He received the Distinguished Flying Cross.

Bud Flagg had a close call during a 1965 mission over North Vietnam:

I was on a photo escort mission up north. We were going to get coverage of a missile site which turned out to be a flak trap. As soon as the RF-8 began his run, he yelled out to

A rare photo of an RF-8G of VFP-62 during the squadron's only Vietnam cruise, in 1966, in the carrier Franklin D Roosevelt. *VFP-62 lost at least one aircraft to enemy action during this deployment*

abort. About that time, I pulled up into a high turn to reverse, and hit burner. I think I took a 37 mm hit in the tail cone at the same time I went into burner. It must have blown the burner out. With the F-8, with the eyelids open and the burner in light, there's an immediate decrease in rpm because there's no back pressure to hold the rpm up.

So, I'm sitting there, I'd heard the boom and felt my plane shudder, and the rpm unwind. I thought I'd been hit. I thought I'd bought the farm—all these puffs appearing around me. The plane seemed to be hanging there. I disengaged burner, out of the throttle detent, which caused the eyelids to close. Now, it was like going *into* burner because there was a sudden increase in thrust. At that point. I began to understand my situation.

The plane began to accelerate, as I stayed in basic engine, a little ahead of the white puffs of flak following me. It was like an eternity. I yelled out to the photo pilot I'd been hit. I guess I had a really high-pitched voice, all the adrenalin and all.

The SAMs

Evidence of Soviet-built SA-2 surface-to-air missiles in North Vietnam was first revealed by an RF-8A from the *Coral Sea* on 5 April 1965. The site was 15 miles south-east of Hanoi, the North Vietnamese capital. However, permission to attack the site was refused, and it was not long until there was a profusion of SAM sites, their definitive six-pointed 'Star of David' layouts easily discernible.

Four months would pass before some form of action against the SAMs was allowed, and then, only after several aircraft had been lost, including two A-4s from VA-23 in the *Midway*, the first official Navy losses to missiles.

Crusaders and Skyhawks formed a unique partnership against the SAMs, under the overall mission codename of Iron Hand. A-4s with AGM-45A Shrike missiles would lead their F-8 escorts in attacks against the sites. These attacks were extremely dangerous, for after the Navy enjoyed initial success with the beam-riding missiles, the communists became adept at turning their fire control radars off, thereby denying anything for the Shrikes to home on to. When the Shrikes were fired, the F-8s would follow the missiles right down toward the site, wait for missile impact, and then open up with their 5-inch Zunis and cannon, creating a one-two punch which was devastating against the target. But many Crusaders suffered major damage or loss during these SAM suppression runs. It was not a mission for the faint-hearted. The SA-2 was a 35-foot long missile with 350 pounds of high explosive in its warhead. Detonation within 200 feet of an airplane usually meant a kill. SAMs accounted for 10 Navy Crusaders.

Dudley Moore had a close encounter with a North Vietnamese SAM in 1966. It was one of those unusually clear days over Pack Six, almost brilliant, not unlike southern California. Boyd Repsher in the lead, and Moore crossed the coast south of Vinh on a MiG. A MiG in those days was a rarity but there was

always hope. After some loose deuce manoeuvring, the two VF-194 Crusaders were down to bingo fuel, but they decided to make one more 180-degree turn before going feet wet.

There was absolutely nothing going on, however, and they turned for home. Moore swung into a tactical wing position. Suddenly, he spotted a large squirt of dust on the ground with a large orange plume rising out of the middle of the cloud. SAM launch!

Simultaneously, Moore hit burner, raised his wing droops up, and keyed the mike.

'Sheepdog, SAM lifting off at 9 o'clock. Get some speed on!' Repsher punched in his afterburner and pushed over in a 40 degree dive. The two F-8s were in a right bank, noses down, and accelerating. By now, Moore was at his lead's five o'clock, watching for the missile.

Both pilots had already seen many SAMs in flight, but this was the first time they had a ringside seat watching the full launch sequence. The SAM was at 3000 feet when the booster kicked off, and the tracking sequence began. But who was it locked on to? There was no way of telling.

Moore flicked an eyeball toward the mach meter— 600 knots. He said to Repsher, 'I'll call the turn'.

The missile was at terminal velocity, shooting a ten-foot flame, and coming fast, a dark telephone pole. As it levelled nearly parallel to the ground, it became obvious that the SAM had locked on to Repsher.

'It's on you, Rep. Break left, hard, now!' Everything seemed to slow down. The hardest part was waiting to time the hard roll so the missile couldn't match the turning angle.

Both Crusaders slammed on 6-plus Gs as their noses went up and over, toward the vertical. The SAM was on them now. It was going to be close. As both F-8s rolled into the vertical 90 degrees, the SAM pulled off Repsher and headed between the two Navy fighters. As the F-8s rolled into the missile, the SAM was right by Moore's canopy. He watched bug-eyed as it zipped across his windscreen, so close he could see big dents on it. As he stared at this beatup missile, all he could think was 'Bad QC! (quality control)'.

The SAM flashed by as they rolled left, standing on left rudder. The Crusaders scooped out, and Moore watched the SAM out of his right side. The missile, with nothing to guide on, tumbled crazily and headed straight up. It climbed about 1000 feet and exploded in a huge cloud of black smoke and flame against the brilliant sky.

The only Medal of Honor to be won in Vietnam by a carrier aviator went to an Iron Hand pilot, Lieutenant Commander Michael Estocin (pronounced Es-*toe*-shin), an A-4 driver with VA-192 aboard the *Tico* in 1967. Estocin received a posthumous award which covered the six-day period of 20–26 April 1967. The last man to see this

An F-8C of VF-24 traps aboard the Bon Homme
Richard *during the 1967 combat cruise. The crewman by
the wing tip is indicating to the pilot he has successfully
engaged one of the arresting cables and can retard his
throttle*

dedicated aviator alive was then-Lieutenant Commander John Nichols, an F-8E pilot with VF-191.

Nichols flew as Estocin's escort during a strike on POL facilities near Haiphong. Estocin got a signal that he was being tracked by one of the many SAM sites in the area. Although the main strike force was turning back toward the water, Estocin remained in position, ready to protect his departing friends.

Finally, a flash below, eight miles away as the SAM launched. Estocin waited for the missile to get within sure range for his Shrike missiles. But the SAM detonated; Estocin had apparently misjudged the distance. His A-4 began to go down, burning and coming apart.

Helpless, Nichols watched as the A-4 seemed to right itself for a moment, even as another SAM shot past them. Although Nichols could see into the battered Skyhawk's cockpit, he could not detect any movement from Estocin. As he crossed over the A-4, Nichols could see the tremendous damage done by the North Vietnamese missile, and knew there was little hope.

At 1000 feet above the water, the A-4 rolled inverted, its centreline fuel tank and Shrikes exploding. The little bomber crashed into the water. Nichols circled but there was nothing he could do.

The MiGs

Although the flak and SAMs were by far the most effective part of the communist defences, the traditionally more glamorous fighter-to-fighter encounters grabbed the headlines. Originally equipped with a mixture of light transport aircraft, the North Vietnamese Air Force received MiG-15 and -17 jet fighters from the Soviet Union and communist China. By the time American attacks began in earnest in 1965, the threat of MiG interception was very real, and taken seriously by every carrier air crew.

As noted, the first appearance by North Vietnamese MiGs came in early April 1965. While the MiGs only damaged one F-8, they shot down two Air Force F-105s the following day.

While there were several engagements between US and North Vietnamese aircraft, the Navy enjoyed very few successes. The first confirmed Navy kills came on 17 July 1965 when two F-4Bs from VF-21 shot down two MiG-17s. Three days later, a MiG-17 was brought down by a flight of A-1s, one of two MiG kills scored by the old prop-driven Skyraider in Vietnam. However, a year passed before the next Navy victories, which would also be the first kills for the F-8. There were a few near-misses for the F-8s, who had to deal, not only with finding and engaging MiGs, but with a constantly evolving long list of rules of engagement. Consider Bud Flagg's predicament:

I recall one BARCAP [barrier combat air patrol] when we nearly ran into MiGs. We all wanted a MiG so bad we could taste it. I was under the control of a destroyer, working south of Hong Ghe. The destroyer told us there was an aircraft coming from Kep, one of the major MiG bases, and he vectored us to within five miles of the bogey, who turned and headed north.

We lit the burners and chased him. But at this time, we weren't supposed to cross the 21st Parallel. Of course, in the air you can't tell what parallel you're crossing, and I was in hot pursuit. We were gradually closing him; I had him on radar. On the APQ-94 radar scope in the F-8, there was a little mark which told you when you were in range for a missile shot. He was about one–two miles above that little

ABOVE
The weather in the South China Sea could be messy. Here, a VF-211 F-8E launches in a tropical rain storm during the 1967 cruise in the Bonnie Dick

RIGHT
Squadrons changed ships occasionally whenever a carrier needed them. Although VF-51 normally cruised with the Ticonderoga *and the* Bonnie Dick, *it also sailed in the* Hancock *in 1967. Here, an F-8E prepares to launch on a CAP mission fully loaded with four Sidewinders. The heavy load imposed more weight and handling problems on the Crusader, resulting in increased fuel consumption*

mark and gradually coming down the scale. All I needed was another 5–10 minutes to close to get a shot off.

But the destroyer yelled for me to break it off since I was approaching the 21st parallel. I pushed it, until they really started screaming at me. I guess I actually did cross the parallel before turning around.

Now was the first time we'd looked at our gas gauges. We both realized we had about 1.5 hours to recover, and had only about 1500 pounds left. So now, not only did we not get the MiG, but our BARCAP ability had been drastically reduced. We were looking for a tanker, and needless to say, the old A-3—one of the best planes to ever serve—came along, tanked us back to 8000 pounds, and we were back in business. But that was as close as I ever got to a MiG.

One of the unique qualities of the entire F-8 fighter series was its claim to being the last gun-armed air superiority single-seat fighter in naval service. Its successor, the highly successful F-4 Phantom II, carried an all-missile armament as a result of a decision in the 1950s to do away with guns in favour of the more sophisticated air-to-air missile. The Phantom, which was originally a single-seater, added another crew member—the Radar Intercept Officer (RIO)—to operate the aircraft's radar system. Ultimately, the RIO's main contribution to the Phantom concept proved to be simply another pair of *human* eyes to help the pilot during aerial engagements. It was not until the development of the Grumman F-14 Tomcat that the pilot truly needed a dedicated, specially trained crewman behind him to operate the weapons radar and to successfully prosecute the fleet defence mission.

Thus, a friendly, but no less heated, rivalry developed between F-4 and F-8 crews. While Navy Phantoms accounted for 36 MiGs and two AN-2 Colt transports, and the Marines got one MiG in a Marine Phantom, the F-8 was credited with 18 confirmed MiG kills, as well as an occasional loosely credited kill in 1972. This last incident involved a MiG-17 pilot bailing out of his fighter as two F-8s approached. Although this nineteenth kill was not officially credited, and rightfully so, it can be interpreted to highlight the Crusader's reputation. Apparently, the MiG pilot had been told by his ground controller the approaching American fighters were Phantoms. However, when he saw their true identity, he threw a few comments into the radio before ejecting.

It is interesting to note that all the Crusader's official kills came within a relatively short two-year period, for after the last score on 19 September 1968, all US Navy MiG kills were by Phantoms. The main reason for this lack of additional Crusader kills, as any Crusader alumnus will confirm, was the lack of 'vectors' for the frustrated F-8 pilots, who spent the last three years of the war flying from the smaller carriers, largely relegated to ground attack duties, with occasional bomber escort duties which meant staying with the bombers even with MiGs in the area.

The powerful Phantom could carry more bombs, in addition to its regular load of Sidewinder and Sparrow missiles, and had taken its intended place as the fleet's main fighter. Thus, the F-8 pilots, though primed and ready to engage the North Vietnamese MiGs, found themselves crying for a chance to go after the MiGs. But, in their time, the F-8 drivers were the leading destroyers of communist aerial hardware.

The Crusader opened its scoresheet on 12 June 1966, when Commander Harold L Marr, commanding officer of VF-211, shot down a MiG-17, while flying escort for an A-4 strike. Watching the Skyhawks make their runs, Marr, his wingman, Lieutenant, j.g. Phil Vampatella, and another two-plane section of F-8s from VF-24, held at 1500 feet, under clouds. As the bombers came off their target and rejoined their escorts, Vampatella called out approaching MiGs from behind, at the seven o'clock position. The four MiGs were at about 2000 feet:

We pull hard into them and the fight's on. Two of the MiGs split off and we pass the other two head on. I fire a short burst of cannon at one MiG, more for courage than anything else—just to hear my four cannons bang.

We're doing about 450 knots and pulling seven to eight Gs and reverse hard right in a sharp scissors. I get a good 90-degree deflection gun shot but my cannon misses again and Phil goes after one and I after the other.

Now I'm at 2500 feet at his eight o'clock and the MiG is down around 1500 feet with nowhere to go. I fire the first of my two Sidewinders but the missile can't hack it and falls to the ground.

The MiG has been in burner for four or five minutes now and is mighty low on fuel, so he rolls and head straight for his base. I roll in behind, stuff it in burner, and close at 500 knots. At a half mile, I fire my last 'winder and it chops off his tail and starboard wing. He goes tumbling end over end. The poor pilot doesn't even have a chance to eject.

The two MiGs which Marr and Vampatella engaged were clean externally, carried no wing tanks or missiles. One MiG was all silver, the other grey; both MiG-17s carried red stars on their upper wingtips, and yellow fuselage markings aft of the wings.

Marr's initial cannon bursts, approximately 150 rounds, fired at the silver MiG which appeared to be

the element leader. Marr's first AIM-9D Sidewinder may have homed in on a cloud's reflection before falling off to the right.

Marr actually fired his second Sidewinder at 4500 feet, one-half mile behind the MiG which crashed at the edge of a small town on the banks of a river.

The second MiG had been the target of one of the other VF-24 fighters, whose pilot, Lieutenant Fred Richardson, had fired both Sidewinders, which missed. His wingman, Lieutenant, j.g. Denis C Duffy, Jr, also fired a Sidewinder at the twisting grey MiG, but although this missile seemed to guide properly, it could not reach the MiG before falling off.

Commander Marr, having destroyed the MiG leader, saw two other MiG-17s orbiting above him at nine o'clock, one grey and the other in the green-brown camouflage usually seen during the war. He climbed to 6000 feet and engaged this second pair of MiGs, firing 25–30 cannon rounds. He saw fragments coming off the right wing of one of the MiGs but he quickly ran out of ammunition, and had to break off, and claim only a probable.

An ecstatic Marr claimed the traditional victory flyby when he returned to the *Hancock*. The F-8 had gained its first kill.

ABOVE
During 1967, VF-111 operated dets aboard different carriers, using two different F-8 models, the C and E. This F-8C gets the launch signal from the Oriskany's *catapult officer during a September strike against targets in North Vietnam*

RIGHT
A characteristic view of the Intrepid *during underway replenishment in July 1968. The three F-8 tails display many markings. On the extreme left, a VF-111 F-8 shows the squadron's Sundowner markings; BuNo 145632 is an RF-8G, while 146951 is another VF-111 F-8. 'Rattler' is the call sign of then-Lieutenant, j.g., Alex Rucker, Tony Nargi's wingman on the mission that saw Nargi make the last F-8 MiG kill*

Vampatella's and Chancy's Kills

One of the most colourful Crusader-MIG engagements followed only nine days later, and involved Marr's wingman on the 12th June fight, Phil Vampatella. On 21 June 11 *Hancock* planes flew a strike into North Vietnam. The group was divided into two groups: a two-plane flight—an RF-8A and its VF-211 F-8E escort—which would make a reconnaissance run of the railway north-east of Hanoi, and six A-4s with three VF-211 F-8E escorts.

The strike group's three Checkmate Crusader escort pilots were Lieutenant Cole Black, Lieutenant, j.g. Vampatella, and Lieutenant Gene Chancy. As the A-4s ran in toward their target, word came that the RF-8A (BuNo 146830) flown by Lieutenant L C Eastman, had been shot down. After making sure the A-4s were clear of their target, the three F-8s hastened to the site of the RF-8A's crash, taking radio cuts on the escort F-8E's radio transmissions. Lieutenant Black and Lieutenant Chancy circled over the site, while Lieutenant Vampatella took the wingman position for the photo escort, whose pilot, Lieutenant Dick Smith, had assumed the role of SAR (Search and Rescue) commander. The four VF-211 F-8s remained at 1500 to 2000 feet above the crash site.

The situation became complicated as the A-4s began calling out SAM launches and MiG warnings. The F-8s began to draw flak, 37 mm, 57 mm and probably 85 mm fire. Lieutenant Vampatella felt his plane shudder as he took a hit, but he remained on station for 10–12 minutes.

Lieutenant Smith and Lieutenant Vampatella sighted the downed photo pilot's chute, and Lieutenant Black and Lieutenant Chancy climbed to gain better radio communication with the incoming SAR helicopter. Reaching 6000 feet, Chancy heard a SAM warning and he and his leader remained at that altitude. Black asked about the F-8s' fuel state, and finally ordered Smith and Vampatella to find a tanker. This left Black and Chancy orbiting at 2000 feet above the RF-8. They spotted an orange signal flare, presumably set off by the photo pilot, about one-half mile from the crash site.

Then, Lieutenant Black spotted two MiG-17s sliding in from the south, out of the clouds at the two o'clock position of the F-8s. The North Vietnamese fighters were very close, perhaps one-half mile distant, and 500 feet above the Crusaders. Black leveled his wings and began firing his cannon, but the MiGs passed close to Chancy, their guns blazing. Chancy quickly fired his own guns as he crossed over his leader, left to right. The MiGs had apparently waited until the Crusaders had left their high altitude station during the A-4 attack, and were in orbit, at low fuel state, above the RF-8 on the ground. The F-8s would be at a disadvantage at such a low height, and also dangerously low on fuel.

Lieutenant Chancy's desperate fire hit the MiG wingman as the section slashed through the Crusaders, blowing a wing off the MiG.

'He was so close', Chancy later recalled, 'I could have counted his teeth. It was a very effective attack'. Chancy also got a harsh tone and fired one Sidewinder, but the missile failed to guide.

It would be a while before Gene Chancy's score would be changed from a probable to a confirmed kill, since the MiG was not actually seen to crash, and other participants in the fight were too busy or too distant to observe the action. However, Captain Jim Donaldson, commanding officer of the *Hancock*, told him to go to Saigon for the traditional press conference which followed every American MiG score. Finally, a Vought rep called Chancy to tell him he owed the lieutenant the special Vought pin which the company gave to Crusader MiG killers. The lapel pin consisted of an F-8 silhouette with a red ruby.

Gene Chancy's kill has always been listed as a missile score, however, he is certain the MiG was downed by his initial gunfire, especially since his single Sidewinder did not guide properly. This would make him one of only two Crusader drivers who could claim a guns kill over Vietnam.

Unfortunately, Chancy's elation at his success changed immediately for he could not find his leader. Lieutenant Black's F-8, BuNo 149152, had been hit by the lead MiG, and he had ejected. To Chancy's dismay, the SAR helicopter, originally sent to recover the RF-8 pilot, got lost and never showed up. Both Black and the RF-8 pilot were captured and remained POWs until 1973. Chancy had to leave his leader on the ground and return to the ship.

'Those guys are what Americans are made of', he said, recalling the trials of all the POWs.

The fight was not over. Hearing Lieutenant Black's call of 'MiGs!', Smith and Vampatella had hauled their planes around and returned to the melée, even though Vampatella's F-8 was damaged. Nearing the action, they saw a section of two MiGs at 2000 feet, in a diving right turn. Smith called a warning.

'F-8, you have a MiG on your tail!' He could see the MiG's guns firing, followed by the F-8 bursting into flames. It was Cole Black going down.

A second MiG section now appeared and Lieutenant Smith tried to engage the leader, but his guns failed while in a high-G turn. Vampatella, meanwhile, had looked back to find another MiG saddled in on his tail, within gun range, and firing. Vampatella tried to scissor with the MiG but had to limit his turns to five Gs because of the previous damage.

The MiG stayed with the F-8, and, although increasingly low on fuel, Vampatella lit his afterburner, disengaging from the MiG, and headed east at 600 knots. Safe for the moment, he found the Crusader getting more difficult to fly. The MiG was more than a mile behind, and the North Vietnamese pilot seemed to have turned back toward home, probably low on fuel, himself.

Seizing the opportunity, Vampatella reduced his speed and turned back toward the departing MiG. At

The Hancock's small flight deck is crammed with aircraft as the veteran carrier sails under San Francisco's Golden Gate Bridge to begin a 1969 Vietnam cruise. Three squadrons of F-8s can be seen, including VF-24, VF-211, and VFP-63. The A-4s are from VA-212 and VA-55, both veteran Skyhawk squadrons

approximately three-quarters of a mile, Vampatella tried one Sidewinder, than the second. The second finally came off the rail and guided straight toward the MiG, detonating immediately behind the enemy fighter, which crashed.

After hitting the tanker, with only 300 pounds of fuel remaining, Lieutenant Chancy escorted Vampatella back to the *Hancock*, 60 miles away. Vampatella tried to refuel, but the tanker could give him only a bare minimum. It was uncertain if he could get back. However, he landed safely, and postflight inspection revealed his plane had been hit in the vertical tail by 37 mm fire, with about 80 small holes dotting the F-8's rear surfaces. Phil Vampatella received the Navy Cross for his courage and skill, the second award of the Navy's highest decoration for Vietnam aerial action. (The first Navy Cross for aerial combat in Vietnam had been awarded to an A-6 bombardier, Lieutenant, j.g. Brian Westin of VA-85, for action on 27 April 1966. The Medal of Honor—the highest *American* award for valour—is given in the name of the US Congress.)

Although these two June 1966 engagements decisively opened the Crusader's score card, the problems encountered with the F-8's armament, especially the troublesome cannon, brought an in-depth analysis of the combats by the Commander-in-Chief, US Pacific Fleet. The study indicated there had been 11 attempts to fire Sidewinders in the two fights, two missiles failed completely, and one experienced a delayed firing. Three attempts to fire the 20 mm cannon resulted in failure, one complete, and two stoppages after only a few rounds. Only Commander Marr was able to successfully expend all his ammunition. The report concluded:

... 13 of the 24 guns experienced some failure. Two of the six aircraft experienced a malfunction on the first round. One pilot voluntarily ceased fire after firing one fourth of his ammunition, and only one pilot was able to expend all his rounds.

20 mm guns in F-8 aircraft have generally been regarded as a weapon secondary to Sidewinder for air-to-air engagements. The results of this study ... show that the opportunities for F-8 aircraft to fire 20 mm in engagements typical in SE Asia may approach the opportunities for them to fire Sidewinder.

That final observation proved unfounded. While the Air Force experienced many successes with 20 mm cannon, particularly with the F-105, which included an integral gun in its original design, the Navy's kills were, with the exception of perhaps two or three F-8 kills, all scored with missiles, predominantly Sidewinders which came to be fairly dependable weapons. The other main missile, the AIM-7 Sparrow which was not carried by F-8s, only by F-4s, while supposedly more sophisticated—and ultimately more expensive—enjoyed relatively little success and subsequently low confidence from the Navy's fighter crews.

Cole Black's loss was one of only three *confirmed*

F-8 losses to MiGs during the entire war. Later, on 14 July 1966, a VF-162 F-8E, and, on 5 September, a VF-111 F-8E, were shot down by MiGs, Air Force Captain W K Abbott, on exchange duty, becoming a POW. It is of interest to report that no RF-8s were lost to North Vietnamese fighters. All 20 VFP-63 and 12 VMCJ-1 combat losses were due to flak and a few SAMs.

Bellinger Gets a MiG

The VF-162 loss to MiGs involved the squadron's colourful skipper, Commander Dick Bellinger. At 42, Bellinger was a little older than the average fighter skipper, but then, he had flown in World War II as a Air Force bomber pilot, transferred to the Navy after the war, and flown combat in Korea. Now in his third war, Bellinger knew this was probably his last chance.

The July shootdown had come after a high speed chase over downtown Hanoi, with one Hunter pilot dragging a MiG which had locked onto his tail. Lieutenant Commander Chuck Tinker only succeeded in evading his pursuer by dodging buildings at 50 feet above the densely populated city. Tinker did not have a working radio—the flight had known this prior to going over the coast—and when he saw yet another MiG on his CO's tail, he could not warn him.

After the MiG peppered his Crusader, Bellinger ducked into a cloud and limped away, trying to make

LEFT
During a mission over North Vietnam in April 1966, Lieutenant Ron Ball's F-8 was hit by groundfire and he was forced to eject. An SH-3A helicopter from the ASW carrier Yorktown *picked him up. His personal flotation bags are inflated around his waist, and his survival radio dangles below the left bag*

ABOVE
An RF-8G launches from the Coral Sea *during the 1967 cruise. Taken in October, this photo shows the pilot's braced position in his cockpit immediately before the cat stroke that sends his plane hurtling off the carrier. The Crusader is also in tension, cocked slightly nose up on the catapult with the bridle attached to the shuttle right behind the nose gear*

Da Nang before his fuel ran out. He was unable to refuel from an orbiting tanker due to the damage to his aircraft, and ejected from his crippled Crusader 40 miles from the mainland.

On 9 October, Bellinger led three other Hunter Crusaders acting as escort for an A-4 strike from the carrier *Intrepid*. An E-1 Tracer vectored the escorts toward incoming MiGs, which turned out to be MiG-21s, only recently entering service with the North Vietnamese Air Force, and representing a considerable jump in technology for the beleaguered communist air service.

One of the delta-winged MiGs split-essed toward the ground, and Bellinger followed, firing two Sidewinders. He was at a dangerously low altitude and could not watch the progress of his missiles as he zoomed over the steaming jungles. But one of the Sidewinders had found its mark and the MiG-21 crashed into the rice paddies below, marking the first Navy kill of the advanced MiG. Dick Bellinger flew back to the *Oriskany* to a tumultuous welcome from his ship and squadron. One week later, Secretary of Defense Robert McNamara, on a Vietnam tour, came aboard the *Oriskany* to personally award Bellinger the customary Silver Star for his MiG kill.

Bellinger had many sides to him, and had as many supporters as detractors. There was very little room for shadings. To many people in his squadron, Bellinger could be a raging, sometimes out-of-control bull, but to many others, his name evokes fond memories.

Lieutenant Bud Flagg—now a reserve rear admiral—recalls that 'Bellinger *was* a colourful character. But he flew the F-8 well and commanded the squadron well. He was always there to do the job . . . He was tops.'

Mrs Dee Flagg, who, like so many of the young wives of the period, lived through her husband's combat deployments with a mixture of fear, courage and ultimate hope, remembers Dick Bellinger and his wife, Norma, as 'great people'.

'He was really a Santa Claus', she recalls of Dick Bellinger, 'although he obviously had a different face when leading the Hunters'.

Bellinger protected Bud Flagg who had two months to go until leaving the last combat cruise. Bellinger would allow his maintenance lieutenant to only fly milk runs, and eventually made him shore det officer, much to Flagg's disgust. But he realized the skipper had his reasons, especially trying to forgo the obvious problems of trying to get Flagg off the ship at the end of his tour, while the *Oriskany* was on the line, in combat.

Bellinger also protected a young Hunter pilot who had two ramp strikes, within three weeks of each other; the last involved a brand new F-8E. The skipper went to bat for the aviator, and he kept his wings.

On another occasion, Bud Flagg's plane had been hit by intense flak, and he barely recovered at Da Nang. Bellinger told him he was grounded and to get his wife over for a visit.

Dick Bellinger, unfortunately, died of Alzheimer's disease, but his wife remained in the Navy family as a full-time Navy Relief representative.

F-8s did not score again until May 1967, by which time, the American bombing offensive against the North Vietnamese was in full swing. Daily strikes seemed to be hurting the North's ability to continue the war, even with major restrictions levied by Washington as to what type of targets could be hit, and where and when. Even with the high number of losses, and the uncertainty as to the fate of the US crews after they bailed out of their stricken machines, the Americans hurled themselves at their objectives.

May 1967 was an especially intense period of activity, and all squadrons from all the ships on the line participated in a number of large raids. The MiGs were active during this time, and the engagements were sharp and intense.

The *Bon Homme Richard*'s Air Wing 21 was in the forefront of Navy successes, beginning on 1 May, the traditional communist holiday. Lieutenant Commander M O 'Moe' Wright, of VF-211, shot down one of three MiG-17s, while he was escorting Iron Hand A-4s 35 miles north of Hanoi. He had tacked on to the MiG's tail as it attacked an A-4. Wright fired a Sidewinder which sent the MiG tumbling into the ground. Air Force Captain Ron Lord, serving an exchange tour with the Checkmates, flew with Wright.

'It was a beautiful hit', Lord said later. 'The MiG just came apart at the seams'. Later, Lord chased a MiG off another A-4 with his cannon.

In addition to Wright's kill, Lieutenant Commander T R Swartz got his A-4C behind a MiG. The VA-76 pilot fired three separate Zunis—normally ground attack weapons—at the MiG which also dived into the ground.

Ted Swartz was actually a Crusader alumnus, having gained 2000 hours in the F-8. He was an instructor and LSO for VF-174, the east coast F-8 training squadron. While at Cecil Field, Swartz instructed many of the Crusader pilots who ultimately fought in Vietnam.

When his tour was about to end, however, Swartz was convinced the Vietnam War would be an attack pilot's war, and he asked to be sent to an A-4 squadron. But, he remained a fighter pilot, and when the opportunity came, he took it, and became the only A-4 pilot to score a MiG kill in Vietnam.

The F-8's best days came next, 19 May and 21 July, when eight pilots shot down eight MiGs, accounting for nearly half of the entire Crusader tally in the war.

The mission for the 19 May involved A-4/F-8 Iron Hand strikes against heavy concentrations of SAM and flak positions, complicated by MiG opposition. Extensive 37 mm, 57 mm, and 85 mm fire was encountered. VF-211 and VF-24 provided the escort. One F-8E from VF-211, BuNo 150930, was downed by a SAM, its pilot captured. Five other F-8s were damaged by flak and MiG cannon fire.

In the air-to-air engagements, the two *Bonnie Dick* squadrons scored two MiG-17s apiece. VF-24's Lieutenant Commander Bobby Lee and Lieutenant Commander Phillip Wood, in F-8Cs, and VF-211's skipper, Commander (later Rear Admiral) Paul Speer, and Lieutenant, j.g. Joseph Shea, each fired Sidewinders. Lee's and Wood's kills were the first for their squadron.

Two months later, on 21 July, four Air Wing 21 pilots scored. While proceeding to their target, a POL storage facility near Haiphong, CVW-21 A-4s were attacked by an estimated force of 10 MiG-17s. The combined VF-24 and VF-211 escort waded into the interceptors. VF-24's newly arrived Executive Officer, Commander Marion H Isaacks, got above and behind one MiG. He tried twice to fire his Sidewinders—he was carrying a full load of four—but the first AIM-9 failed to guide, and the second malfunctioned and didn't fire. Frustrated, he tried once more. This time the third missile came off the

A railway and highway bridge in Haiphong receives attention from aircraft of Coral Sea's *CVW-15 during a 1967 air strike. While these strikes could have helped bring the communists to the peace talks much sooner, the incomprehensible bombing halt instituted on 1 November 1968, by US President Johnson, undid everything the intense bombing campaign accomplished, and kept the war going for at least another four years*

An RF-8G took this BDA (Bomb Damage Assessment) photo of CVW-15 strikes on a railway yard near Haiphong, North Vietnam, in 1967. BDA was essential to determine the success of raids, and the need for return strikes. BDA was the RF-8's bread and butter, but due to the predictability of its role after the strike, the photo Crusader could usually expect a hot reception from gun and SAM batteries on the ground

rail and tracked perfectly, right up the MiG's tailpipe. The enemy fighter went down in a fireball.

Staring at the fireball, Isaacks nearly became someone's kill, himself, when one of the MiG's wingmen drove in, firing all the way. Isaacks kicked right rudder, turning to meet his attacker. With his windscreen full of MiG intake, the VF-24 XO gaped as the North Vietnamese pilot turned away at the last moment and snap-rolled for the deck, leaving Isaacks with a badly damaged Crusader.

His F-8 had a small fire going near the right aileron, fed by hydraulic fluid. However, the blaze remained confined to the small area on the wing and after the fluid had been burned, the fire extinguished, as Isaacks flew back to the carrier.

Isaacks summed up the air war during a visit to LTV soon after his MiG kill.

'The MiGs are good for morale, I guess. There's more glamour in shooting down a MiG than shooting up a SAM site.' But, he added, missile and gun emplacements caused more concern for pilots than MiGs in the air.

Lieutenant Phil Dempewolf also scored a probable with a Sidewinder. Positive confirmation could not be made because two other MiGs attacked after Dempewolf's MiG went down.

Lieutenant Commander Robert Kirkwood became one of two Crusader pilots who could claim a much-desired 'guns only' kill, firing his 20 mm cannon at a MiG-17. Lieutenant Commander Kirkwood was the leader of the second section flying TARCAP for 15 A-4s. He had fired a Sidewinder at Isaack's MiG, but the executive officer's missile got there first. Kirkwood manoeuvred behind another MiG and fired another AIM-9. The MiG turned left as the Sidewinder exploded, and Kirkwood closed to gun range. At 600 feet, he opened fire and the MiG went down.

Lieutenant Commander Tim Hubbard of VF-211, flew an F-8E which had included a Sidewinder along with Zunis, and he used both types of missiles as well as 20 mm cannonfire to down another MiG-17, which brought his squadron's total to seven, making it the highest scoring Navy squadron at the time and, ultimately, the highest scoring Crusader squadron.

CVW-21 was now the highest scoring air wing. Only in 1972 did *Constellation*'s Air Wing 9 tie with the *Bon Homme Richard*'s record with nine kills from January to May, including the four MiG-17s and one MiG-21 attributed to the Navy's only aces, Cunningham and Driscoll, of VF-96.

The Air Wing 21 cruise report—part of the massive amount of paperwork required by every combat deployment—attributed the wing's success against the MiGs to using the F-8s in their designed role as fighters:

One radical deviation made by this Air Wing in contrast to others was the employment of F-8 aircraft. The F-8s were used primarily as fighters. Wing bomb racks were never installed. As a result, nine MiG-17s were confirmed shot down, plus one probable and nine more damaged in the air. When air-to-ground ordnance was desired, Zunis were used . . . which mount on the Sidewinder missile stations. In certain cases, six Zunis and one AIM-9D were carried. F-8s in this configuration had two confirmed MiGs . . .

All the CVW-21 F-8 MiG killers received the traditional Silver Star for their achievements. Lieutenant Dempewolf received the lesser Distinguished Flying Cross for his probable. Commander Speer also received the second Navy Cross awarded to a VF-211 pilot. The Navy's highest award was given for his having 'contributed greatly to the successful execution of this mission' by protecting the A-4s from the determined enemy attack.

The Crusader had established its credentials as a MiG killer, and was eventually tagged by zealous Vought public relations officials as 'the MiG Master', a name it wears to this day. But time was growing short.

The final US Navy MiG kill for 1967 was registered by a VF-162 F-8E. Lieutenant Richard Wyman launched on 14 December, as a spare. Three other Crusaders had been scrubbed for mechanical reasons, and Wyman and Commander Cal Swanson, who had assumed command of the Hunters a year before, headed inland. Swanson's radar was down and so the lead fell to the junior pilot.

The pair spotted an A-4 with a VF-111 F-8 escort. The A-4 pilot, Lieutenant, j.g. Chuck Nelson, told them there were MiGs nearby. The F-8s quickly closed on the fight. The MiGs were all over the lone Sundowner F-8C, flown by Lieutenant Commander Dick Schaffert.

Finally, the Hunter flight got within range, and Swanson tried to manoeuvre with one of the MiGs, but the North Vietnamese pilot got on his tail. Wyman shot a few bullets toward the MiG in an effort to save his skipper. Apparently, the MiG got the message and broke off. The fight developed into a dogfight. Each time Wyman tried to fire a Sidewinder, the MiG would shake him off in a tight turn.

Another Crusader pilot, Commander Bob Rasmussen, CO of VF-111, the Hunters' sister squadron, already in the fray, fired a Sidewinder, but missed. The fight was now down to the trees; it had started at 16,000. Finally, Wyman got behind the MiG and fired another Sidewinder. This time, the AIM-9 guided perfectly and took off the MiG's left wing. The enemy fighter dived into the ground only 50 feet below.

The fight had shown there were good pilots on the other side, too. It had taken four F-8s, twisting and diving all over the sky, to bring down one MiG. Wyman recalled the climax of the long fight.

'The wing fell off. Red fire streaked along the left side of the plane as it cartwheeled into a rice paddy.'

Cal Swanson commented, 'That was probably the longest MiG engagement of the war. That MiG pilot was a tiger. He was there to fight . . .'

Chapter 6
The Last MiGs, 1968

MiGs were scarce for the next six months, at least for the Navy. The next kill did not come until June 1968, and, again, the victor was an F-8. Commander L R Myers, skipper of VF-51, on his one hundred and eighty-second mission over Vietnam, used a Sidewinder to blow the tail off a MiG-21 on 26 June. The MiG made a head-on pass against the three VF-51 fighters. Myers wrapped his Crusader into a turn which put him at the MiG's six o'clock, and he fired his Sidewinder. It was the first of two kills for the F-8H model of the Crusader.

John Nichols got the next kill which gave a good illustration of why no RF-8s were brought down by MiGs. On 9 July, Nichols escorted an RF-8 on a low level photo mission south of Vinh. The two *Ticonderoga* Crusaders launched for the afternoon mission, and ran in toward the target, drawing anti-aircraft fire all the way.

Lieutenant William Kocar brought his RF-8 down to 2000 feet, while Nichols remained at 3000. As Kocar made his runs, Nichols spotted a camouflaged MiG-17 streaking toward the photo plane. Shouting a warning to Kocar and the controllers on the *Tico*, Nichols followed the RF-8 into a hard turn, just as tracers streamed past him. He had not seen the first MiG's wingman.

Nichols focused on the lead MiG and fired a Sidewinder. But he was too high, and the missile could not guide properly. The MiG pilot suddenly stopped his turn, rolled wings level and lit his afterburner. Nichols saddled in and fired a second Sidewinder. This time, the missile hit the MiG causing major damage. The fighter remained in air, however, to Nichols' amazement and he began firing his cannon, obtaining a few hits. The MiG was mortally wounded, and eventually disintegrated. Lieutenant Kocar in the RF-8 excitedly confirmed the kill.

After the Crusaders recovered aboard their

MiG Master insignia. The F-8 was dubbed the MiG Master by zealous Vought representatives, and for a time, it was the leading destroyer of the North Vietnamese fighters. Eventually, it was overtaken by the F-4, but in its heyday, the Crusader was the MiG Master

carrier, the intelligence department presented Nichols with a biography of the young North Vietnamese pilot of the downed MiG. He had only about 450 hours total time, with 250 hours in the MiG-17.

'Not a great deal, but it should have been enough to hack the programme with his initial advantage', Nichols later wrote.

On 27 July, Lieutenant Commander Guy Cane of VF-53, leading four F-8Es, met four MiG-17s, and shot down a MiG with a Sidewinder. Meeting a two-plane section head-on, Cane, and his wingman, Lieutenant, j.g. Dexter Manlove, ended up turning

ABOVE FAR LEFT
Commander Hal Marr preflights his VF-211 F-8E. Marr scored the first MiG kill by an F-8 on 12 June 1966. He was also credited with a probable after he fired his 20 mm cannon at a second MiG-17

ABOVE LEFT
Lieutenant, j.g., Phil Vamaptella (centre) listens to a preflight brief in the VF-211 ready room. He scored a MiG kill on 21 June 1966, and received the Navy Cross

BELOW LEFT
The third F-8 MiG score went to Lieutenant Gene Chancy, also of VF-211, when he shot down a MiG-17 on 21 June 1966, in the same general action in which Vampatella got his kill. Chancy is shown in 'his' F-8, although it is not the Crusader in which he actually scored his kill which he claims was made with 20 mm cannonfire, and not a Sidewinder as is usually listed

ABOVE
Commander Dick Bellinger leaves his VF-162 F-8E in September 1966. He scored the first MiG-21 kill by the Navy a month later. His camouflaged flight suit was a squadron novelty obtained through a trading deal with a US Army unit in South Vietnam

with the enemy fighters until Cane got one missile off which detonated just behind the MiG's tailpipe. 'I thought it had missed until a chunk of his starboard wing came off and the MiG went into a nosedown spiral', Cane said. It was his one hundred and eighty-sixth combat mission, and his first encounter with a MiG.

The Crusader's next kill followed only five days later, on 1 August. Again, it was a photo escort mission, or at least that's how it started. Lieutenant Norm McCoy, of VF-51 was in an F-8H, paired with Lieutenant Jay Miller in an RF-8G from VFP-63's Det 31. (The photo dets were now designated by the hull number of the carrier to which they were assigned. Thus, Det 31 signified the *Bon Homme Richard*, CVA-31.) Miller, now on his second combat tour, had returned from his 1967 *Coral Sea* cruise and had been assigned as the communications officer for VFP-63. The interminable paperwork got to him and he told his OINC to send him out again to fill a hole in the *Bonnie Dick*'s photo det left when another RF-8 pilot had been shot down. At first, the OINC, Lieutenant Commander John 'Dutch' Schulze, denied the request, but soon told Miller to pack his bags. ('Dutch' Schulze was a character in the squadron, and would later command VFP-63 in June 1972. Almost predictably, his det called themselves 'Schulze's Flying Circus', and Schulze occasionally sported a red German helmet, even on the flight

ABOVE

Three MiG shooters from VF-24. Left to right, Commander Marion Isaacks, Lieutenant Robert Kirkwood, and then-Lieutenant, j.g., Phil Dempewolf. On 21 July 1967, while Isaacks and Kirkwood received confirmed kills over MiG-17s, Dempewolf did not. Thus, he also received a Distinguished Flying Cross and not the customary higher Silver Star given to those pilots who scored confirmed kills

LEFT

Captain S W Vejtasa, himself a highly decorated ace of World War II, awards the Silver Star to Commander Marion 'Red' Isaacks (centre) and Lieutenant Commander Robert Kirkwood (right) for their two MiG kills on 21 July 1967

Five CVW-21 pilots return from the 1967 cruise in the Bon Homme Richard. *Left to right Commander Paul Speer, Lieutenant Commander M O Wright, Lieutenant, j.g., Joe Shea, Lieutenant Commander R G Hubbard, and Commander Marion Isaacks*

LEFT
Five MiG killers pose in this CVW-21 photo following the highly successful 1967 cruise. Left to right Air Force exchange pilot Major J A Hargrave (he did not score a kill), Lieutenant Commander T R Swartz (who scored a kill in a VA-76 A-4C; note the A-4 behind the group with Swartz's name below the canopy), Commander Paul Speer, Lieutenant Commander M O Wright, Lieutenant, j.g., Joe Shea, Lieutenant Commander Bobby Lee, and Lieutenant Phil Wood

ABOVE
Lieutenant Commander Bobby Lee (extreme left) shot down a MiG-17 on 19 May 1967. He is shown with other pilots checking out in the first F-8Hs

RIGHT
Commander Paul Speer (left) talks with Lieutenant, j.g., Joe Shea following their two kills on 19 May 1967. The two VF-211 pilots each shot down a MiG-17

ABOVE
Lieutenant Dick Wyman of VF-162 scored a kill over a MiG-17 on 14 December 1967. He is shown here in VF-33's ready room as the squadron's operations officer during the America's *1973 Mediterranean cruise* (Dana Barclay)

TOP RIGHT
Commander L R 'Moose' Myers of VF-51 describes his MiG kill on 26 June 1968. His sweat-stained fatigues indicate the intensity of the moment as well as the humidity in the close spaces aboard an old carrier

ABOVE RIGHT
Commander L R 'Moose' Myers tells Captain T P Dankworth, skipper of the Bon Homme Richard, *about his MiG kill on 26 June 1968*

OPPOSITE TOP LEFT
Lieutenant Commander John Nichols (right) is congratulated by VF-191's Commanding Officer, Commander C H Tuomela, after Nichols' MiG kill on

9 July 1968. Nichols eventually commanded VF-24 and became one of five 3000-hour F-8 pilots

OPPOSITE TOP RIGHT
Five years after his MiG kill in 1968, now-Commander John Nichols, Commanding Officer of VF-24, sits in his squadron ready room during the Hancock's *1972–3 combat cruise*

OPPOSITE CENTRE
Lieutenant Norm McCoy (second from left) and Lieutenant George Hise (third from left) tell two other MiG shooters about their encounter on 1 August 1968. Commander Moose Myers, (left) and Commander Guy Cane (right) each got MiGs on this cruise

OPPOSITE BELOW
Lieutenant Tony Nargi of the VF-111 det in the Intrepid *scored the last F-8 MiG kill when he shot down a MiG-21 on 19 September 1968. Here, Captain Vincent Kelley, Commanding Officer of the carrier congratulates Nargi after the pilot's return*

Lieutenant Tony Nargi (centre) and his wingman, Lieutenant, j.g., Alex Rucker (right) pose with the Intrepid's *XO, Commander Thomas D Brown, after Nargi's F-8 kill*

deck.) Jay Miller's account of transpacing in the F-8 will bring a smile or two from many Crusader drivers:

Ron Sonniksen and I transpaced two F-8s all the way to the ship over 10 days. We went to Hawaii, and then the PI. Moose Myers—a MiG killer and eventual flag officer—met me and took me out to the ship from the PI.

Sonniksen and I led ourselves out to Hawaii from San Diego. Just the two of us, with only our compasses. We were 600 miles out and we met a Marine KC-130 whose radar was skewed in the plane, so we spent all our bingo fuel going around in a circle trying to find him.

They'd get a lock on us and say, 'Okay, you're 30 degrees from us', but their radar scope was skewed—and they didn't know it. So what they were reading as 30 was actually another 30! So we'd head off in that direction, and meanwhile they're going in a different direction.

So, pretty soon, Sonniksen told them to shut up and start counting. We homed on them and found them. I was already 200 pounds under bingo to get back to California. I wasn't very comfortable at that point. I plugged in, and then we sent the tanker back, and we were by ourselves again.

The next 400 miles were by ourselves, and we picked up another KC-130 1000 miles out of San Diego on their regular station. We went over Ocean Station November, a ship which sits out there, and talked to them on the radio. They wished us good luck, and finally about 250 miles out of Hilo, Hawaii, we picked up the Hilo TACAN. Here we were, two F-8s, and we were circling over Hilo. Barber's Point, our destination, was farther out, on Oahu. We had already been five hours in the air and had eaten the lunches Ron's wife had packed for us, *and* used the garbage bags we'd brought as portable 'toilets'. I was numb and frustrated. I wanted to get out of that airplane so bad.

Then they started giving us traffic vectors, taking us further out. Finally I keyed the mike—they acted like they didn't even know who we were, I don't know where they

thought we came from—so, I said, 'Be advised Barbers, I'm single engine'.

He came back, 'Roger, understand you're *single engine!* You're cleared straight in!' Of course, we hadn't told them we were F-8s anyway. We landed, taxied in, shut down, got disorganizedly organized, somehow.

I stepped over the side of the cockpit, and my legs were so numb from the cold and the long flight, they collapsed and I fell from the cockpit all the way to the tarmac. When the plane captain came up, I told him there was a bag under my seat. Even in the heat, the bag was still frozen, which shows how cold it had been during the flight. The heater in the F-8 came from bleed air from the engine. By the same token, when you were at real low level, out in the desert, the air conditioning wasn't enough.

Then we took off from Barber's, and half way from there to Wake, we found an A-3, but we left him while he was tanking someone else, and went into Wake ourselves. Then from Wake to Guam, we were supposed to have A-3s, but an F-4 which desperately needed the A-3s couldn't get started. So we decided to press on rather than waste fuel waiting for the F-4s and the A-3s. And we took off for Guam. That was kind of scary. Guam isn't a big place, and we had to rely on those old F-8 TACANs.

Joining his det on the *Bon Homme Richard*, Miller began his second combat tour. At the time of McCoy's kill, the F-8s had lost several airplanes, and didn't always have enough for all the missions. Miller's account of Norm McCoy's MiG kill on 1 August follows:

Norm was on a photo escort mission with me. There were probably two airplanes for either a BARCAP or FORCECAP between the boat and the beach. Usually, if things got out of sorts, the controllers just paired up who was left, and make a complete mission.

George Hise was by himself. His wingie went down or

ABOVE
A sequence of photos taken during one of the most hectic F-8-vs-MiG encounters. In December 1967, Crusaders from VG-111 and VF-162 engaged a flight of MiG-17s in a violent, twisting low-level fight. Eventually, Lieutenant Dick Wyman shot this MiG, but only after other pilots tried. Top to bottom, the green MiG dives away, followed by a Sidewinder that explodes harmlessly, too far from its target

ABOVE
The Enemy:
In characteristic poses near their MiGs, these North Vietnamese pilots exhibit the drastically different styles of headgear worn by communist aviators. The older MiG-17 required only a cloth helmet, but the newer MiG-21 pilot wore the more modern hard hat with European-style sun visor outside the helmet

something, and he was on his own. When Norm and I coasted out, after my mission, someone came up and asked us if the escort had enough gas to join up with Hise to take over the CAP mission.

I don't believe we got chased off the beach by MiGs. We'd finished our mission and were headed back. I remember it was a short mission and I had so much gas. It was not unusual for the RF-8 to have 6500 pounds *after* the mission, which was enough to fly to the Philippines. And the fighters would be down around 4500, because of their higher drag and lesser drag and lesser fuel quantity to start with.

McCoy joined up with George and they got a vector toward a MiG from Red Crown—the ship which functioned as a radar picket and kept a watch for MiGs. I think there was also another section of F-8s from the *Intrepid*. And they took out after the MiGs. Then McCoy and Hise got a vector. And for some reason, the first section broke off, and Hise made contact, and fired a missile. He called a hit. Within seconds after that the MiG went into a cloud and the F-8s lost sight of him.

When they reacquired him, McCoy was in the driver's seat, close to a minute after Hise's call. He pickled off a 'winder and nailed him. Bang! right there. Then, someone asked his state, and he came up with something ridiculous, 14- or 1600 pounds. They gave him a tanker call, and he refused. He later told me he was following the MiG down taking pictures with his Super 8 movie camera mounted on his glare shield. He chased the MiG to the impact and got pictures of the smoke and flames. I think the MiG pilot ejected, but I'm not sure. When McCoy crossed the beach, he had about 800 pounds of fuel.

He reached the A-3 tanker about 30 miles off the coast with about 4-500 pounds, and plugged on the first shot. That always amazed me. Because when you were just tanking for practice, it usually took you two tries, but it seemed every time you needed it, bang, it was always the first try, at least with the F-8 pilots.

When he got back to the ship, the CAG listened to the tape of the kill I'd made in the plane, and determined that since the MiG was still flying a full minute after Hise's hit—which apparently knocked off a piece of the MiG's wing—it was still manoeuvrable until McCoy's hit which was fatal. He got the kill. But they both got to go to Saigon for the usual MACV briefings which followed a kill.

The Crusader's last kill went to Lieutenant Anthony

J Nargi of VF-111's Det 11, operating from the veteran 27C carrier *Intrepid*. The old ship, which had suffered a major kamikaze strike at the end of World War II in 1945, and was finishing its days as an antisubmarine carrier (CVS), had been drafted to serve as a modified attack carrier with a small attack air wing, using A-4s and a detachment of Sundowner F-8Cs.

Nargi and his wingman, Lieutenant, j.g. Alex Rucker, were on a CAP mission on 19 September, when they were alerted to incoming MiGs, headed for their A-4 strike force. The two F-8s climbed to meet the threat which turned out to be MiG-21s.

'I think the MiG pilot saw me about the same time', Nargi reported. 'I called 'MiG-21 high' to my wingman. The MiG pilot started taking evasive manoeuvres immediately. He climbed and went into a loop, and I was able to get into position behind him'. Nargi fired a Sidewinder which blew the MiG's tail off, and the enemy fighter went down in a fireball. The North Vietnamese pilot ejected and floated down under an orange and white parachute. It was the Navy's twenty-ninth MiG kill of the war, and the F-8's eighteenth confirmed score.

Nargi and Rucker engaged a second MiG. Both F-8 pilots fired missiles which exploded close to the MiG, but the enemy plane seemed undamaged and quickly headed north to escape the VF-111 fighters.

When all the numbers were tallied, for the loss of three F-8s, the Crusader racked up a 6 to 1 kill-loss ratio. Oddly enough, Navy F-4s gained 36 kills for the loss of six Phantoms, creating the same ratio, 6 to 1.

Pickings were lean for the next three years, with only one Navy F-4 crew scoring in 1970. It was not until the heavy combat in the spring of 1972 that US crews began to score again. Carrier-based Phantoms shot down 26 MiGs from 1970 to 1973; they had scored 10 times during 1965–68. For the F-8, however, Nargi's kill represented the end to a relatively short, but intense, list of victories. But that did not mean the Crusader's war was over.

Though this F-8E carries six North Vietnamese flags on its fuselage strakes, it was not a MiG killer. Both VF-24 and VF-211 advertised their exalted status as the Navy's premier Crusader squadrons by painting flags and MiG silhouettes on various squadron aircraft. This aircraft was photographed at NAS Dallas in 1967, probably right after its return from CVW-21's cruise (Via Jim Sullivan)

Chapter 7
The End of the War, and Retirement From the Fleet, 1969-82

The Photo Birds

The reader can see from previous pages, how active a role the RF-8 detachments played throughout Vietnam. While their more glamorous fighter pilot compatriots shot the guns, dropped the bombs, and downed the MiGs, the men of the light photo dets fought their own dramatic and highly dangerous war. 'Unarmed and unafraid', was the reconnaissance pilot's motto. Jay Miller once said, 'Well, I sure was unarmed, but I don't know about the second part'.

VFP-63 lost 20 RF-8s to the deadly North Vietnamese flak and SAMs, though not one photobird was downed by a MiG, testimony, in part, to the teamwork between the photo pilots and their fighter escorts, as well as the intensive training and planning conducted by the crews. Light photo, indeed, all photo reconnaissance, was a dangerous proposition. Other squadrons in other carriers flying the more sophisticated RA-5C Vigilante and special reconnaissance versions of the big A-3 Skywarrior, also suffered many losses, way out of proportion to the size of individual dets, and the overall number of the specific type of aircraft eventually produced.

RF-8 drivers were among the most highly decorated of all military service pilots, and the most skilled in a speciality requiring mastery of a demanding aircraft, an occasionally temperamental and complicated camera system, and, not the least, a large helping of intestinal fortitude:

Here is a quick glimpse of an RF-8 mission from the February 1969 issue of *Crusader Fighter Report*:

600 Seconds Over North Vietnam

American jet aircraft launched from a Task Force 77 carrier in the Gulf of Tonkin, streak in from the sea. One of these planes is a photo-reconnaissance bird. Guarded by two fighter aircraft, the photo plane dashes in over the coast to the heart of the Vietnamese panhandle.

Across roads, along a river, cross and recross a railroad, the photo plane, cameras whirring in its belly, covers a predetermined area of the countryside.

Below, hidden in bunkers, in stands of trees, along river banks, anti-aircraft gunners attempt to down the aircraft. Rounds of anti-aircraft fire burst in the path of the speeding planes.

Unscathed, the photo plane and its escorts turn back to the beach and home—a Seventh Fleet attack carrier. Time over the beach was only 10 minutes—600 seconds.

The PIs

One unusual aspect of the RF-8's mission was the close relationship between the pilots and their ground team, especially the small group of specialists who looked at the mission film. Each det included, in addition to the complement of pilots and normal maintenance and administrative personnel, four or five specially trained individuals. These enlisted men and officers planned, briefed, debriefed, and reported the flights of their RF-8 pilots, showing a close involvement with the overall mission not found in other squadrons.

The enlisted men were Photographic Intelligencemen (PTs), while the junior officers who accompanied the det in the intelligence departments were designated Photographic Interpreters (PIs). These intelligence specialists were a vital part of the overall mission and they assumed responsibilities out of proportion for their relatively junior years.

Louis R Mortimer served two long cruises in Vietnam, one in the *Coral Sea* and one in the *Ticonderoga*. He had enlisted in the Naval Reserve at 17, and maintained his affiliation while going through college. Following his commissioning in 1966 through the Aviation Officer Candidate School (AOCS)—of 'An Officer and a Gentleman' fame—he received orders to attend the joint service school for

intelligence officers at Lowrey Air Force Base, near Denver, Colorado. During this intensive six-month course, he was taught various disciplines including basic photo interpretation, weaponeering—which instructed the requirements specific targets dictated in choosing the proper ordnance for their destruction—as well as briefing techniques:

I always laugh when I think how I got to light photo. I got low grades in photo interpretation. Two of us wanted photo squadrons. The other man went to heavy photo, VAP, the A-3 units on Guam.

Originally, I thought I was best suited to a fighter squadron, but they told me they want a more mature, sophisticated individual to work with the pilots and shoulder greater responsibility. I didn't know how true that was, but later, I thought you needed that maturity.

After Lowrey, we went to a three-week school at FITCPAC—Fleet Intelligence Training Center, Pacific—located, at the time, at Alameda, near San Francisco. This course gave us attack intelligence training for carrier operations as carried out by CTF 77, the main component of the on-going carrier presence in the South China Sea, on Yankee and Dixie Stations, rules of engagement, Southeast Asia geography, culture and history.

Then they sent me to San Diego to VFP-63. I checked in at night. The first guy I met was Jay Miller, who was going through the RF-8 training syllabus. I signed in with the duty officer, and in came Jay, fresh from a flight.

'Christ, I really scared myself. This night flying's for the birds. Hi, I'm Jay Miller.' And he stuck out his hand. I came back the next morning. We had an interview with the CO of the squadron and he introduced me to the department heads, and told me I'd be working in the Fleet Photo Lab. It was then I learned the difference between an Air Intelligence Officer (AIO) and Photo Interpretation Officer (PIO). The AIO never went to sea. I would be the junior PIO for my det and would go almost immediately to sea, to Vietnam aboard the Coral Sea.

We were trying to learn the RF-8's camera system with the pilots. The pilots would fly the mission and we as PIOs would grade the film. So, we were teamed very early with

ABOVE
An F-8J of VF-211 refuels from a KA-3B during a CAP mission over the Gulf of Tonkin in 1972. The A-3, originally a carrier-based nuclear bomber, found its most enduring role as an aerial tanker. The KA-3s made hundreds of saves of battle-damaged aircraft struggling toward their ship

RIGHT
The veteran carrier Hancock *during a 1968 cruise. The* Handjob *first fought in World War II and found herself at the spearhead during the Vietnam War. Part of the so-called 27-Charlie class of refurbished carriers, she had two bow catapults, and a centrally located elevator. An A-4 rests on the lift which was in a strategic location if the carrier sustained combat damage, or the elevator became stuck in the down position*

the junior pilots. We spent six months at Miramar learning the cameras before going to sea.

We formed the det early and integrated with CVW-15 to go to workups in Fallon, Nevada. Boy! It was cold up there! Interestingly enough, the film was processed right at Fallon, contrary to the situation after the war where all photo mission film went to San Diego. That's when I learned how important it was to have a good working relationship with the people in the photo lab. They could make or break you many times over. You had to be firm, but *enlightened*, humane. If you screwed with the photomates, your whole mission could be destroyed, everything a pilot risked his life for.

Mortimer worked through an intense period of combat operations, learning his job, and working with the many individuals in his det, and in the air wing. He went through the turmoil of experiencing the loss of his OINC shortly after the Coral Sea arrived on the line:

Lieutenant Commander Jim Vescelius became our OINC. Originally, he was going to be the second in command,

because he was junior. Lieutenant Commander Ron Sonniksen was supposed to be our OINC. But, there was a problem with the OINC of another det in the *Oriskany*, and they sent Sonniksen to the *Oriskany*, and Vescelius took over as the senior guy.

We had our Operational Readiness Executive (ORE) off California, then we sailed to Hawaii from Alameda where we had our Operational Readiness Inspection (ORI). These determined our readiness to go on cruise. We did pretty well.

We always used to joke, 'What happens if we flunk? Are they going to send us to Vietnam?'

Then we stopped in Japan, then to Cubi in the Philippines. From there to the line, right up north to Yankee Station.

We decided to break up the duty section to include a day and a night officer. There was so much film coming in. Naturally, as the junior guy, I got to be the night person, look at the film and write the many reports.

We had three PTs, a 2nd class, 3rd class, and a striker, a non-rated sort-of apprentice PT. We had five pilots. The senior PI would interact with the Strike Ops Department, which determined which targets would be hit by the air wing. He also handled daily messages.

Most of the times, we PIs assigned the targets to the pilots, as the flight schedule came out for the following day.

Then, we would work with the pilots, briefing them on the mission requirements and enemy defences. We'd research the target, trying to find previous photos, so they'd know what it looked like. Our pilots would also listen to the briefing given by ship AIs for the whole air wing.

One distinction was that all the other air wing pilots were debriefed by the ship AIs, but we in VFP-63 debriefed

ABOVE
John Glenn's Project Bullet Crusader continued to serve until 1972. Remanufactured as an RF-8G, BuNo 144608 was eventually assigned to VFP-63's Det 4 in the Oriskany, *off South Vietnam. Lieutenant Thomas B Scott returned from a reconnaissance training mission on 13 December 1972, and during his landing approach to the carrier, struck the deck, short of the arresting wires. He ejected, but Glenn's faithful Crusader wound up at the bottom of the South China Sea*

RIGHT
Shown at NAS Miramar in May 1973, shortly after returning from one of the last combat cruises, this RF-8G has been cleaned up. It carries a popular cartoon character of the time on its tail, the Playboy *'Horny Granny' (Peter Mancus, via Jim Sullivan)*

our own pilots. Debriefing was a tough act because some pilots tended to look down on the poor AI trying to get information from the pilots who had been on the mission while he was safe on the ship. But, there were only a few of those types.

Our photo pilots were always anxious to talk to us, however, because they understood the need for the information to look at their film. Photo pilots were more sophisticated than other wing pilots, because the photo pilot was the flight leader, even though he might be junior—*way* junior—in rank to his escort. Even if the escort pilot was the skipper of the fighter squadron, the jaygee in the RF-8 was the flight lead. Sometimes it would cause friction.

We read the mission film for BDA—bomb damage assessment—after a strike to see if another strike was needed. The air wing would hit a target, closely followed by our photobird. That was something we told them not to do, because the Vietnamese knew that the unarmed photo bird would come along, fly straight and level, and they could blow him away. But they did it that way. That's how our OINC, Lieutenant Commander Vescelius, got bagged on 21 September 1967, during a strike over Haiphong. We needed immediated BDA, right after the bombs, showing the bursts, and he flew way too low in an effort to get really good coverage. He broke the 3500-foot altitude minimums.

When we got back into port, we picked up another experienced pilot, Lieutenant Andre Coltrin, as our OINC, to finish our first line period. Later, on our second line period, Bill Rosson became our OINC. One of the nicest guys you'd ever want to meet.

Unfortunately, with all the heroic and dedicated efforts of the men and ships of TF 77, the communists were in no mood to talk, and the war continued. By late 1967, the North Vietnamese embarked on a huge supply operation, sending huge amounts of supplies south for a big military offensive in early 1968. The photo reconnaissance squadrons were in the front lines for this one. With a holiday standdown and peace bargaining schemes emanating from Washington, most of the intense strikes ceased. But the RF-8 dets flew on and on, and on.

Christmas, 1967

Because of the holidays, we thought everyone would enjoy a standdown. But, not us in photo. I never worked so hard in my life. We flew mission after mission. Before, I would look at film and never see anything. But during the Christmas Truce, it was open season. The roads were full of trucks, even during the day, all moving south. We reported all that, projecting where it would be at nightfall. While the air wing flew mainly around the ship, like on CAP missions, our RF-8s were flying regular missions. I looked at stacks of film, wrote my reports, only to look up and find more stacks waiting for me. One day, I worked 24 hours around the clock to get the film out during that period.

Of course, all this stuff went to supply the 1968 Tet Offensive, an all-out communist drive against the South. During Tet, the ship went south from Yankee Station to support defences against the Tet drive, on Dixie Station. That was the time the A-1s got back into the action since they had been prohibited from flying strikes on Yankee Station. They were too vulnerable to the heavy flak, and could only be used to cover Search and Rescue operations. But they earned their keep down south.

The huge communist offensive finally began on 30 January 1968, throughout South Vietnam, and the intensity of the attacks still evokes strong emotions 20 years later. This period of intense fighting included the legendary defence of a small US Marine outpost at Khe Sanh, six miles from the Laotian border. And

much of the supplies for the communist drive came
down the trails from the north, watched and reported
by the faithful RF-8 photo dets.

However, the communist offensive failed, and the
strike continued as before. The American government was determined to bring the North Vietnamese
to the peace table, and several so-called 'bombing
halts' were instituted as inducements. The most far-
reaching of these pauses was the halt begun on
1 November. President Lyndon Johnson decreed
there would be no further strikes into North
Vietnam. It was a desperate gamble by a president
who had decided not to seek re-election. But that
gamble also failed.

Again, while the other squadrons in the carrier air
wings reoriented their attentions to the south, or
withdrew from combat entirely, the light photo dets
continued flying missions to monitor communist
compliance with the truce. There were reprisal raids,
authorized only after the RF-8s and RA-5s had been
shot at. After an RF-8 had been downed in June, a
full-scale attack went north on 5 June 1969.

A major development in the RF-8 community was
the decomissioning of VFP-62 on 5 January 1968.
Although VFP-62's usual duties kept it with the
Atlantic Fleet, one det had made a Pacific combat
deployment in the *Franklin D Roosevelt* (CVA-42)
as part of CVW-1. VFP-62 Det 42's cruise from June
1966 to February 1967, saw the combat loss of at least
one RF-8G. And, of course, the 'Fightin' Photos'

*An F-8J, the last fighter model of the Crusader to see
widespread fleet service, is seen about South China Sea
clouds in March 1971 during the* Hancock's *cruise. The
VF-211 fighter is armed with two AIM-9 Sidewinders*

*Lieutenant Henry Livingston goes through pre-start checks
in his Juliet before a mission in 1972. His VF-211 F-8 is
armed with Sidewinders, as well as the plane's 20 mm
cannon*

finest hour came in 1962 during the Cuban Missile
Crisis. But, after more than 100 detachments in 22
carriers, in 19 years of service, VFP-62 was retired.

This change seemed to affect the entire reconnaissance community as other squadrons were
decommissioned, including VAP-62, on 15 October
1969, and its sister squadron, VAP-61, on 1 July
1971. These squadrons had given yeoman service in
Vietnam with their RA-3Bs.

With the demise of VFP-62, VFP-63 now
assumed responsibility for providing RF-8 dets to all
the Navy's carriers world-wide, but the emphasis
remained in Vietnam. In 1971, the squadron was
restructured to include a permanent shore
command—the 'home squadron'—and five numbered detachments, with two dets for Atlantic
operations, and three for the Pacific Fleet.

ABOVE
1972! More, intensified combat. Here a VF-211 F-8J is seconds away from launch from the Hancock. *The flight deck crewmen holds his thumb up to indicate everything is in place and the Crusader is properly positioned on the catapult*

RIGHT
Representing an F-8 carrier squadron in combat in 1972, this photo of the officers of VF-211 in the Hancock *is typical of such lineups. The squadron CO, Commander Jimmy Davis, is fifth from the left, rear row, and Lieutenant Henry Livingston, is fifth from the right in the front row. Several people sport large moustaches, a trademark of the carrier fighter pilot. Note the infra-red bubble protruding from the squadron F-8J, and the pitot tube at the centre of the nose (via Henry Livingston)*

In addition, on 1 September 1972, VFP-63 assumed responsibility for all F-8 training in the Navy. VF-124, long known as 'Crusader College', began to gear up for the F-14 Tomcat, then in the early stages of flight testing. VFP-63 had received F-8Hs in 1969. The idea was to provide RF-8s with their own escorts. However, the requirements in the fleet necessitated redistributing the Hotels to fighter squadrons, and VFP-63 had to wait until the mid-70s to get fighters once more. By that time, however, the F-8 had left the fleet, and the fighters served as squadron hacks and currency trainers.

The RF-8A eventually gave way to the updated RF-8G, the first of which had been modified from existing As in 1963. The RF-8G joined the fleet in October 1965, and made its first cruise beginning in July 1966 aboard the *Coral Sea*. The Golf was immediately distinguishable from the Alpha by the long ventral strakes mounted on the rear fuselage. The strakes had actually been introduced on the F8U-2 (F-8C).

The RF-8G did carry a lot of internal modifications, including an up-rated engine, the Pratt & Whitney J57-P-22, offering 16,000 pounds static thrust, hard-harness electrical wiring, and various avionic updates. The RF-8A's cameras were also changed in the G, and better ECM gear was installed.

Renewed Combat: 1972

The interim period of 1969–71 came to a dramatic end on Easter weekend 1972 as hordes of North Vietnamese troops and VC guerillas poured across the South Vietnam border, catching the South Vietnamese by surprise. Divested of much of the American protection they had enjoyed in the first part of the war, the Republic of Vietnam's troops reeled backward from the onslaught. Finally, they established some organization and eventually halted the enemy advance, at least enough to allow American units to come to their aid.

While the carrier task forces had been reduced, those that remained on station in the South China Sea had not been idle and had supported several operations. By late 1971, however, the pace had begun to increase, and following the Easter Invasion, the United States scrambled to reinforce the small number of squadrons and personnel still in South

THE END OF THE WAR

Vietnam, or off the coast. By July, there were six carriers on the line. For many aviators who had served earlier cruises in the 1960s, nothing had really changed.

Will Gray had served in VFP-63's Det 43 during the *Coral Sea*'s busy 1967–68 cruise. He had remained in F-8 squadrons in the States, but eventually returned to light photo, flying from the *Midway* during 1972:

When I returned to Vietnam in 1972, in the *Midway*, VFP-63 Det 3. I was the replacement OINC for Lieutenant Commander Gordie Paige—my roommate for my first two cruises—who had been shot down on 22 July and captured. I think he was the last F-8 POW. The war was just the same as it had been in 1967. If I had saved my maps I could have used them all over again. I always used charts even though I knew the country like my own farm in Louisiana. I had a full set of charts, in every scale (1:5,000,000, 1:1,000,000, 1:250,000, and 1:50,000) for the target areas. There was no storage place for all that in the Crusader's cockpit so I sat on the pile and kept the one I needed up in the windscreen.

The only difference between my 1967 cruise in the *Coral Sea* and the 1972 cruise in the *Midway* was time and a few minor equipment changes. I still flew the RF-8G, with different cameras and newer ECM (Electronic Counter-

measures) gear. The escorts were still F-4s with the same fuel problems.

The F-4 was a hindrance to the mission since it was short on fuel. And with his large radar cross-section and smoking exhaust, he alerted the enemy defences. When we had photo-on-photo escorts, we drew little fire. We flew erratically and fast, and our small radar cross-section did not present an offensive threat to the enemy so he could not always come after us with his best shot.

There were three carriers in the Gulf of Tonkin that had RF-8 dets, so I had to use a new callsign for my det. Instead of the familiar 'Corktip', we were now 'Baby Giant'. And our familiar Papa Papa (PP) tailcode letters were replace with November Foxtrot (NF).

The North Vietnamese defences were virtually the same except for one encounter I had with a ZSU-23. I was running a section of railroad that crossed the Thanh Hoa Bridge. I approached the bridge from the north at about 600 knots and 4500 feet. I had my eyes on the viewfinder, following the rail line. I looked up to see a stream of red coming right at me from a point on the ground right by the railroad. It looked like a solid red line. I just about broke my right leg getting in rudder to break away. They missed! It was over in a second, but I was impressed. It took me a couple of miles to get back on the route and continue south until my Phantom escort ran low on fuel and called 'Bingo!'

One of the nicest features of the RF-8G was its great fuel

load. With 10,152 pounds of JP-5 and a very low drag airframe, it had the perfect combination for photo work. The maximum trap fuel was low in those days due to older landing gear so you could only bring back about 2000 pounds of fuel.

We always started late in the launch to save fuel and took virtually no time to call 'Up and ready'. We had no INS [Inertial Navigation System] to align and no crew to coordinate. Since the RF-8 was lighter than the fighter F-8 we generally made military power cat shots which saved even more fuel.

Saving fuel has to be a philosophy. We met our escorts on the KA-3—the greatest tanker ever built—and waited for the F-4 to take on about 2000 pounds to top off. The cruise out to the coast-in point was made at about 31,000 feet at max endurance speed to save fuel and eat up the clock. When we had the coast-in point located, we pushed up the power and dumped the noses to gain speed before

A view of the 27C class carrier Oriskany *during her last deployment in 1975. It was also the last cruise for the fighter Crusader. An F-8J of VF-191 is on the number 1 catapult, just ahead of the island. The ship's H-2 plane guard is slowly keeping pace with the old carrier*

Some time shortly after returning from their 1975–76 cruise, the F-8Js of VF-194 indulged in FCLPs at NAS Miramar, although they would never again deploy. Here, a Red Lightning Crusader sails past the watchful LSO monitoring the practice carrier approach. Note the raised wing, and large flaps of the F-8, as well as the deflected horizontal stabilizers (Author)

THE END OF THE WAR

entering any SAM envelopes.

I raised the droops passing about 400 KIAS, and the Crusader would run right up to Mach 1 at military power. The F-4 would generally have to go in and out of burner and play the inside of our turns in order to keep in position.

Flying combat is the ultimate experience you can have in an aircraft. Being allowed to perform a mission you have trained very hard for is extremely satisfying. It is a mix of sickening fear and satisfaction. I know what it feels like to be a dove in a corn field on the opening day of hunting season, and after flying to the end of the field safely calling 'Corktip . . . feet wet'.

As the massive infusion of US airpower continued, the F-8s were back in the thick of the fighting, although they would be denied an opportunity to add to their MiG-kill list. While the RF-8s, who had never left the front lines, flew an intensive string of reconnaissance missions, the fighter 8s flew from the smaller-deck 27C carriers. The build-up of assets had been fast and heavy, in both aircraft and men. The intensity of the war's violence had also come as a surprise.

Lieutenant Henry Livingston was a first-tour aviator with VF-211 during this hectic phase of Vietnam. He joined the Checkmates in April 1971

and remained with the squadron until December 1973. He was very busy in 1972:

On 20 June 1972, Commander Jimmy Davis, VF-211's skipper, got shot down over Mu Gia Pass, one of three major exit routes from North Vietnam into Cambodia and Laos. He spent a harrowing two days and one night on the ground before he was rescued.

He had made a strafing run on an area he had just bombed, violating one rule literally written in blood: never fly over the same ground twice. The 23 mm flak sounded like someone knocking on his door. His F-8's hydraulic system came up red and the stick died. He ejected in a flat spin. When his chute opened, the shock was so strong it paralyzed one-half of his body.

Fortunately, the jungle was deep, but the karst ridges were also very steep. We kept an airborne vigil, with A-4s in orbit and an occasional F-8 working with the on-scene commander to sanitize the area. The Sandys—the Air Force A-1 Skyraiders from Thailand—finally arrived and I was on my way to the scene when one of the Sandys called, 'I'm hit. I'm losing it!' He bailed out, and now, there were *two* pilots on the ground.

The Jolly Green Giants—the Air Force rescue choppers—came in and got the Sandy pilot, but could not retrieve Jimmy. Then, on the following day, the Jolly Green started his run down a valley. Jimmy was flashing his

mirror and, in accordance with Murphy's Law, the sun went behind a cloud. The helo turned the wrong way, but the on-duty A-4 figured it out and reoriented the helo pilot. Davis caught the jungle penetrator hoist and was returned to the *Hancock*, a bit too stiff to fly for a while.

Shortly after Davis' return, an Army general, bedecked with pearl-handled pistols and a big brass belt—we thought he was the son of George Patton, but who was probably Major General James F Hollingworth, who was responsible for the defence of the An Loc region—came aboard the carrier and strode into our ready room. He demanded 'who the son of a bitch was' that had diverted air strikes from his military zone, III Corps in South Vietnam. We had all stood up and come to attention, but Jimmy had remained seated due to his wounds. He simply answered the irate general.

'I did, sir!'

The general looked at him for a moment in total silence. Then he said, 'I'm damn glad to have you back, but next time, don't cost me so many air strikes'. He then began to describe what an incredible job the F-8s had done bombing the town of An Loc, north of Saigon, near the Cambodian border. Surrounded by three North Vietnamese regiments, 100 mm guns and tanks, the South Vietnamese had held the town for more than 60 days, from early April to mid-June. It was the first battle where the communists used tanks. Every tactical Navy aircraft, including Crusaders, had been stacked up three or four flights high as they waited their turn for the Forward Air Controllers to bring them down to bomb the town's perimeter.

I had been in that circus over An Loc. Brian Foye and I were a section of F-8Js, toting Mk 83s and 20 mm. We checked in with the Pave Nail OV-10 FAC. When we arrived, there were already several flights on station, and the FAC worked them around the southern perimeter.

'Wind about two knots from the south-west. Best bail out position is due south about 20 miles. I can't work you down unless you can give me precision'. He was trying to lay down ordnance on a column of tanks approaching the town wall on the eastern side. The lead tank had come out of the jungle and started toward the wall.

Brian had the lead and the FAC called us down on that lead tank. Brian rolled in, diving down between columns of white clouds, and I watched him until I lost him through a hole in one of the clouds.

I arced around to the roll-in point at 12,500 feet, 220 knots, and could see the concentric shockwave of a Mk 83 detonation. I watched the tank still moving sluggishly into a crater filled with water. I lined up my fixed reticle and adjusted the sight to 107 mills. A quick glance showed about 65 degrees on the artificial horizon, but it was virtually useless at such a steep dive angle.

My speed increased toward 400 knots and my altimeter staggered around the dial, plunging toward a 6500-foot release point. All the numbers looked good. The clear air and blue sky between the towering cumulus gave me a false sense of bliss.

Suddenly, my F-8 gave its characteristic wing flex as a half-ton bomb released from a wing. After a slight pause, the Gs began as my nose came across the target. I could see the broken trees, craters—and a tank. The air was dark under the clouds, but the smoke was thick and I thought I was going through the gates of Hell.

I pulled harder, knowing I had stayed too long over the target with a classic case of target fixation. Unknown to me, the North Vietnamese tank commander had abandoned his

tank, and ran toward the jungle. But his crew had been chained to their positions. Brian's bomb had fallen so close that it rattled the tank commander and he knew that another bomb would hit within 20–30 seconds. My bomb upended the tank, and blew the escaping commander away.

General Hollingsworth handed out pictures blown up to 3 feet by 2 feet of the tank. The tank was captured and eventually set up on a cement block in Saigon as a memorial to the Battle of An Loc.

In the escort role—bomber and photo escort—the F-8s usually carried only two Sidewinders since a full bag of four AIM-9s placed demands on the fighter, making it nose heavy and reducing its maneouvrability. The supply of Sidewinders had been low during the early stages of the war. Often, F-8s would carry the same missiles through several missions.

Lieutenant Livingston escorted A-4s regularly. There was plenty of action:

Both VF-24 and VF-211 were used as bombers in 1972, but only in the South. Up North, we did not bomb, but were fighters, doing escort or BARCAP, TARCAP, MIGCAP, photo escort or Iron Hand SAM suppression missions. We could also be assigned as flak suppressors, going in ahead of the strike force, then reverting back to TARCAP duties. I also escorted an A-4 occasionally who ended up solo on an Alpha strike. The Skyhawk had a special role away from the main formation in flak suppression.

I also got called to strafe up North but this was rare. It was also rare to find yourself as on-scene commander for a downed aviator. But that's just what happened. I was with Lieutenant Commander Boyd Repsher on TARCAP during one afternoon. The weather was lousy as we chased a bunch of A-4s which had diverted to their secondary target since the primary target, a bridge, was obscured by overcast. After the abort, the Alpha formation broke up into sections and turned south.

Route One north of Vinh usually had something going on, and was a visible landmark, though the flak and SAMs were always present. We tried to keep track of the scattered Skyhawk formation. Rolling through layers of clouds and popping out over the rain-soaked rice paddies and hamlets below, we could hear clipped radio chatter as one section or another found an opportunity. It reminded me of a bunch of young hunters noisily scrambling into the woods after their quarry. Clearly, the big risk was hitting each other.

Suddenly, there was a mayday call. Repsher and I were jinking in tight combat spread, less than three-quarter mile abeam. We were loaded with two Sidewinders each and 20 mm. Boyd and I were roommates as well as assigned wingmen. Good deal for me because he was the third or fourth senior officer in the squadron, and I was a junior lieutenant. This was his second combat tour.

Lieutenant Commander Tom Latendresse had ejected in a wild spiralling ride from his disintegrating A-4. Number two on a flak site, he had taken a direct hit and when he landed after his ejection, his right arm was wrapped behind his back, his right hand on his left shoulder. As he lay on his back, chest heaving from shock, near his parachute, in the muck of a green rice paddy, his leg had almost been severed at the knee. He managed to push out his PRC 90, the small personal survival radio each air crewman carried, and began a laboured transmission on the common emergency frequency. After initial difficulty in making a clear call, he finally came through.

'I'm surrounded . . . send some ordnance down!' Repsher and I were first on the scene, and by coincidence, were already in a 10-degree strafing perch, 180 degrees left turn toward the firing position. Sheepdog called in hot—he was entering a firing position—and I began to set up the SAR effort.

Finally, Repsher and I rolled in side by side at only 800 feet above the ground. Through my gun sight, I adjusted with rudders to avoid Tom and his chute, and try to walk a burst of 20 mm cannonfire at the approaching black pyjama-clad troops I saw approaching his position. We watched the enemy closing in through the waving grass and Boyd and I heard Tom's last transmission.

'I'm surrounded. Don't shoot. Tell my wife I love her!' Then it was quiet.

All of us aviators had the idea that if nothing else made sense, we were sure going to try to get our POWs out. So much of lives were wasted by the political leadership; the only morals left were our own. In other words, instead of Washington fragging bridges and suspected truck parks from photos, the leaders should have gotten a fix on winning the war, and not with a half-and-half military-political response.

Latendresse was eventually released in 1973 after becoming one of the last POWs of the war. He is now a captain and one of the Navy's 'Super CAGs'.

Much to the Crusader pilots' frustration, they seldom got any MiG vectors in 1972. They firmly believed that the North Vietnamese would not engage Crusaders and would wait until the F-8s were out of the area before launching to pounce on other American aircraft, especially the Air Force F-4 bomber formations. Although the F-8s flew with the large Alpha strike formations, they were never attacked by MiGs, yet the USAF formations were constantly engaged by enemy fighters.

In February 1972, a month before the major Easter Invasion, two VF-211 F-8Js relieved the VF-24 BARCAP. Lieutenant Livingston takes up the story:

The *Chicago* immediately turned us south toward a 'bogey' and asked us to come up on secure voice. Checking in again, we were advised that a 'Red Bandit' was headed towards us from the Haoi/Haiphong area. (Red Bandits were MiG-17s; Blue Bandits were MiG-21s.)

I asked my flight lead, Ed Schrump, if he didn't smell a rat because the North Vietnamese never sent a solo 17 out over the water. Since it was early in the revival of hostilities, Nixon still had us contained below the major heartland area of North Vietnam.

The *Chicago* came right back with 'Oh, yeah, there are six Blue Bandits in trail'. Ed and I thought it sounded like a fair fight. Since my radar was the only sweet one, he passed me the lead, at which point I went under the hood, buster, and back to our clear combat frequency. Buster was the term for top speed to get from one point to another, in this case, the interception point.

Colonel R F Conley, commanding MAG-11, stands beside his appropriately decorated Studebaker and an F-8E of VMF-312 in 1964 at NAS Atsugi, Japan. After demanding permission to go into combat, 312 went to South Vietnam for a few months, although, unlike the other two F-8 squadrons, 232 and 235, it never returned for a second tour

An F-8E of VMF(AW)-235 takes off on a mission in South Vietnam on 12 April 1967. The Crusader carries 5-inch Zuni rockets on fuselage racks and underwing rocket pods. Note the characteristic raised wing of the F-8

RIGHT
VMF(AW)-232 took over 235's aircraft. Here, seconded F-8Es, now wearing Red Devil insignia, prepare to take the runway for an April 1967 mission from Da Nang. Note the widely-differing bombloads of the two Crusaders

As our two heavy F-8s, armed with Sidewinders and cannon, blasted head-on toward the MiG gaggle, the MiG-17 began a slow port turn, effectively crossing our bow—a perfect rear aspect intercept, except we were still 40 miles away. We were really closing, and I was out of the cockpit looking at a grey overcast with about three miles visibility. I shut down my radar at 10 miles.

Now the MiG-17 was dead ahead, but running away. At seven miles, we were still not getting good visual identification, and at five, the *Chicago* ordered us to break it off because we were crossing the magic no-go line. We pressed it a few seconds more, but then began our break-away about 2½ miles, just out of 'winder range.

During this time, Lieutenant Commander John Nichols, who had shot down a MiG-17 in 1968, was ordered to the Air Force base at Udorn, Thailand, to instruct the frustrated F-4 crews in air combat manoeuvring (ACM). USAF fighters were only breaking even against the North Vietnamese MiGs and were looking for help. Accordingly, Nichols took another VF-24 pilot, and two pilots from VF-211, along with their fighters. The plan was to fly strikes up north with the Air Force Phantoms, tank, and then get in some ACM practice before recovering at Udorn. This pace kept up for several days and each day, the Navy pilots destroyed their USAF brethren, to the obvious delight of the F-8 drivers and the continued frustration of the USAF.

Nichols was not too happy, however, at constantly beating the Air Force, and he was annoyed at their apparent lack of ACM training and expertise. He chastised them, none too diplomatically at times, for not using the vertical plane—the F-8's speciality—during engagements. It seemed the Air Force had completely forgotten the lessons of earlier conflicts.

Even Robin Olds—the Air Force's top MiG killer in Vietnam at the time—was angry. He heard about the Navy's visit and wangled a few rides with the Udorn F-4s. Nichols recalls that after one mission and subsequent ACM session, the Phantom with Olds in the back taxied in. The canopy barely opened when Olds' helmet flew out, followed by the irate colonel. He was furious at the poor performance of his pilots.

As a parting shot, the Air Force tried to keep Nichols from flying any more missions. Why? Because, he was told, the grey F-8s looked too much like MiGs and were confusing the USAF pilots. The only way he could go was to allow his four Crusaders to be camouflaged. At first, Nichols was amenable until he asked how much weight the new paint job would add. About 1200 pounds. No way. The F-8 normally recovered with about 2000 pounds of fuel. With a new paint job, this would cut the allowable fuel to 800 pounds, totally unsatisfactory. Nichols and his detachment returned to the *Hancock*.

The bitter feelings between the Air Force and the Navy, as they struggled to help contain the communists, continued. The simmering pot occasionally boiled over. One senior F-8 pilot collided with an Air Force KC-135 tanker. The USAF had so many planes based in Thailand, they had to swing out over the Gulf to form up before their missions. Some people in the Navy considered this an intrusion into their territory. Thus, feelings ran high when the F-8 unexpectedly met the 135. His right wing missed the tanker by a scant three inches—by later measurement—but his ventral fins scraped the big Boeing. The Air Force complained about what it felt was harassment.

By 1972, the F-8 had rapidly begun to disappear from fighter squadrons. Some squadrons tran-

sitioned to Phantoms; some even made the change early enough to fly F-4s in combat in 1972. By the last full year of the war, only four fighter squadrons flew the F-8: VF-24 and VF-211 in the *Hancock*, and VF-191 and VF-194 in the *Oriskany*. All four squadrons flew the F-8J. And, to course, VFP-63's detachments continued to fly the RF-8G.

The 27C carriers had largely been retired by this time, too, which limited the deck space available to the Crusader. The older ships like the *Ticonderoga*, *Intrepid*, *Shangri-La*, and *Bon Homme Richard*, had retired from service, leaving only the *Hancock* and *Oriskany*. Also, Crusader squadrons, especially those in the Atlantic Fleet, were simply decommissioned. VF-62 and VF-13, longtime Atlantic Crusader units, retired in 1969.

In keeping with its long period of service, and sterling combat record, the Crusader eventually boasted five pilots who attained over 3000 hours in various models of the F-8. The first man to gain the magic number of hours was Commander Richard A 'Pete' Peters, who flew his three thousandth hour in the F-8 in November 1971. Peters also accumulated nearly 800 carrier landings in the F-8, more than any other Crusader pilot. Commander (later Rear Admiral) David R Morris followed in July 1972. MiG killer Commander John B Nichols III flew his three thousandth hour in August 1973. Lieutenant Commander (later Rear Admiral) Jerry Unruh got there in September 1974. Commander (later Rear Admiral) W F Flagg became the fifth and last 3000-hour Crusader driver in 1978, and with 3272 hours, also garnered the high-time slot of all F-8 pilots.

The F-8's final hours in the fleet are filled with amazing stories. But none are more incredible than two which involve Commander John Nichols' VF-24 in the *Hancock* in 1973. While the ceasefire of January 1973 had ended the fighting in Vietnam, the old carrier continued making deployments to the South China Sea. A few months after the ceasefire, VF-24's Executive Officer hit the ramp when trying to land, which is called a 'ramp strike' in carrier aviation. The XO hit the deck so hard, he also hit his head on the canopy, breaking the plexiglas, and rendering himself unconscious during that critical stage of the landing sequence.

Fortunately, his F-8J flew itself off the deck and somehow maintained reasonably level flight until its pilot regained his senses, and landed at Da Nang.

Following the ceasefire, North Vietnamese observers were stationed in South Vietnam to administer portions of the agreement. The arrival of the Checkertail Crusader, armed with 20 mm ammunition, caused great concern. In Washington, diplomatic messages flew and the North Vietnamese exhibited righteous indignation.

It was finally decided to helicopter the XO out, and simultaneously bring in an 18-year-old plane captain who had volunteered to rig a tow so that the F-8 could be dragged through Da Nang to the piers where a US freighter, which had been detoured by the US State Department, would take the fighter aboard and eventually bring it back to the Philippines. The plane captain, an Alaskan Aleut Indian named Guest, with the inevitable nickname of 'Eskimo', was unceremoniously dropped off and left to his own devices for two days.

Unsupervised and without provisions—except from the local prostitutes who 'took the youngster under their wings and fed him . . .' Guest rigged a tow and the fighter made the trip through Da Nang in the early morning. However, while the freighter captain did take the plane aboard, he had his regular tour to make, and after leaving Da Nang, he made his scheduled run through Cambodia and other parts of SE Asia before arriving in the Philippines 30 days later.

The young American plane captain had plenty of tales to tell, not the least of which was being the last American fighting man—except for embassy Marines—in South Vietnam, with the last US fighter plane. The F-8 was so badly damaged during its ordeal that it was finally struck off register in the Philippines.

Hancock conducted normal operations in the Gulf of Tonkin throughout the summer and early autumn of 1973. But she received orders in late October to go south toward the Indian Ocean, then to the Arabian Sea. She began the transit on 29 October and arrived at the southern end of the Red Sea as the third Arab-Israeli War was in full swing.

Finally, the commanding officers of the squadrons of Air Wing 21 listened in amazement as they were told to stand by to fly their A-4s and F-8s to Israel and turn them over to the hardpressed Israeli Air Force. CVW-21 included three A-4 squadrons—VA-55, VA-164 and VA-212—and the two veteran F-8 squadrons, VF-24 and VF-211. A-4s were coming from the United States, through transoceanic flights, including stops on carriers in the Mediterranean. But the plan to completely turn over an air wing's assets to the Israelis seemed incredible to the pilots of CVW-21.

They began to ask questions. 'Will we be armed during the flight? Can we shoot back at the Arabs? What'll we do after we arrive?' The briefers did not, or could not, answer the questions satisfactorily, and the air in the ready rooms was tense. However, the Israelis gained the upper hand in the war, and eventually, the *Hancock* was sent on its way back to the United States. It was nearly the last cruise for the fighter Crusader.

The F-8 Retires

While VF-24 and 211 prepared to transition to the F-14, VF-191 and VF-194 stayed with the *Oriskany* for one more Westpac cruise. The 'Mighty O' began her sixteenth Westpac deployment on 16 September

TOP
The carrier Marines of VMCJ-1 line up in front of their aircraft during the busy 1964 deployment in the Bon Homme Richard

ABOVE
An RF-8A of VMCJ-1 in mid-1964, immediately prior to the unit's deployment to South Vietnam. The RF-8A did not have the familiar fuselage strakes behind the main gear that appeared on the RF-8G

ABOVE
VMF(AW)-333 did not go to Vietnam until a cruise in the America in 1972, by which time the squadron had changed to Phantoms. However, Trip-Trey flew F-8Es in 1967 in the US. Here, a squadron Crusader carries underwing bombs as it stands on the flight-line at MCAS Yuma, Arizona. The pilot, Captain Corbett, soon went to Vietnam with VMF(AW)-235 to fly combat (Clay Jansson, via Jim Sullivan)

RIGHT
The mid-1970s were a time of change for the Navy's last fleet Crusader squadron. VFP-63 took over fighters, now without squadrons, to provide aircraft for new F-8 pilots. This F-8J gets attention from maintenance personnel on the squadron flight-line at Miramar in June 1976 (Author)

1975. CVW-19 included the two F-8J squadrons, and three A-7 squadrons, as well as Det 4 of VFP-63.

The majority of the air wing had been craned aboard the old carrier at NAS Alameda, and had not been allowed to fly during the transit to Hawaii, presumably to reduce wear and tear on the carrier's gear and her aircraft. When the *Oriskany* arrived in Hawaii and began flying, the standdown had serious consequences. One of the RF-8 pilots flew into a mountain during a photo mission. And later, when the ship reached the Philippines, VF-194 lost an F-8 during a night carrier landing when the pilot landed

too far right and clipped aircraft spotted at the bow. He ejected and was recovered, but his F-8J was lost.

The following night, another VF-194 Crusader touched down during a landing which was made too far *left* of centreline, even though the pilot had been waved off. The F-8 took out the lens, and the pilot ejected as his plane slid off the deck. He was recovered by the ship's helicopter. Following two night losses, night recoveries for the Crusaders were halted. If night flying was scheduled, the F-8s would launch and land at Cubi in the Philippines. The planes would then recover aboard the *Oriskany* the next morning.

CVW-19 operated off the Philippines in the Scarborough Shoals area, participating in several exercises with the Air Force. The Crusaders flew ACM against Marine AV-8A Harriers, recent additions to the Corps on deployment to Cubi.

One problem during this period were the local salvage hunters on the weapons range. These people would hover nearby in small boats and move right in with divers to recover expended ordnance, much to the annoyance of the carrier pilots.

Lieutenant J 'Chuck' Scott flew with VF-191 on this, the last F-8 fighter cruise. Although the communists had accomplished their final takeover of South Vietnam the previous April, and the last-minute flail of the so-called *Mayaguez* Affair in May had seen a short, sharp fight between the Marines and Cambodians, the South China Sea was relatively tranquil in the autumn of 1975. Nevertheless, the *Oriskany* treated its deployment to this once war-torn ocean with the appropriate attitude:

On another line period, we deployed to Yankee Station and flew some sorties along the southern coast of Vietnam. Of course, this was very exciting for me as a nugget, but I also remember how much of a workload it was. Not having any combat experience meant my neck hurt from 'checking six' even when I didn't have to, and always being the first one to run out of gas because I was raging around at 250 knots.

A typhoon cut the deployment short, and the *Oriskany*, having returned to the Philippines, was ordered home early. Avoiding the Malaccan Straits because of pirate activity, the carrier fought heavy weather throughout her transit. Eventually, on 3 March 1976, the old ship tied up at the Alameda piers and was retired shortly afterward. Commander Jack Hamilton, CO of VF-194, made the last trap in a fleet F-8.

A traditional part of any cruise, and one eagerly anticipated by air crew and families alike, is the flyoff. This involves the air wing's aircraft making formation flights from the ship to their home airfield, a sort of mini-airshow for the folks on the ground. CVW-19's 1976 flyoff is described by Chuck Scott:

Man-up on a frigid wintry flight deck in anti-exposure suits, 300 miles off Alameda. Twenty-one F-8s launched, but one couldn't get his gear up and he diverted to LeMoore with a wingman. So, 19 F-8s arrived over Miramar. All the planes recovered safely and parked at the end of the runway with the engines turning so the pilots could change from the bulky wet suits into their sexy blue flight suits. There was a large press corps in attendance on the ramp. We taxied to the ramp by rocket numbers—the pilot's pecking order within the squadron determined by seniority. Richly enjoyed by all participants.

With the end of the cruise, the F-8 retired from the fleet, and VF-191 and VF-194 transitioned for a short while to Phantoms. Then, these two veteran squadrons also retired. (But were eventually reborn as F-14 squadrons in the 1980s—only to be decommissioned after only a few months as a part of deep cuts.) All Navy Crusader activity now centred on VFP-63 which maintained its responsibilities supplying light photo dets.

Another final milestone came on 26 August 1975, when Lieutenant Jerry Tucker became the last of 1630 graduates of Crusader College, now transferred to VFP-63. Already an experienced F-8 pilot with 235 combat missions with VF-211 during the 1972 cruise in Vietnam, Tucker went through the photo training syllabus.

On 19 May 1976, the Navy's last fighter F-8 lined up on Miramar's Runway 24-Left. Lieutenant Frank Meyers was at the controls of F-8J BuNo 149215 as it began its last flight to the storage facility at Davis Monthan Air Force Base. Although the Juliet was assigned to VFP-63, it still bore the familiar red-and-white checkerboard markings of its original squadron, VF-211. Originally built as an F-8E, 215 accumulated a respectable 3707 hours in the air over a 14-year career, and had been turned over to VFP-63 after VF-211 began its transition to the F-14 in September 1975. With the departure of 215, the fighter Crusader had, at last, retired from the Navy. (Actually, *the* last flight by a fleet F-8 was probably made on 6 October 1980, when Commander Joseph T Phaneuf, commanding officer of VFP-63, flew his F-8J to Davis Monthan for storage.)

Leatherneck Crusaders in Vietnam, 1965-68

While Navy squadrons flew the major portion of Crusader sorties in Vietnam, there were five US Marine Corps squadrons which saw a great deal of combat. As previously mentioned, VMF(AW)-212 was the second fighter squadron during CVW-16's 1965 cruise in the *Oriskany*. The Lancers' CO, Lieutenant Colonel Charles Ludden, took over the wing when Commander James Stockdale was shot down in September. It was the first time since World War II that a Marine commanded a carrier air wing, and the last time a Marine squadron flew from a carrier as part of the embarked air wing until 1971.

During their tour with CVW-16, the Lancers flew 3018 combat hours and 1588 combat sorties over

North and South Vietnam. One Marine, Captain Harlan P Chapman, was shot down and captured. Chapman ejected from his F-8E on 5 November 1965, 30 miles east of Hanoi, and was repatriated seven and a half years later in February 1973, having been promoted to lieutenant colonel during his imprisonment.

However, most of the Marines' activity came from shore-based squadrons. In Vietnam, the fixed-wing jet squadrons operated mainly from two bases, Da Nang and the smaller, but important, base at Chu Lai, 55 miles south of Da Nang.

As the influx of squadrons continued throughout 1965, VMF(AW)-312 brought its F-8Es to Da Nang on 19 December, as part of Marine Aircraft Group (MAG) 11. 312 had fought to come to Vietnam after the squadron had learned it was to be rotated back to the States. Lieutenant Colonel R B Newport and his men demanded a chance to join their fellow Marines and eventually got the chance, flying 718 combat missions by February 1966.

VMF(AW)-312 returned home to transition to F-4s, but left its F-8Es in Vietnam for its replacement, VMF(AW)-235, led by Lieutenant Colonel George A Gibson. The Death Angels, whose squadron motto was *Ride Nunc*, 'Laugh Now', quickly became the most recognized of Marine Crusader squadrons, sporting bright red noses with white stars. Arriving at Da Nang on 1 February 1966, 235 quickly got into the action.

During this early stage of the war, not all the

fighting was between the Americans and the communists. The South Vietnamese, unused to taking orders from their American allies, occasionally resisted. A rebellion in April 1965 by a small faction in the South Vietnamese Army precipitated a confrontation between the 9th Marine Regiment and a well armed South Vietnamese force at a bridge.

The arrogant South Vietnamese commander threatened to use his 155 mm howitzers against the Marines. Undaunted, the American Marine CO, Colonel John R Chaisson, looked up just as a flight of VMF(AW)-235 Crusaders, armed with bombs and rockets, roared overhead. Looking the Vietnamese commander in the eye, he growled,

'I'll see those 155s and raise you two F-8s.' The South Vietnamese backed down.

VMF(AW)-235 was relieved by VMF(AW)-232, under Lieutenant Colonel N M Trapnell, Jr, on 15 November 1966. The Red Devils of 232 took over 235's veteran F-8Es, and began flying combat missions in December. The F-8E's were heavily involved in ground support missions, the Crusader being the only type which could carry 2000-pound bombs which were very effective against the enemy concentrations in the dense jungles of the area.

VMF(AW)-232 suffered its first combat loss on 4 May 1967, although its pilot was rescued. Captain H J Hellbach was not as fortunate after he radioed he had taken flak hits during a mission on 19 May. His Crusader exploded before he could eject. The Red Devils left South Vietnam on 30 June 1967, after flying 5785 sorties.

The Death Angels of VMF(AW)-235 were, after all, the most active of the three in-country Marine fighter squadrons, returning through 1968 to fly combat. In May 1967, the squadron flew a record 854 sorties in support of Marine ground forces. The squadron eventually flew a total of 9140 day and night combat missions in both North and South Vietnam.

An RF-8G of VFP-63's Det 1 shows its Bicentennial markings in April 1976. This photo shows the Crusader's wing down. The pilot, in the cockpit as he begins his pre-taxi checks, will eventually raise the wing before he reaches the runway

ABOVE
During the frustratingly long period of the Iranian Hostage Crisis, 1979–80, Navy carriers steamed in and out of the Indian Ocean, as close as they could to the outlaw nation of Iran. VFP-63's photo detachments did yeoman service during the long cruises. A Det 2 RF-8G recovers aboard Coral Sea *in February 1980 during the old carrier's IO deployment. Soon,* Nimitz's *Det 5 would join Det 2, and the two photo dets would remain together until the* Coral Sea *returned to California in June 1980*

RIGHT
An RF-8G of VFP-63 sits on the wet flight-line during an April shower at NAF Washington, DC. The plane is well maintained, but wears very simple markings. By this time, 1981, there was only one photo det on cruise, and the squadron would be gone within a year (Author)

Then-Captain David C Corbett remembers 235 as including 'the wildest bunch of crazies I have had the pleasure to serve with . . . that last bunch of drivers were kicked out of practically every O-Club in the Orient during 1967–68, but how they could fly the F-8'. Corbett also fondly remembers his time in the Crusader. 'I would have been happy to fly an entire career in the F-8; it was a pilot's aircraft.'

During the 1968 Siege of Khe Sanh, VMF(AW)-235 flew in support of Operation Niagara, the massive air operation which included Navy, Marine and Air Force aircraft in a continuous attack against communist positions. Now-Colonel Corbett recalls that period:

Tet '68 had just started, and to read the papers, we were losing our butts. In reality, the Marines in I Corps kicked tail, not the least of that action took place at Khe Sanh. The F-8 was the only aircraft which could carry the monster 2000-pounders, and we did a lot of helo landing zone clearing.

During a period of about three weeks, we worked very closely with the grunts defending Khe Sanh. They were in a bad way because it was difficult to resupply them. The bad guys were attacking them in every possible way. The most effective method was to tunnel toward the perimeter wire, pop up, and attack the Marine positions. This had to be stopped. Someone decided to use our F-8s.

We flew mission after mission, dropping our big bombs only about 300 feet from our own positions, the closest we'd ever tried. The bombs had delayed fuses which allowed them to penetrate two or three feet into the ground before they exploded. When they went off, whole sections of the tunnels would collapse. The plan worked better than we expected and the enemy's drive to take Khe Sanh was squashed. I can't imagine how the grunts felt about us dropping so close, but they apparently had a lot of confidence in us, and it paid off.

Corbett had a lot of experience with the huge Mk 84s.

Although he complained the F-8's bomb sight was not very good, he recalled that he and other pilots used a simple grease pencil mark on their sights which, when properly aligned in conjunction with the individual pilot's most comfortable seat position, gave fairly consistent results:

The F-8 was one of the few aircraft which could carry the 2000 pounders. When four Crusaders were loaded with two Mk 84s fused with 36-inch Daisy Cutters, the devastation to the landscape was incredible, to say the least. On one mission, I remember that with a total of eight 2000-pounders, we completely levelled an entire mountain. I was so impressed that I actually went down low and slow to see the results. It was terrible, but very effective.

Another time, I dropped these same weapons on troops in the open. The enemy was literally cut in half. The Daisy Cutter exploded 36 inches above the ground, and in my opinion, against troops in the open and for clearing landing zones, there was no more effective weapon.

Besides the four Marine squadrons that flew F-8s in SE Asia, a fifth squadron, VMCJ-1, flew the RF-8A.

One of three Marine composite squadrons, VMCJ-1, also operated the Korean War-vintage Douglas EF-10B Skyknight. Both aircraft performed yeoman service throughout the 1964–68 period of the war. The photo Crusaders supported Navy and Air Force, as well as Marine, operations, flying missions over North and South Vietnam and Laos.

As mentioned earlier, VMCJ-1 also sent personnel and aircraft on detachment to several Navy carriers immediately after the Gulf of Tonkin incident in August 1964 to bolster VFP-63's dets. During 1966, in a time of intense operations and combat, VMCJ-1 flew over nearly 1800 reconnaissance sorties.

By October 1966, however, the RF-8A was supplanted by the RF-4B Phantom, and the Marine photobird quickly disappeared from service, leaving the F-8Es of VMF(AW)-232 and VMF(AW)-235 to carry on the Crusader name in SE Asia.

The Marines lost 12 F-8Es to flak in Vietnam, plus two during enemy rocket attacks on bases. Eight Echoes and one RF-8A were lost operationally in SE Asia. (Operational losses are considered to result from non-combat related problems, such as system malfunction, weather-related, and pilot error.)

By comparison, the Navy lost 10 fighters to SAMs and 42 to flak and small arms—hand-held weapons. Twenty Navy RF-8s were lost to flak. Thus, including three confirmed losses to MiGs in 1966, and one possible in 1967, the Navy lost 56 F-8s and 20 RF-8s in combat. Operationally, 58 fighters and nine photos were lost. Overall, a little over 13 per cent of all Crusaders manufactured were lost in SE Asia. Again, Bud Flagg:

At the end of the first cruise, every time we went across the beach, I'd get very nervous and break out into a cold sweat. Once we crossed the beach, and got involved in the heat of battle, we did what we were supposed to do, but we constantly asked ourselves who was going to get hit, or come back.

Every strike we flew, we lost at least one plane, sometimes the pilot. It was an eerie feeling at the briefs. Both A-4 squadrons, especially, took heavy casualties in planes and pilots. The Marines lost four planes—two in combat—and one pilot.

The second cruise, in 1966, VF-162 went through 12 F-8s and five pilots. That was within three and a half months since that was the cruise which was cut short by the *Oriskany*'s fire in October. The losses were not all in combat, some were operational—ramp strike, bridle slaps—as well as flak and SAM losses. Four were actual combat losses.

I think it was a war everyone would like to forget. All the young guys, myself included, thought it was something we had to get into, wear medals, the glory side, never realizing what a major part this would be of our lives, the stress and strain we were under, and how, in later years, this stress would surface. When you've been scared out of your wits, I'm not sure you ever fully recover from it. When they began using missiles, that was another type of sheer terror. You knew you could avoid the missiles, but to see these huge things coming at you was awesome, and your heart stood still. It was hard, sometimes, to even call out the

missile. I think the Vietnamese sometimes just 'lobbed' the SAMs at us to see if they could hit anything.

It was amazing that during the Alpha strikes we didn't have any midairs, and the A-4s could put their bombs on target in all the confusion, the shooting, drop, get out on your own, and find your way back to the ship.

The atmosphere changed during the cruise, from the regular laughing and scratching to tense, raw emotion in the ready room. The playfulness and boisterousness of the legendary fighter pilot changed. Our tempers became short, and more than once we were involved in shouting matches. There was a certain amount of fatigue—battle, or otherwise—and we all had trouble sleeping. Whether anyone admitted it, we were all scared and wondered if we would survive. Now, looking back after 20 years, I can admit it to myself. I hope we've found a better way 20 years later.

VFP-63, The Eyes of the Fleet, Carries On, 1977-82

When the last fighter Crusaders left the fleet in 1976, only one regular Navy squadron continued to operate the F-8. VFP-63, with its five detachments, settled in to fly the faithful RF-8G to the end of its career. Although the RF-8G's retirement had been scheduled to coincide with the retirement of the *Essex*- and *Midway*-class carriers, VFP-63 continued to provide dets for the Navy's carriers, throughout the late 1970s, even as plans for the retirement of its sometime-competitor, the RA-5C Vigilante, were solidified. The Vigi left in 1979, and suddenly, the only operational tactical reconnaissance system, ready and able to deploy in carriers, was the venerable RF-8G. (The long-nosed RF-4B employed by Marine squadron VMFP-3 occasionally deployed in the *Midway* and *Coral Sea*, but the photo-Phantom's limited numbers did not allow for greater use.

The F-14 Tactical Airborne Reconnaissance Pod System (TARPS) was on the way but it would have to overcome not only the normal introduction problems but stiff resistance from the fighter crews in the Tomcat squadrons already in the fleet. No fighter pilot or Radar Intercept Officer (RIO) wanted to admit any interest in taking pictures, and no fighter skipper wanted to waste any of his valuable aircraft on special outfitting to carry and operate the expensive camera pod. It would take time for the F-14 TARPS to earn a place in the air wings of the 1980s.

Meanwhile, the RF-8G kept flying, assisted by modifications, including an engine change. With the release of many fighter engines, a plan was devised to replace the J57-P-22 engines of the remaining photobirds with the powerful J57-P-429 engine of the Juliet. Begun in February 1977, and called the Power Eye Mod, this upgrading gave the old RF-8Gs nearly a third more power, and the old airframes literally leaped off the runways much to their surprised pilots' delight. In addition to the engine change, the modifications also included new electrical wiring, as well as the installation of new ECM equipment.

By mid-1977 the Power Eye Mod programme was in full swing. The modified RF-8s could be readily identified by the two large air intakes mounted on their tail cones. The change did not mean just replacing one powerplant with another, but required reams of instructions and lists of parts for the wiring, clamps and monitoring devices for the actual installation and operation of the P-429.

The period 1975–81 was a climactic and hectic time for the light photos. Problems with the ageing Crusader were subjugated by the need for its proven tactical reconnaissance capabilities, especially as the RA-5C retired. VFP-63's Det One, with Lieutenant Commander Kevin Smith as OINC, deployed with CVW-9 in the *Constellation* in April 1977. The det received its aircraft a month prior to workups at NAS Fallon, and major efforts were needed to bring the equipment to operational conditions. Although the Fallon workups went well, a series of mishaps focused attention on the RF-8s. Although the exact cause of these accidents—many of which were due to flameouts—could not be determined, several experienced Crusader pilots tried to find the reason. They finally found that a specific seal in the engine fuel control units was breaking down because of age. The faulty seals were immediately replaced and no further flameouts occurred.

Because of the *Connie*'s status as the 'ready carrier', CVW-9 participated in a larger-than-normal number of at-sea periods. Det One's pilots gained over 75 traps each, *before* deployment. (Det One's total flight time for 1977 was 830 hours, nearly 200 over Det Five in the *America* with 643.) However, though Det One was doing well, trouble still hounded the parent squadron at Miramar.

Another string of accidents, resulting in 11 aircraft lost, so alarmed senior Navy officials that they tried to shut down VFP-63. Since Det One was already deployed in the Pacific, the approval from the Commander, Seventh Fleet, was needed, and he turned the request down flat because of his pressing operational commitments. Thus, for a time, *Connie*'s Det One was the only RF-8 outfit conducting normal operations. However, the Commander, Pacific Fleet Fighter Wing, sent a message to the commanding officer of the *Constellation*, and the commander of CVW-9, requesting they assess their VFP det's capabilities in light of the RF-8 community's excessive mishap rate.

Operating under the glare of this unusual spotlight, it was apparent to Det One that one essential ingredient was missing: an adequate supply of spare parts of high-usage items. The det then came up with a list of crucial spares which was maintained throughout the remainder of the cruise. In addition, selected enlisted men were eventually obtained to fill in in key electrical and mechanical maintenance areas. Det One's performance so impressed Navy leaders

Four former VFP-306 skippers stand with the Crusader Sword during the squadron's decommissioning ceremony in September 1984. Left to right Captain R F Norrell (1979–81), Captain T C Irwin (1977–79), Captain R G Hoch (1975–77), and Commander A E Wattay (1973–75). The sword is a real twelfth-century crusader's sword and was previously owned by VFP-63 (Author)

that it was awarded a Seventh Fleet citation 'for outstanding superior performance . . . achieving aircraft readiness levels that surpassed all other air wing units while flying an impressive number of flight hours in support of Seventh Fleet Reconnaissance Operations'. By the end of the decade, VFP-63 had completely reversed the downward spiral with revamped training, and was awarded a Meritorious Unit Commendation.

By 1979, VFP-63's complement, which at one time had numbered some 700 officers and men, had been reduced to 300. But the photo dets still served. In 1979, the Iranian Hostage Crisis brought a greatly increased US presence in the Indian Ocean. Long, boring deployments were the norm, and the carriers and their supporting task forces settled into one dreary cruise after another.

VFP-63's Det 5 left Miramar in August 1979 before the crisis. The det flew east to serve with the new nuclear carrier *Nimitz*'s air wing. But when the crisis began in November, the *Nimitz* sailed from the Mediterranean to the Indian Ocean where she remained for several months. The abortive rescue attempt in April 1980 brought H-53 helicopters to the *Nimitz*. Det 5 gave up its spaces, including the ready room it shared with the carrier's EA-6B squadron, and cross-decked to the smaller ship to serve alongside *Coral Sea*'s own Det 2, which had left Miramar in November. The two dets remained with the *Coral Sea* until her return to the States in June 1980. What had begun as a six-month cruise for Det 5 became a 10-month, 325-day, two-ship deployment which took the members around the world.

Then-Lieutenant Donnie Cochran, an RF-8 pilot in Det 5, commented, 'It got old very fast.'

Eventually, the date was set for the last RF-8 cruise and the retirement of the fleet's last Crusader squadron. Again, the *Coral Sea* figured in Crusader history as Det 2 sailed in Air Wing 14 for an Indian Ocean deployment. On 22 March 1982, the carrier and its photo det arrived home, where RF-8G BuNo 144618 landed at Miramar to formally end the cruise, and the last regular deployment of a Crusader squadron. In January, the squadron had received notification that 30 June would be its last day. Even before the ceremony, the last fleet RF-8G flew to Davis Monthan on 28 May. Included in Det 2's final cruise was the last Crusader 'nugget', a first-tour aviator, Lieutenant John DuGene, who, in 1980, had been the last RF-8G Fleet Replacement pilot to be trained in the Crusader. He commented: 'I'm part of the history of a great airplane. The RF-8 is a fun plane to fly . . . It creates a sense of responsibility and confidence'. During the cruise, DuGene, who would soon transition to the F-14, flew an airplane older than he, BuNo 144607, then the oldest supersonic aircraft serving in the Navy, built in 1956 several months before DuGene's birth.

Part of the VFP-63 retirement ceremony included passing the famous Crusader Sword. Purchased in March 1967 by then-Lieutenant Commander Bruce Moorehouse of VF-124, the thirteenth-century antique weapon had actually belonged to a *real* crusader. Leaving VF-124, Moorehouse decided Crusader College needed something more fitting than another ugly trophy. A New York antique dealer found the sword, and soon, VF-124 had one of the most appropriate symbols of any military squadron. The sword even came with the motto 'Draw Me Not Without Reason, Sheathe Me Not Without Honor'.

The sword remained with VF-124, then with VFP-63. In June 1982, with the disestablishment of VFP-63, the Washington reserve squadrons, VFP-206 and VFP-306 assumed joint custody of the priceless relic.

After 33 years of providing photo reconnaissance to the Navy, VFP-63 retired, the last dedicated photo reconnaissance squadron flying the last dedicated reconnaissance aircraft in the Navy: the RF-8G Crusader. Commander David M Beam, the last skipper of the Eyes of the Fleet, declared: 'It seems like I've been here forever. I came as a nugget in 1966 and now I'm here closing the door.'

But the Crusader still had a few good years left in her, and she had been busy carving another career in the reserves.

Chapter 8
A Second Life: The Reserves, 1965-87

The reserves are a navy within a navy, which is true of other auxiliary components of the US military establishment. However, the Navy has usually treated its reserves with modified disdain, allocating only the barest of essentials, operating funds and equipment. But it is a fact that without the vast number of reservists who augmented the relatively small number of regulars in World War II, the overwhelming victory over the Axis Powers would have been impossible. Korea saw the recall of thousands of reservists, and although Vietnam relied less on the reserves, the auxiliaries were still there and were always considered an asset to their assigned activities.

The Naval Air Reserve dates back to August 1916, and many of the first American naval aviators came from this enthusiastic band of young college men who made up the initial cadre of pilots immediately before America's entry into World War I. Following the war, the 1920–30 period saw the reserves slip into the doldrums of lethargic activity and funding, although the reserves did maintain their existence—just barely. The Axis—Germany, Japan, Italy—did not have this reservoir of additional manpower, and this lack of reserve personnel played a large part in their ultimate and resounding defeat.

Until Vietnam, the Naval Air Reserve continued using obsolescent aircraft in a country-wide array of scattered squadrons which could, as in the case of Korea, be called up for active duty. During Korea, entire carrier air wings were composed of recalled reserve squadrons. The American author James Michener's popular novella *The Bridges at Toko-ri*, subsequently made into a Hollywood movie starring William Holden and Grace Kelly, told the story of Lieutenant Harry Brubaker, a Denver lawyer recalled to combat duty.

In January 1968, the North Koreans captured the US intelligence ship *Pueblo*, and imprisoned its crew. In response to the crisis, the Navy mobilized six reserve squadrons, including three F-8 squadrons, VF-703 in Dallas, VF-661 at Andrews near Washington, DC, and VF-931 at Willow Grove, near Philadelphia.

The F-8A and B Crusaders had been serving with the reserves since 1965. Originally, the squadrons shared the planes and flight time between the Navy and Marine Air Reservists which operated at the same bases. The planes, in fact, carried a joint NAVY/MARINE marking on their fuselages.

The 1968 recall was a disaster. VF-931 and VF-661 went to Cecil Field in Florida, while VF-703 travelled to Miramar, to transition to the latest fleet models of the F-8, the Charlie and Echo. But the problems encountered in training, maintenance, and availability were so great that by November, the units were still not operational. The ultimate resolution of the *Pueblo* Crisis allowed the deactivation of the reserve squadrons, and gave the Navy much to consider.

By 1970, the Navy had come up with a major revision of the tactical reserves which would mirror the fleet organization. The far-flung squadrons were re-established as members of two reserve carrier air wings, CVWR-20 and CVWR-30, which would mobilize with the Atlantic and Pacific Fleets respectively.

In addition to the administrative reorganization, the new squadrons would also receive fleet comparable aircraft which would allow the reservists to maintain their currency in the event of recall. Each CVWR included eight squadrons; two fighter, three attack, one early warning, one tanker and one light photo. At the time, the Crusader equipped three of the squadrons, the fighter and light photo. Eventually, the original A-4s in the three light attack units were replaced by A-7A and B Corsair IIs, creating a nearly all-Vought air wing.

The combined Navy and Marine Air Reserve unit at NAF Washington, DC, was one of the first reserve organizations to get Crusaders. Here, an F-8B sits on the flight-line in 1967 (Clay Jansson via Jim Sullivan)

LEFT
An F-8J of VF-301 is positioned on the catapult while an RF-8G of VFP-306 flies overhead. The photobird has apparently made an unsuccessful attempt to land, evidenced by the lowered arresting hook, and has 'boltered', going around for another try

VF-201 and VF-202 in Dallas, Texas, and VF-301 and VF-302 at Miramar, flew the F-8H and later the Juliet, while VFP-206 and VFP-306, both located at NAF Washington, DC, on Andrews Air Force Base, flew RF-8Gs. Even VC-13, a composite squadron, received F-8Hs when it was formed on 1 September 1973, at New Orleans. However, the Saints exchanged their Hotels for A-4Ls in April 1974. In the middle of the Vietnam period, all air reserves boasted a high level of combat experienced pilots, and it showed. To the amazement of the fleet, the reserve aviators continually demonstrated their proficiency, whether operating around carriers or in bombing and fighter competitions. An advertisement in *Naval Aviation News* magazine declared 'Naval aviators can still fly—in the Naval Air Reserve'. The accompanying photo showed A-7s of VA-303 flying over the

Golden Gate Bridge in San Francisco. The draw was irresistable.

VF-201 and VF-202 quickly qualified their pilots with CQs (carrier qualification periods) on the super carrier USS *John F Kennedy* in 1971. VFP-206 and VFP-306 also conducted their initial CQs on the USS *Franklin D Roosevelt*. The two reserve VFP squadrons also made generous use of the facilities at Miramar which, besides their own small lab at Andrews, was the only base which could support the photo mission with proper film processors.

The VFPs also established themselves by responding to requests from various government agencies for photographic coverage. The Blue Angels flight demonstration team came to rely on the two RF-8G squadrons to provide pre-show photography of the airfields the team visited. Using the air-to-ground views provided by the RF-8s, the team analyzed the approaches and surrounding areas of each field to determine the best routes and form-up areas, as well as the location of obstacles and checkpoints.

The fighter squadrons differed from the light photo squadrons, not only in models of the F-8 and mission flown, but the actual size, number of aircraft, and personnel complement. Whereas the fighter squadrons might include 10–15 reservist pilots, with perhaps 100–150 maintenance, administrative and support troops, the VFP squadrons were essentially dets, with no more than five aircraft, and perhaps

50–60 people, including six or seven pilots. The smaller size of the VFPs made for increased workload for the squadron members, which highlighted the dedication needed to be a naval air reservist.

In addition to the required two-day weekend per month, and two-week period of active duty—Active Duty for Training (ACDUTRA)—squadron members usually found themselves spending at least one more weekend, and not a few extra nights after their regular job, at the base. Special ACDUTRAs, above the required annual two-week period, were also necessary if the reservist was to be considered in good standing. An example of these Special ACDUTRAs was VFP-306's one-week cruise to MCAS Yuma in December 1981.

Commander L E Johnson wanted to give his squadron, especially the three new pilots he had recently been assigned, an uninterrupted period of good flying weather to get to really know their planes. As the squadron's five RF-8s flew cross-country, a C-9 airlift brought the remaining pilots and ground troops. Executive Officer Commander John Kuchinski found himself the centre of attention when he arrived at Yuma in his black-tailed Crusader. Throughout the period, Marine aviators and troops called the squadron expressing both pleasure and envy at seeing the Crusaders on the flight line. Until the end of its career, the Crusader constantly drew stares as it taxied in, its unique wing raised above the fuselage.

Once a year, the squadrons of the two CVWRs got together, as a wing, on the annual 'cruise', usually conducted at the air station at Fallon, Nevada, 60 miles east of Reno. It was the only time when the CAG—there were, of course, wing commanders, just

ABOVE
VFP-206's first CQs, on the FDR, in 1971. AF 632 snags one of the wires as the flight deck crewman signals a successful engagement to the pilot

ABOVE RIGHT
Beginning a 1982 training mission from NAF Washington, VFP-306 CO, Commander L E 'Rocky' Johnson exchanges pre-start signals with his plane captain (Author)

BELOW RIGHT
This RF-8G of VFP-306 shows the flat bottom and many windows of the photo Crusader. Note the square windows for stations three and four, the vertical cameras, and the blister directly below the national insignia which houses the station one forward fire camera

like the fleet—could see his air wing as a total operating unit.

One minor problem was the fact that Fallon had let its photo facilities go, and thus, the RF-8s could not remain at Fallon. The VFPs cruised at Miramar, to the delight of the reservists, especially the non-pilot members. The photobirds would make their runs up north as far as Washington State, east as far as Salt Lake City, and more operationally, through the twisting, mountainous routes of the Fallon ranges, and bring their mission film back to San Diego. Eventually, someone got the idea of installing film processors at Fallon in 1977, and the VFPs found themselves back in the fold.

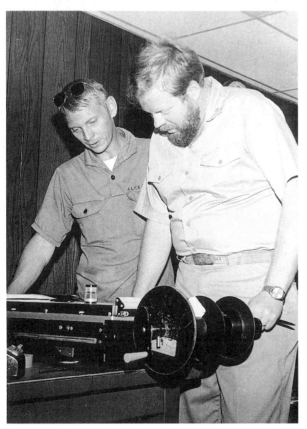

ABOVE LEFT
Lieutenant Commander Bob Norrell waits to be brought up the flight deck to the catapult during carrier qualifications aboard the John F Kennedy *in 1978. Today, his highly decorated flight helmet would not be allowed since it decreases the helmet's visibility in the water after an ejection* (Author)

BELOW LEFT
*The mission wasn't over after the RF-8s returned to base.
Lieutenant Commander Louis R Mortimer (right) reviews
mission film with PH1 Lee Alexander on a portable light
table. A magnifying tube sits at the ready on the table*
(Author)

ABOVE
*Engine changes are a fact of life for military squadrons,
and the process is usually involved. Here, a crew of
VFP-306 mechanics prepare to pull the tail off one of their
RF-8Gs to effect an engine change. Having jacked up the
dolly under the aft fuselage, the mechs carefully separate
the tail, exposing the Crusader's engine* (Author)

November 1976: The Reserve TACAIR Test

One thing the reserves can always count on is constant criticism from political opponents, anti-military lobbyists and irate citizens who consider the money used to operate the reserve air wings a proper waste. The danger of disestablishment is always present and the reserves must continually prove themselves to justify continued existence.

In November 1976, CVWR-30 deployed aboard the *Forrestal*-class carrier USS *Ranger*. While the carrier's regular air wing remained ashore, the reserve wing took its place for a one-week period to test the effectiveness of the 1970 reorganization. The ship left the North Island pier and sailed into the Pacific Ocean off the California coast. For many of the reservists it brought back not too distant memories of other deployments to a war now slowly fading from the public conscience.

After initial carrier landing qualifications, CVWR-30 conducted several exercises, earning the hearty endorsement of the ship's captain and crew. The fighters and light attack bombers flew their missions, while the VFP-306 RF-8Gs got a lot of operational training.

By this time, the F-8Js had also retired. In 1975, both the Naval and Marine air reserves transitioned to F-4B Phantoms, leaving only the photo Crusaders. Aboard the *Ranger*, the F-4s of VF-301 and VF-302 flew CAP and escort missions. The black-tailed RF-8s of VFP-306 earned high marks for their performance. The test was a resounding success and silenced critics, but only for a while.

Throughout the late 1970s and early 1980s, the RF-8Gs continued flying. The draw to fly the Crusader brought many young aviators, fresh from the fleet, to Andrews. They waited for months for a chance to fly the legendary F-8, even the non-fighter recon version. With the Power Eye Mod, the old jet's performance was, indeed, impressive, and even the jaded youngster who just left an F-14 cockpit, had his enthusiasm rekindled after his first flight in the Crusader.

During a 1978 CQ on the *Kennedy*, Lieutenant Commander Eliot Tozer, who had recently joined VFP-306 and made his first carrier landings in the Crusader, entered the squadron ready room, his flight gear still buttoned and zipped and his face aglow: 'Damn, I got all my traps. I'm a qualified F-8

Lots of action on the Ranger's *flight deck in November 1976 during the Reserve TACAIR Test which proved the validity of the reserve air wings. As steam from a previous launch surrounds the flight deck, a VFP-306 RF-8G waits on Cat 4 while an A-7B of VA-304 also waits its turn* (Author)

ABOVE
*A fine example of black and white aerial photography by
RF-8s. Two VFP-306 RF-8Gs begin refuelling operations
from a KA-3B of VAK-308 over Fallon in 1983*
(Lieutenant Commander John Cotton)

ABOVE RIGHT
*A Crusader from VFP-306 whistles past the landing signal
officer (LSO), its arresting hook ready to grab one of four
wires to bring the RF-8G to a halt on the flight deck of the*
Ranger *in November 1976. The crowded area of the
forward flight deck is readily apparent, and illustrates the
value of the angled deck developed by the British* (Author)

BELOW RIGHT
*A favourite bit of 'trick' photography practised by every
reserve photo pilot. Over the Grand Canyon in Arizona,
an RF-8G of VFP-306 looks like it's about to make a
very tricky landing on one of the mesas*

ABOVE LEFT
VFP-306's officers in 1983. A unique organization permitted two active duty reserve officers and a cadre of enlisted to administer the unit during the week, while the remaining officers—as well as enlisted personnel—worked during weekends, coming together as the entire squadron. Left to right (rear row) Lieutenant Commander Mike Campbell (Safety), Lieutenant Commander John Cotton (Operations), Lieutenant Commander Dave Strong (Maintenance), Lieutenant Commander Craig Grover (Asst Maintenance); (front row) Lieutenant Commander Henry Livingston (Admin), Commander Rocky Johnson (CO), Commander Gary Reise (XO), and the author (Air Intelligence). Commander Reise and Lieutenant Commander Grover were the active duty reservists who kept the squadron running on a daily basis. Commander Reise eventually became the squadron's last skipper. Lieutenant Commander Strong would become the last F-8 skipper, in command of 206 in 1987. Except for Lieutenant Commander Cotton, an A-7 pilot, all these pilots had extensive fleet F-8 experience, three with Vietnam combat time

BELOW LEFT
Without a doubt, one of the most striking schemes applied to reserve Crusaders belonged to VMF-321 at NAF Washington. Originally called the Black Barons, the squadrons applied a black-white star coloration to the entire dorsal area of their F-8Ks, as well as the fuselage strakes. This 321 bird's oxygen system is being serviced. The fighter carries empty Zuni tubes (J W Kinnamont)

ABOVE
Returning from one of their final detachments to Miramar, four VFP-206 Crusaders show varying styles of markings in 1987, just before the squadron's decommissioning. Although the planes are roughly 30 years old, they are well maintained and able to perform their mission (Frank Mormillo)

ABOVE
The final launch. Five catapult officers stage a dramatic send-off for Lieutenant Commander Barry Gabler as he gets ready for the last carrier launch of a US Crusader, in October 1986, from the America *(David Casper)*

LEFT
The first and last F-8 drivers. Commander Dave Strong (left) greets John Konrad, the Vought test pilot who took the XF8U-1 on its first flight in 1955. The meeting occurred during the retirement ceremonies for the F-8 and VFP-206, the last Crusader squadron on 29 March 1987 (Author)

ABOVE RIGHT
Getting ready for the last flight, Commander Dave Strong, CO of VFP-206, the Navy's last Crusader squadron, runs through his pre-start checks on 30 March 1987

driver!' Although he was an experienced A-4 pilot with many combat missions in Vietnam under his belt, it had always been Tozer's dream to fly the F-8, and he had finally realized it.

Then-Lieutenant Wally Baker remembers the F-8 could be a handful during the landing because of its relatively narrow-tracked main gear and long fuselage. Having made the first east coast cruise in F-14s in 1975 with VF-32, Baker was an experienced aviator, but for the first flights in the Crusader, he tried to land the plane as gingerly as he could so as not to burst a main tyre.

'The landing was an indicator as to how comfortable you were in the Crusader', he recalls. The F-8's lack of landing parachute and its lengthy rollout after touchdown required constant attention, especially from newly-qualified Crusader pilots.he Marine Air Reserve included several Crusader squadrons which became the prime operators of the Kilo and Lima versions, except for a few of these conversions which flew with fleet VC squadrons for a short time. These models retained the Echo's ground attack capability which was at the heart of all Marine aviation, supporting the troops on the ground.

VMFA-112 in Dallas and VMFA-321 in Washington operated much the same as their Navy sister squadrons, usually at the same fields. But, instead of Fallon, the Marines took their ACDUTRA at the desert air station at Yuma, Arizona, in the south-western corner of the state. The weapons ranges and good flying weather were perfect for training. Along with the Navy, the Marines traded in their F-8s for Phantoms, in 1975.

The Photo Derby

The reserve VFPs continued flying, keeping their collective hands in during periodic competitions such as the Photo Derby which was open to all comers. Actually, the correct, and more expansive, title was 'The World Famous Open Class Photo Derby', and entrants included reconnaissance squadrons from the Air Force, Air National Guard, a Canadian F-5 squadron, VF-124, the Navy's west coast F-14 training squadron which also included TARPS training, and, of course, the two VFP Crusader squadrons.

The Photo Derby had been the idea of Commander Doug Simpson, a Vietnam-experienced RF-8G pilot, now serving with the reserve VFPs. Simpson tried to include as much realism as he could, with challenging routes and 'bad guys', waiting to pounce on the speeding competitors as they flew their missions. Normally, another reserve squadron, VC-12, from NAS Oceana, Virginia Beach, Virginia,

CRUSADER

provided the interceptor threat with their specially trained pilots in A-4s and TA-4s. E-2 Hawkeyes would also participate, monitoring the action and providing the recon aircraft with threat warnings, just as they would in real combat.

While the Photo Derby enjoyed some popularity in the 1980s, eventually, the event became part of a larger Air Force-sponsored competition. It was just as well, for the Crusader's days were, indeed, numbered.

The Last Squadron

In a continuing effort to maintain the momentum established by providing the Naval Air Reserve with modern equipment, the decision was made to transition the four reserve fighter squadrons to the F-14 Tomcat, with one squadron from each wing being designated as the TARPS squadron. VF-301 and VF-302 were chosen to be the first to change, with 302 taking over TARPS duties; 201 and 202 would transition later, with 202 becoming the TARPS squadron for CVWR-20.

As the plans solidified, so did the date for the decommissioning of VFP-306. On 30 September 1984, Commander Gary W Reise, the last of VFP-306's seven commanding officers, ordered his squadron's colours struck, as hundreds of observers, officials and squadron alumni watched. The Hawk-eyes of VFP-206 were now the sole remaining US Navy Crusader squadron.

For the next two and a half years, VFP-206 flew its RF-8s all over the country, and conducted CQs, all business as usual, even though the writing was on the wall. Their disestablishment was coming: March 1987.

In October 1986, the Hawkeyes joined other fleet and reserve squadrons for a CQ on the USS *America*. Coincidentally, it would also be the last CQ for the F-4, with VF-201 and VF-202 making their final traps before transitioning to the F-14.

On 18 October Lieutenant Commander Barry D Gabler manned RF-8G BuNo 145633, and launched from the ship:

It was a beautiful day at sea as I rolled into the groove for the Crusader's last trap. I saw the deck, the wake, the wires, and the people. It was over too quickly. I got an OK-3 Underlined grade, the best you can get. Moments later I was up on Cat 4 where *all* the catapult officers were ready to fire me off for the last F-8 launch.

A good runup, a quick check of my instruments, a salute, and then the massive acceleration of the cat. We were airborne and climbing out in full afterburner. Number 145633 and I did one roll and joined up with the flight for a diamond fly-by. For both of us, it was the end of our carrier careers.

Finally, on 29 March 1987, the last Crusader squadron retired, along with the last US RF-8.

BuNo. 146860 had been built as an F8U-1P (RF-8A) in 1959, and served with Marine squadrons VMCJ-1 and VMCJ-3. Later, assigned to VFP-63's Det 19 in the *Hancock* in 1970-1, it accumulated 200 hours in combat. Stored at Davis Monthan in June 1971, it was later reassigned to VFP-206 in 1973. Now, as AF 701, this veteran Crusader served as a focal point during a weekend of memories.

Displayed with 'One-X', the first XF8U-1, BuNo 138899, loaned by the Smithsonian National Air and Space Museum, 860 provided a backdrop for one more picture for the many F-8 alumni, pilots and ground personnel. Retrieved from years of storage, One-X was lovingly restored by the members of VFP-206, repainted and polished so it gleamed in the sunshine which graced this important milestone in the Crusader's career.

Commander David Strong, the last of VFP-206's ten commanding officers, and the last Crusader CO, officiated at the ceremony, calling for his squadron's colours to be struck and the unit to be retired. Strong also held the somewhat dubious honour of making the final ejection from a US Crusader in 1985, for which he received a rare peacetime Distinguished Flying Cross from the Secretary of the Navy. (See Chapter 10 for the story of the last F-8 bailout.)

On the following day, Monday, 30 March, Commander Strong made the last take-off in the last Crusader. This time, the weather did not cooperate and the clouds were thick and low. Undaunted, Strong made three low, fast passes over the Naval Air Facility, then stood his plane on its tail and rocketed up into the clouds. It was a fitting end to the Crusader's career after so many years, when as many as 71 Navy and Marine Corps squadrons flew the Crusader, an incredible number considering that only 1261 of them were built. The last Crusader's last flight lasted only 20 minutes as Commander Strong brought it to the Smithsonian's storage park at Dulles International Airport in Virginia to await restoration and display at a future date.

Reserve Captain Tom Irwin, himself a 2800-hour F-8 pilot who participated in some of the first combat missions over North Vietnam in 1965, and a former commanding officer of VFP-306, wrote a fitting epitaph for the Crusader in the July 1982 issue of *Naval Aviation News*:

Its record of achievement will never be diminished as it moves from active service into retirement. It will always be the plane that moved Naval Aviation to the forefront of supersonic tactical flight. Those who flew the Crusader—loved it. Those who didn't—respected it.

Chapter 9
The Crusader in Foreign Service

Besides the F-4 Phantom and the Bell H-1 series of helicopters, and somewhat unexpectedly, no American combat aircraft of the immediate post-Korean timeframe had as long, though geographically limited, a foreign career as Vought's F-8 Crusader. Indeed, the Crusader has enjoyed nearly as long a career with France's Aeronavale as with the US Navy. This success is all the more remarkable in view of the fact that only 42 F-8s entered French service. Even today, in the late 1980s, though the American Crusader is gone, the French fighter continues to serve, perhaps into the mid-90s, even though speculation had determined a 1985 date for its retirement.

The French had been impressed by the TF-8A's performance at the 1962 Paris Air Show. The Two-sader had been on a road trip to drum up business for Vought's pacesetter. At one point, the British evinced strong interest in the two-seater which offered supersonic performance ashore and aboard carriers, as well as the opportunity to train pilots and navigators in an advanced aircraft. However, the British ultimately chose the more expensive Phantom since they could re-engine the McDonnell fighter with their own Rolls-Royce engines.

The French were more determined, and wanted a replacement for the ageing first-generation jets which flew from their two new carriers, the *Foch* and *Clemenceau*, generally comparable to the US 27C class aircraft carriers. The Crusader's high approach speed gave cause for concern in operating from the small French decks.

Vought agreed to rework the F-8's wing extensively and to incorporate the new arrangement of boundary layer control which blew hot engine air over the wing control service, creating more lift, and thus reducing the approach and stall speeds. The horizontal tail was also enlarged for better stability. The stall speed dropped from 113 to 90 knots. An

F-8D, BuNo 147036, was used for the test airframe and flew in February 1964. Although the test F-8D crashed in April, the first production F-8E(FN) flew that June.

Initial CQs were held aboard the *Shangri-La*, with US Navy pilots coaching French aviators. Eventually, a group of Vought and US Navy pilots went to France for a year's duty to help the French transition. In May 1965, the first CQs aboard a French carrier had been completed.

The production run was completed in January 1965. Originally, 46 single-seaters and six two-seaters had been ordered, but when the Two-sader's development was cut short, the French reduced their order.

Although the F-8E(FN) retained the US armament of four 20 mm cannon, the external mission load changed to accomodate French missiles, primarily the Matra R. 530 and 550 air-to-air missiles. Sidewinders could be carried, but the Matra was the first choice.

American instructors were very impressed with their French pupils during the initial indoctrination at Cecil Field even though there were problems with language. John Nichols was one of the Landing Signal Officers who 'waved' the French aviators. 'They were magnificent, skilled pilots', he remembers. Once they got to sea, the French also exhibited a high degree of facility, at one point making 90 landings without a waveoff.

Two *flottilles de chasse* roughly equivalent to fighter squadrons, were equipped with the F-8. 12F and 14F had flown another Vought product, the F4U-7 Corsair, in then-Indochina from the carrier *Lafayette* in 1952–53, in the 1956 Suez Crisis from the *Arromanches*, and finally, during the Algerian Crisis in 1961 from shore bases. 12F had been decommissioned in 1963, and 14F in 1964, but the squadrons were recommissioned in October 1964 and

ABOVE LEFT
A prototype F-8E(FN) with a huge Matra missile during testing

BELOW LEFT
Lieutenant James Flatley (later Rear Admiral), scion of a famous American naval aviation family, prepares for a launch from the Shangri-La *in 1964 during initial testing of the French Crusader. His aircraft carries US Sidewinder missiles, although the nationalistic French seldom carried this American armament* (via Jim Sullivan)

TOP
An F-8E(FN) of 12F in England in June 1981, seen just at touchdown (Russell-Smith, via Jim Sullivan)

ABOVE
During an airshow in 1987, a French Crusader exhibits the darker slate grey colour scheme now applied to French Navy aircraft (Peter Foster)

A typical deck scene aboard a French carrier. The light grey Crusader joins an Alize (right), Etendard (left) and Alouette helicopter (far left). Note the larger horizontal stabilizers of the F-8E(FN) than those of its US cousin (via Norman Polmar)

March 1965, respectively, to re-equip with the Crusader.

French naval aviators took enthusiastically to their new mounts. By 1970, 12F and 14F had each logged over 20,000 hours in their F-8s. Premier Master Pilot Roland Peltre became their first 1000-hour pilot in 1969, and was duly awarded an aircraft tyre around his neck. In a more serious vein, he said, 'I consider the Crusader an excellent fighter and one that brings much satisfaction to its pilot'.

14F eventually transitioned to the Super Etendard in May 1979, its F-8s going into storage to be used by the sole remaining French Crusader squadron, 12F. The F-8s not in service were placed in huge plastic bags at the large base at Landivisiau, near Brest on the Atlantic coast of Brittany. Although 26 F-8E(FN)s survive, only 14 are in service in dets assigned to the two French carriers. The Crusader's colours and markings were fairly reserved, the American grey and white scheme being the normal paint scheme,

although in the twilight of the French fighter's career, it appears that a slate blue-grey colouring will slowly be applied as each aircraft goes through maintenance. The F-8E(FN)s were retrofitted with F-8J wings.

As active as the Crusader was, the only combat it saw in French service was during the tense period in September 1983 in the Eastern Mediterranean. The *Foch* arrived off Lebanon on the 6th, and on the 22nd, French Crusaders from the *Foch* flew CAP for a Super Etendard strike force which struck rebel gun positions in Lebanon. The French seemed reluctant to publicize the American aircraft's role, and only covertly mentioned F-8s in newspaper stories, simply stating the Crusaders 'were charged with protecting the bombers', the Super Etendards. The *Foch*'s air group transferred to the *Clemenceau* when she relieved the *Foch* in early October. Several recon missions were flown, along with a relatively unproductive reprisal raid by 14 Super Etendards on 17 November. It might be assumed that this raid was covered by an F-8 CAP.

Now expected to serve into the 1990s, until the introduction of a follow-on aircraft designated *Avion de Combat Marine* (Naval Combat Aircraft), French F-8s may well prove to be the longest serving of the entire F-8 line. At the time of writing, several options are under discussion, including a life extension program for the F-8E(FN) which would permit it to serve into the late 90s, as well as the purchase of McDonnell Douglas F/A-18s, a more costly, and only interim solution. In early 1988, a French team even visited Davis-Monthan Air Force Base in Arizona to inspect the lines of stored F-8s. Were they looking for spare parts to keep their F-8s flying well into the 1990s?

In the summer of 1987, when world attention focused on the Persian Gulf, France sent a carrier task force as part of the western naval presence. The *Clemenceau* carried a contingent of Crusaders of 12F, along with Super Etendards and Etendard IVP reconnaissance aircraft.

Although the deployment was in deadly earnest, the French occasionally met their American counterparts in ACM engagements. In August, two F-14s from the *Constellation* tackled a 12F Crusader. The US fighter crews had fought F-8s before, and expected their adversary to come in high and fast, but the lone Frenchman surprised them and came in low. It took both Tomcats to win the engagement over the aggressive Crusader driver.

Then, as the three aircraft joined up for a few pictures, the F-8 pilot led them back toward his carrier. He dropped down to 200 feet, at 600 knots, heading for his ship, going even lower, to an estimated 50–60 feet above the water. As he drew near his ship, the French aviator pitched up and slightly left in a vertical manoeuvre, and punched in his afterburner. The American F-14s broke off, their crews shaking their heads and wondering about the sanity of the *Clem*'s traffic control.

TOP LEFT
A VF-154 F-14 joins on a 12F F-8E(FN) after air combat manoeuvring over the Persian Gulf in 1987. The French pilots fly their 25-year-old fighters with considerable Gallic élan, much to the delight and amazement of the American flight crews (Bruce Greer)

CENTRE LEFT
This view of a French Crusader clearly shows the more shapely nose of the later models of the F-8, as well as additional dorsal and ventral antennae

BOTTOM LEFT
An F-8E(FN) carries one Magic air-to-air missile on its starboard cheek mount

TOP
An F-8H of the Philippine Air Force in November 1980 (Russell-Smith, via Jim Sullivan)

ABOVE
Two F-8Hs of the 7th Tactical Fighter Squadron of the 5th Fighter Wing at Basa Air Base, Pampanga, Philippines. The open hangars are typical for the humid surroundings

Crusaders in the Philippines

In late 1977, the Philippines government purchased 35 F-8Hs, 25 to be completely refurbished by Vought, and the remaining ten to serve as replacement aircraft. The Hotels had been in storage at Davis-Monthan. The aircraft sold for $11.7 million, with an additional contract for $23 million to cover the refurbishing by Vought and training of Philippine Air Force pilots and maintenance personnel. As noted earlier, the two-seat TF-8A had been used to indoctrinate the PAF pilots, but was lost on 28 July 1978, when the Vought pilot and his Filipino student ejected, and the TF-8A crashed in a farmer's field.

Although the Philippine government had really wanted F-15s or F-16s, the 'sale' price of the F-8Hs was too good to pass up. The Hotels went to the PAF's 7th Tactical Fighter Squadron, 5th Fighter Wing at Basa Air Base, Pampanga, in northern Luzon. The 7th TFS had been established in October 1957, flying F-86F Sabrejets.

Vought sent a training and administrative team which remained in the Philippines for a year in an effort to get the Filipinos to become self-sustaining, particularly in the maintenance area. Initial attempts to change engines were tough going, but eventually, the Filipinos became fairly proficient in maintaining and flying their new aircraft. They participated in the US Air Force's Cope Thunder exercises, earning high praise from American officials.

In March 1984, Vought sent a contingent to help the Philippines Air Force refurbish their remaining 19 F-8Hs. The Crusaders had begun to show drastic deterioration in the humid Philippine environment.

For the next year, the Americans helped the Filipinos patch up their F-8s. The metallite had actually begun to disintegrate and the Vought team glued together several layers of local plywood, covered them with aluminum, and fitted the pieces to the area on specific airframes. Finally, only 12 F-8s remained, with the other seven being cannibalized for parts. By 1987, however, the availability rate had plummeted, and of the 12 Crusaders remaining in service with the PAF, only eight were fully mission capable at any one time.

During the expulsion of Philippine President Marcos in 1986, the Crusaders were flown to the US Air Force Base at Clark near Manilla to protect them from saboteurs. The F-8s were intended for Air Defence and ground attack duties, but they also stood alert duties alongside the PAF's F-5s. PAF F-8s intercepted many Soviet bombers which over-flew the north-western area of the Phillippines. In a surprise move, the PAF phased out their remaining Crusaders on 23 January 1988. The reason was the lack of qualified replacement pilots. Thirty-one PAF pilots had flown the F-8 in nine years; 38 had gone through ground training.

Only Major Pascualito R Ramos, who ended up the high-time PAF F-8H pilot with 2037 hours, was qualified for maintenance check flights at the time of the phaseout. First Lieutenant Marcelino L Ben, Jr, became the last PAF F-8 driver.

In nine years, the PAF had suffered only five major accidents, losing two pilots, the others ejecting safely. Not a bad safety record.

Eventually, the Phillippine government hopes to buy more F-5s, or perhaps British Hawks, to replace the Crusaders.

An F-8H of the Philippine Air Force touches down at its base at Basa. Only one squadron, the 7th Tactical Fighter Squadron, flew the refurbished Crusaders which were eventually retired in January 1988

Chapter 10
Ejections, Near Misses, and Narrow Escapes

A ride in a Crusader was always a thrill. But sometimes, the pilot got more than he originally signed the yellow sheet for. Here is a sometimes humorous, sometimes harrowing look at the experiences of aviators who had to 'step out' of their F-8s, or found themselves in unique situations in their Crusaders.

Nylon Letdowns: When Your Landings Don't Equal Your Take-offs

By the time the Crusader retired, pilots had made 493 ejections from all models of the F-8. Overall, 517 of the 1261 Crusaders built had been lost, a loss rate of 41 per cent. Eighty-four Crusaders had been lost in Vietnam as a result of flak, SAMs, and small arms, plus three or four, to MiGs. There was a period where at least one ejection from an F-8 occured each month, from June 1957 to February 1969, with a break for March, then began again in April 1969 until May 1970. As the Crusader began leaving the fleet, the pace accelerated as the Reserves picked up more F-8s.

VFP-63 experienced 15 ejections from October 1973 to July 1981, and was the front-runner, with 60 ejections, followed by VF-124 with 42. VF-194 totalled 31 bailouts, VF-211, 22 and VF-162, 21, just to name a few. The numbers and comparison lists could go on and on.

Thirty F-8 drivers were double winners, making two ejections, and four individuals liked it so much they opted for a third rocket ride. Of course, many of these emergency egresses were in combat, and the choice was limited: stay and die, or eject and survive, even if it meant as a POW.

The first ejections from an F-8 occurred in 1956. During an evaluation flight, Marine Captain James Feliton punched out on 4 May. Veteran test pilot

John Konrad, the first man to fly the F-8 in March 1955, was forced to eject when his plane's engine failed at high altitude on 14 August. Bob Rostine, another Vought test pilot, left his F8U-2NE prototype later in the year.

The first fleet ejection came on 30 January 1957, when Captain Bob Dose of VX-3, had his engine come apart at 10,000 feet. After trying six times to restart his engine, Dose ejected to be rescued from the chilly Atlantic by an Air Force amphibian. It was only the beginning.

From 1957 to 1960, F8U-1s dropped from the air with frightening and frustrating regularity. The first F8U-1P ejection was on 24 July 1958, when a VFP-63 aviator left his aircraft. Every unit recorded at least one punchout, whether it was a fleet squadron, Navy or Marine, or a specific facility such as the Naval Air Test Center at Patuxent, China Lake in California, or a Naval Air Rework Facility. VF, VFP, VMF, VMCJ, or VC, it made no difference. The F-8 played no favourites. And once Vietnam got rolling, well . . .

Then, there were the early days when ejection was not always a viable option and you just had to stick with the airplane. Commander Chuck Deasy, the Executive Officer of VF-142, led four F8U-1s back to the *Ranger* on 11 March 1959. The carrier was 90 miles south of Atsugi, Japan, and the weather was fine. Deasy and his planes entered the break and confidently began setting themselves up for their approaches. Deasy crossed the rounddown, but instead of catching the wire and stopping, his Crusader skewed down the angled deck. He rammed the throttle forward, but his plane was too slow and dropped off the deck.

As the pilot fought to hold his staggering plane in the air, the *Ranger* deck crew ran to the edge, gesturing wildly, trying to 'help' the fighter back into level flight. The Crusader threw a rooster tail of water

ABOVE LEFT
Veteran F-8 driver, T C 'Cat' Irwin in the cockpit of his RF-8G while CO of VFP-306 in 1978. Notice the simple cloth strap by which the pilot pulled the canopy down before locking it in place. Irwin enjoyed a full career in Crusader, having flown with VF-24 in Vietnam, as well as both Naval Air Reserve VFP squadrons, accumulating over 2800 hours in the F-8

BELOW LEFT
After his tailhook failed, forcing him to ditch his D-8C in the South China Sea, Lieutenant, j.g., Tom Irwin signals for the helo to come get him. His VF-24 Crusader stayed afloat long enough for the young fighter pilot to scramble over the cockpit side, which is now underwater. The Crusader sank minutes after this photo was taken

ABOVE
Lieutenant Commander Tom Tucker, VFP-63 det OINC, is hauled into the SH-3 SAR helo after being shot down over Haiphong Harbour in August 1966. The daring rescue was made under intense fire from North Vietnamese positions in the harbour, and underscored the lengths to which all US SAR crews would go to rescue downed aircrewmen

as it 'walked' barely above stall speed. Finally, Deasy gained enough flying speed to come out of afterburner, return to level flight and land back at Atsugi.

When he returned to the carrier the next day and took a look at the movies which recorded his incredible experience, he could see that his tailhook had grabbed two wires and the shock had ripped the hook shoe from the shaft. He had been flying a new F8U-1 which had an afterburner with a new nozzle modification which gave near instantaneous burner ignition. The extra thrust had saved him and his aircraft.

Ditching an F-8

Zero-zero ejection capability did not arrive until the mid-60s, and out-of-the-envelope ejections were not advised. While Chuck Deasy had been fortunate, Lieutenant, j.g. Tom Irwin had to make the decision to stay and ditch in his doomed F-8 in 1965.

On 13 January 1965, Irwin returned from a daytime air intercept training mission. VF-24 was part of *Hancock*'s CVW-21 off Vietnam but the war had been quiet. Irwin snagged the carrier's number four wire and the rollout seemed normal. He was about to retard the throttle when he suddenly realized he was not stopping. The F-8C, BuNo 147011, was headed for the edge. His aircraft did not have the afterburner arrangement of Deasy's aircraft, and Irwin had to consider the two-second delay between selection and burner light.

The young aviator could not know that his hook point had sheared from the shank. He selected burner, but the Crusader floated over the angle, the indicated airspeed below the 80 knots needed for a successful ejection. Irwin pulled the canopy jettison handle, but although the latches released, there was not enough airspeed to carry the canopy away and it stayed on the rails.

In the limited time remaining, he considered an out-of-the-envelope ejection but decided to stay with the plane. He had enough airspeed for limited pitch control, at least until his main wheels rolled over the deck edge. By using the rudder to keep his wings level, he was able to enter the water more or less level, rather than nose first or in a cartwheel.

As the F-8 hit the water, the afterburner ignited, causing the engine to explode. The splash also carried away the canopy. Although the Crusader entered the water upright, water immediately began pouring over the cockpit sill. Irwin pulled the ditching handle which released him from the seat and he bobbed out of the cockpit just as a wave splashed over him.

The oxygen hose from the seat pan to his mask was entangled on the canopy handle on the right canopy rail. While awash and laying on the rail, Irwin separated the connector at the end of the mask hose and quickly rolled over the side of his fighter. The

Commander Chuck Deasy nearly had to go for a swim, but was able to keep his F8U-1 out of the water

forward end of the center section of the Crusader's two-position wing, and most of the vertical stabilizer were all that were above the water.

Having inflated his life preserver, Irwin swam away as his Crusader finally sank out of sight. The *Hancock* had stopped close to his position and the ship's H-2 helicopter plucked him from the South China Sea. The time from the deck to the water was two seconds; from the water to the flight deck, safe and sound, two minutes. He noted later: 'I was never able to duplicate my emergency egress time from a cockpit onto a work stand in the hanger.' Only one of

the five F-8 pilots who experienced a 'controlled collision with the water' survived.

Vought initially installed its own ejection seat but changed to a Martin-Baker seat which had earned a good reputation in England. The Mk 5 did not have a zero-zero—zero airspeed, zero altitude—capability, and eventually, the Mk F-7 Zero-Zero seat was installed in late model Crusaders.

The Martin-Baker seats performed even during underwater ejections, perhaps the most frightening type of emergency egress, which has very limited chance of success. Two of four underwater ejections in Crusaders were successful, one in 1965 and one in 1967. One in 1962 and one in 1969 were not. The 1969 underwater ejection saw the pilot survive, although his seat failed to fire. He succeeded in popping the canopy, freeing himself from the seat, and floating up to the surface.

In 1967, a complicated, somewhat odd area of concern was the 'anthropometric limitations' of jet pilots using the Mk 7 seat. The problem related to the optimum body position during ejection. The force of ejection occasionally compresses the pilot's body, resulting in spinal injuries. Thus, proper position is important before initiating ejection.

During this period, concern surfaced about large pilots sitting in the Mk 7 seat, without the proper clearance from the canopy. The maximum height was dictated to be 6 feet 1 inch at 185 pounds. In 1969, the thickness of the seat pack, which contained important survival implements, was reduced by one inch, along with the seat cushion. (The author knew two F-8 pilots who, at 6 ft 4 inches and even 6 feet 5 inches, were obviously well above the stipulated height.)

Besides ejecting and ditching, a third alternative awaits the carrier pilot: the barrier. Essentially a nylon webbing quickly strung across the flight deck, the barrier has saved many planes and pilots from a cold swim. But sometimes, a barrier engagement had an unexpected variation.

On 5 March 1958, Lieutenant, j.g. John Miottel of VF-154 had watched helplessly as a squadron mate rode his F8U into the water during a bad weather approach to the *Hancock*. With 730 hours total flight time, and 140 hours in the Crusader, Miottel did not have a lot of experience to call on. His depleted fuel state—only 850 pounds—and the fact he was beyond the point to head for land, made it necessary to recover aboard the ship.

After boltering twice, he was told it appeared his hookpoint had been twisted and was not picking up the arresting cable. There was little choice but to rig the barrier. As the barrier came up, he circled, burning down to below 500 pounds. His situation was beyond critical.

Finally, the ship called him down, and Miottel started his approach; his extremely low fuel allowed only one pass. With the LSO guiding him, he flew into the barrier and seemed to be stopping, but his aircraft suddenly swung to the left and hung up on the port deck edge. It stopped, then rolled 60 degrees to the left. Miottel jettisoned his canopy as the plane rolled over onto its back and fell toward the water 70 feet below.

He looked up to see the ship's wake, as he groped for the ditching handle and braced himself to hit the water. As the water poured in, he pulled the ditching handle and was thrown clear of the Crusader which had become entangled in the barrier webbing. Struggling to free himself of his parachute, with a faulty oxygen mask, as he went periodically underwater in heavy seas, Miottel finally inflated his life raft and was soon picked up by the ship's helo.

The barrier, and the collapse of the F8U's left main gear had combined with an unexpected roll of the carrier to nearly finish Miottel's young flying career.

Stupid Stuff

As most aviators know, there is enough in flying to kill you without any human assistance. But, somehow, many folks never get the message. Consider John Nichols' experience in 1962. Life in the Crusader community at Cecil Field was great. All the squadrons, in Nichols' words, 'were full of wonderful pilots'. It was not unusual for COs to challenge each other and their squadrons to meet over the field for a little ACM, the winner to be published at the O-Club.

However, an admiral's aide with very low time was given command of VF-62, and life deteriorated for one of the Atlantic Fleet's premier F-8 squadrons. One day, eight Crusaders were readied for a flight to the base at Guantánamo, Cuba. One of the planes went down with a hydraulics problem. The remaining seven took off. Nichols and two other pilots made up one section, while the CO and three others were in the four-plane. The weatherman had forecast a line of intense thunderstorms between Cecil and Gitmo, and sure enough, they were huge.

Instead of turning around, the skipper pressed on, followed by the other six. Even though the Crusaders had climbed to 40,000 feet, the cumulus towered far above them. Nichols and his two mates flew into the storm at 30,000, having descended and sped up to Mach 1.1. The skipper's section remained high and immediately ran into trouble.

As Nichols exited the clouds, battered but safe, he heard the high-pitched voice of the CO calling, 'I'm disoriented, I'm ejecting . . .' His wingman also called that he was bailing out, and then there was silence.

Five hundred miles from Gitmo, Nichols called Miami Center for a radar fix on the CO's section, but there was nothing. Landing at Guantánamo, Nichols and the other two pilots waited. Finally, two men from the other section landed, their Crusaders barely flyable after multiple lightning strikes which completely fried their avionics. Three days later, after the storm had dissipated, a search was begun. The CO was found floating in his life raft. His jaygee wingman was never found; only the young pilot's helmet. VF-62 soon had a new commanding officer.

And then there are the folks who insist on discovering new ways to fly, new aircraft configurations, and just tempting fate. One characteristic of many naval aircraft is their folding wings to facilitate storage below decks. A few enterprising aviators have occasionally tried to take off with their wings folded—and succeeded. The F-8 has had more than its share of such incidents, seven to be exact.

One of the most famous ejections—perhaps because it was so well photographed—was VF-11's Lieutenant, j.g., John Kryway's mishap in October 1961 aboard the FDR. When the deck dropped out from under him, he landed hard,

breaking his starboard main gear. The magnesium strut caught fire. Although the tailhook had caught a wire, the hook parted from the shaft due to the strain, and Kryway ejected as his F8U-1 left the angle. He was rescued shortly after entering the water. Note in the third photo, as he leaves the deck, Kryway's hands are reaching for the ejection face curtain over his head

The first incident occurred on 2 August 1960, when a VF-11 F8U-1 pilot took off from Naples, Italy, and flew for 24 minutes before landing safely, his wings still folded. Five F-8Es did the wings-folded trick, one in 1964, one in 1966, two in 1967 and one in 1968.

Lieutenant Commander Tom Hudner took off at night in an Echo. Hudner, who had won the Medal of Honor in Korea trying to rescue a squadron mate who had been shot down, climbed to 10,000 feet and rocked his plane from side to side in a successful effort to force the wingtips down.

Two Marine pilots of VMF(AW)-235 at Da Nang made wings-folded take-offs in 1966 and 1967. The last was with the Crusader fully loaded with two 2000-pound bombs, six Zunis and a full bag of 20 mm ammunition. The pilot jettisoned his load and made an uneventful recovery. While the pilot in the 1966 incident also recovered, he also forgot to lower his landing gear, probably not one of his better days.

The final Crusader wings-up take-off involved a Juliet on 28 January 1969, during carrier landing practice. As the pilot reached rotation speed, the LSO called to tell him his wings were still folded. He quickly came out of burner, lowered his hook and engaged the arresting gear.

Vietnam Stories

Combat in SE Asia, while giving the F-8 a chance to show its capabilities, also set the stage for combat losses, ejections and incredible variations on the theme. As previously noted, VFP-63 suffered the first combat loss of a Crusader in June 1964, when Lieutenant Charles Klusmann ejected from his RF-8A, and spent three months as a POW before escaping. A VF-111 F-8D was shot down the following day, the squadron CO, Commander Doyle Lynn, being rescued by a Marine H-34 helicopter.

As the pace of Vietnam combat intensified, so did the losses and ejections. VF-154 in the *Coral Sea*, experienced several losses in the first half of 1965. On 29 March, the skipper, Commander Bill Donnelly, ejected after his F-8D had been hit by ground fire during a strike. He parachuted into shark-infested waters off Bach Long Island, and drifted for 45 hours in his damaged raft, which he had to blow up every 20 minutes. Twice during the night, he was forced to go below the surface of the water to evade a North Vietnamese patrol boat which was searching for him.

Finally, an F-8 from the *Hancock* spotted the weakened pilot and radioed his position. An Air Force Albatross amphibian rescued Donnelly and brought him to Da Nang.

One of the most famous of shootdowns involving a Crusader took place on 31 August 1966. Lieutenant Commander Thomas Tucker, the OINC of the *Oriskany*'s photo det, ejected from his VFP-63 RF-8G at only 1500 feet after being hit by 37 mm fire over Haiphong Harbour. The photo pilot came down only 100 yards offshore, in full view of the communist defenders, including six North Vietnamese junks which quickly got underway to retrieve the American aviator. (The North Vietnamese offered a $200 bounty on captured US pilots.)

An SH-3 Sea King helicopter of HS-6 in the ASW carrier *Kearsarge* (CVS-33) sped to the scene. Its pilot, squadron skipper Commander Robert S Vermilya, and his crew had been loitering on their designated SAR station, and aimed their armoured helicopter for Tucker.

Overhead, Tucker's escort Crusader pilot Lieutenant Commander Foster Teague, was the only cover because the time was too short to wait for a backup. The helo's gunners provided suppressive fire, while Teague strafed the oncoming junks, as the SH-3 drove toward Tucker, eventually scooping him up from under the enemy's nose, and retreating amidst a hail of gunfire.

In the 'Hope-the-New-Year-Gets-Better Department', Lieutenant, j.g. Craig Taylor was on his first combat mission, flying an F-8C of VF-111 from the *Oriskany* on 2 January 1968. He was flying escort for an RF-8 and was hit by ground fire. He landed seven miles off the North Vietnamese coast, and saw a posse of junks heading for him. A-4s appeared and chased the enemy flotilla away, allowing a rescue helo to retrieve Taylor.

Two VF-162 Crusader pilots shared a unique distinction as the first pilots to make two combat ejections. Twenty-five year-old Lieutenant, j.g. Rick Adams had been shot down by a SAM in October 1965, ejecting over the water. He was rescued by a helicopter and quickly returned to the *Oriskany*. In July 1966, Adams' plane was hit by flak, and the young pilot ejected for the second time, landing in dense jungle. Lieutenant Commander Butch Verich, one of the Hunters' more senior pilots, directed the SAR effort. Finally, with A-1s laying down suppressive fire, the helo found Adams and pulled him out. The Navy decided that after two shoot-downs, a pilot should be transferred back to the US.

Butch Verich would soon join Rick Adams. At 40 years of age, Verich was somewhat old to be flying combat, but like his CO, Dick Bellinger, 42, he brought a wealth of experience with him. Verich was shot down in August 1966, the victim of small arms fire during an attack on river barge traffic.

In July 1967, Verich, along with two other VF-162 F-8s attacked enemy flak sites ahead of an A-4 strike. Verich's Crusader was hit by a SAM, and he punched out. As he floated down, he could see his squadron mates laying down suppression fire for his protection. He landed near the wreck of his burning fighter.

Verich landed in jungle and he eluded enemy troops for 15 hours, waiting for rescue. The SAR effort had to be suspended as night came, but soon after dawn, F-8s, A-1s, and A-4s swept in.

'They tore the place up pretty well', Verich recalled. 'It was a little scary but my friends were out

This VF-24 F-8J has a precarious position aboard the Hancock *during a 1971 cruise. Apparently, the pilot made a barricade engagement—note the spent strips around the fuselage. The plane has climbed up onto a convenient bomb stowage crate, and, with its port outer wing gone, hangs over the water awaiting rescue*

A classic barricade sequence. This VF-191 F8U-1 is approaching the Bonnie Dick's *barricade in 1962, and, although proper contact is made, the hapless Crusader goes through the webbing and over the side, as a deck crewman—probably the hook runner—watches helplessly*

there and I knew things would be all right.'

Verich fired a flare which directed the rescue helicopter from HS-2 in the carrier *Hornet* (CVS-12) to his position. The helo pilot and his crew braved intense enemy fire to finally drag Verich up into the quivering aircraft. It took 20 minutes and three tries to grab the helo's rescue sling, but Verich finally grabbed hold. The helicopter pilot, Lieutenant Neil Sparks received the Navy Cross.

VF-211's Gene Chancy, who would score a MiG kill on 21 June 1966, also had to eject twice from Crusaders. The first time came in 1963 during peacetime, the second in combat.

In December 1963, Chancy had just finished the training syllabus at VF-124. Before joining his fleet squadron, he tried to keep his new skills sharp by being available for any flights which might need a new fighter pilot. On Friday the 13th, his CO asked if he wanted one more flight before going to VF-211. It was to be a short hop to pick up an F-8C, BuNo 145577, at a rework facility at North Island.

A helicopter ferried Chancy from Miramar and he took off soon afterward, anticipating a happy hour's flight time wringing the plane out before returning it to Miramar. After 'a few aerobatics and wifferdills' he headed back when an explosion rocked his aircraft. The startled young pilot checked his gauges as he listened to an unwinding sound. At first, he thought he'd lost his engine, but the dials told him he was still flying. Finally, he was able to determine he had had a complete electrical failure, and had lost two of the plane's three hydraulic systems. This time, the usually dependable ram-air turbine (RAT) was not working.

As he tried to go through emergency procedures, Chancy found he could not lower his landing gear, and because his gauges were not working, he could not tell how much gas he had left:

Ooomph! That smarts. A classic ramp strike. This VF-13 Crusader hit the flight deck well short of the arresting wires. This type of mishap can end in fire, ejection, and loss of aircraft and pilot

After two low passes in front of the Miramar operations tower, rocking my wings, I saw two F-8s enter the break and turn off the 180 for final. I was frustrated at the tower for ignoring my frantic attempts to be noticed so I flew directly in front of the second F-8 . . . he got the message and joined on my wing for a bit of hand signalling . . .

By now, Chancy knew he was going to have to eject from his crippled fighter and with the two other F-8s trailing, he flew out toward the desert west of El Centro, climbing to 20,000 feet. Finally, the little formation reached a good spot, and after positioning himself, Chancy pulled the face curtain. The ejection went well, and he had a long time to consider his options as he fell toward the ground four miles below.

His chute opened at 10,000 feet and he floated down, watching the column of smoke rising from where his Crusader had dug a hole in the desert floor. Although the cause of his mishap could never be specifically determined, the best guess was that the pressurization turbine exploded.

Lieutenant Chancy's second ejection was not made under as 'calm' a set of circumstances as his first three years before. Now in the middle of a combat cruise in Vietnam, he and his flight leader launched from the *Hancock* for a BARCAP on Monday, 3 May 1966. He flew an F-8E, BuNo 149169.

After the two Crusaders joined up, they spent 20 minutes on CAP station, and then were vectored toward a suspected enemy radar site located on an island. They approached the island and spotted a small building. Chancy followed his leader as they rolled in to strafe the target.

As Chancy lined up for his turn, he felt his plane shudder, and saw a fire warning light. His utility hydraulic pressure went to zero, and he called his flight leader. His in-flight refuelling probe had extended and other lights were lit. It was time to go. The decider came when his control stick locked dead centre and the plane snap-rolled inverted.

He pulled the curtain, inverted, at 5000 feet and 300 knots. His chute opened and he watched his plane crash into the sea. Preparing for water entry, he noted his position from the enemy island as he inflated his life preserver.

Entering the water, he released his torso harness fittings and tried to climb into the small personal one-man life raft each aviator carried in the seat survival pack. However, the raft had been punctured and was useless. Chancy then saw he was drifting toward the island and began backstroking toward the open sea.

After several minutes, he was relieved to hear the beating of the rotors of a little H-2 SAR helo. He was not looking forward to spending a night struggling to stay afloat and away from the island. As the helo crew flew him back to the *Hancock*, they told him they had been under fire from the island. Chancy had seen nothing.

Commander John Dixon, skipper of VF-191 during the 1965 cruise on the *Bonnie Dick*, had a one-of-a-kind experience during a mission in Laos. With another F-8, he flew along a river in Route Pack IV, nearly as bad an area as the infamous Pack VI. With his mission fuel nearly gone, Dixon finally found what he thought was a truck and dove on it, but it turned out to be a hill. He had gone so low that he did not enough power to climb as he bottomed out of his dive.

He impacted the tall elephant grass, skidding along the ground until he could get the power up to take off again. Dixon recovered successfully, but the ground crew found bits of grass in the Sidewinder rails, chunks of dirt embedded in the fuselage, and the entire belly of the Crusader turned from the normal off-white to green.

The Last Ejection

Following Vietnam, the Crusader entered widespread service in the reserves. The reserves had contributed to the ejection rate on many occasions, although until the demise of VFP-63, the fleet photo squadron experienced many more times the number of bailouts. From March 1975 to July 1981, VFP-63 tallied 14 ejections, some in the continental US and others on deployment; some in training and some in operational mishaps.

The first ejection from a reserve Crusader occurred on 9 January 1965, when the pilot of a Dallas F-8A punched out. A Washington reservist left his VF-661 F-8B the following month. While the reserves enjoyed a fairly good reputation and a commensurate loss rate, it fell to a reservist to make the last ejection from a US Crusader.

Commander David Strong, the Executive Officer, of VFP-206, was number two in a two-plane flight from NAS Miramar on 11 March 1985. The squadron was conducting one of its ACDUTRA cruises. After preflighting his RF-8G, BuNo 146855, AF 606, Strong climbed in and he and his lead taxied to Runway 24 Left.

Immediately after take-off, both pilots came out of afterburner, but Strong felt and heard an explosion and his power began to quickly decay. Failing to relight his engine, he turned his attention to steering his plane away from an office park near the runway, toward the ocean. He couldn't make it, and initiated ejection at 170 knots and 250 feet above the ground, with his aircraft in a right roll, outside the envelope of the seat.

The ejection went well, however, and deposited Strong in a street 200 feet from the crash site. Divesting himself of his parachute and flight gear, Commander Strong began helping fire crews to fight the fire begun by the crash. Secretary of the Navy John Lehman awarded Commander Strong a rare peacetime Distinguished Flying Cross for his courage in staying with his plane beyond the limits required in order to keep away from a populated area.

With Commander Strong's ejection, the long list of emergency exits was finally completed. One more experience needs to be told, however. That of then-Lieutenant Commander Robert G Hoch of VFP-306.

During a cross-country on 14 July 1973, Lieutenant Commander Hoch experienced a flameout. After several attempts to relight the engine of his RF-8G, BuNo 145615, Hoch ejected at 10,000 feet above the Arizona desert floor. He floated down circled all the way by his wingman and friend Lieutenant Commander Robert Norrell. (Both men would eventually command the squadron, Hoch in 1975, and Norrell in 1980.)

Hoch touched down safely and after taking off his chute and flight gear, waved at Norrell who eventually had to leave his friend as his fuel diminished. At something of a loss as to what to do next, Hoch was taking stock of his situation when he heard the rumble of motorcycles in the distance.

The noise finally grew nearer and evolved into a father and son out for a day's dirtbiking. They rode up to the downed pilot as a reserve C-130 flew over, the crew kicking out a cold six-pack of beer. Things were looking up as Hoch climbed aboard one of the bikes with a can of beer in one hand, and holding onto the driver with the other.

The bikers took him to a military hospital where Hoch knew he would have trouble explaining the alcohol in his bloodstream. Drinking and flying are frowned on, always have been. Somehow, he got through the doctor's exam.

Chapter 11
Variations on the Basic Theme

Besides the six basic models of the F-8 (A through E, and RF-8A), the four remanufactured fighters (H, J, K, L), and RF-8G, the French E(FN), and the one-off TF-8A Two-sader, a few additional variations were built.

The XF8U-3: What Could Have Been

By 1955, with much of the experimentation and knowledge of captured German research assimilated and incorporated into many of the world's air forces, a unique argument was raging in the United States. Main points of contention revolved around two important aspects of tactical jet aircraft. The first involved the need for two crewmen, as opposed to the more traditional single aviator, the fighter pilot who did everything—fly, navigate, and fight.

The second consideration centred on the use of missiles instead of a fixed gun armament. The two areas were linked, it was felt, because if future fighter aircraft were to be armed solely with missiles, then it would take a specialist—another crewman—to operate the system, while the pilot could concentrate on flying the aircraft. Things were getting too complicated. There was also the belief that two pairs of eyes were better than one in a dogfight.

Sandwiched in between these main points was the fact that fighter pilots wanted more speed included in the increased performance of any new fighter. The Air Force's F-105 and ultimately abortive F-107—a development of the F-100—were attempts to give the desired increase in speed. The Navy had its designs, too.

There were other areas as well. Although single-seaters would probably be lighter, new fighters would probably use two engines, making the airplane heavier, but providing an attractive safety factor. And the cost, that was a separate area, too. The entire

military was learning valuable but painful lessons about the skyrocketing cost of designing, building, developing, and producing new aircraft. In the late 1950s, North American's A3J Vigilante carrier-borne atomic bomber was 'costing its weight in 18 carat gold, at the then-current price of $35 an ounce'.

Two companies, Chance Vought and McDonnell, had been working on separate private developments for the Navy. Vought, fresh from its triumph with the F-8, had begun to redesign the Crusader, coming up with a sharply altered shape, but using a lot of Crusader-derived experience. McDonnell, with only limited experience in military aircraft, was a young company. However, though its big XP-67 twin-engine prop fighter of World War II, and the postwar FH-1 twin-jet Phantom had been its only real aircraft programmes, McDonnell was deeply involved in its AH-1 attack aircraft.

In July 1955, in an effort to choose one aircraft and save money, the Navy brought the two programmes into direct competition with the issue of an interceptor design requirement. Vought and McDonnell quickly entered the competition with their current designs and soon, the field was narrowed to these two examples. The AH-1 had been redesigned and redesignated from a single- to a two-seat, twin-engine fighter, the F4H-1 Phantom II.

Deciding not to call its entry the XF9U, Vought merely designated the aircraft the XF8U-3 Crusader III. (The best explanation for the 'III' designation is that the F8U-2 (F-8C) was considered such a major upgrade that it was initially called the Crusader II. Thus, when the F8U-2 was quickly followed by the first example of the F8U-3, it was logical to call the latest aircraft the Crusader III.)

The Dash 3 was an extremely advanced aircraft whose possibilities were stillborn as the Phantom eventually won the competition and the Vought development contract was cancelled in December

Not just another F-8 derivative. The Crusader III stands with an F-8A during flight testing. Although the family resemblance is obvious, the -3 was much, much more

dedicated to the Phantom, and the other responsible for testing the Crusader III. The Flight Test Division of the NATC organization provided several experienced test pilots, including then-Commander Donald D Engen. Commander Engen flew both the Phantom and Crusader III, and while he knew the F4H was a winner, he was more impressed by the Vought aircraft, if only by its size:

The airplane was *big* and the only similarities to the earlier Crusader were in the systems within the aircraft. It was a greatly different airplane and that was evident from the time you first saw the large protruding lower lip of the intake and the sheer size of the fuselage. The plane was more slab-sided than the F8U. The cockpit was roomy with a much greater slope to the forward windscreen. The controls, cockpit layout, and instrument panel immediately made the pilot more comfortable.

The XF8U-3s, three of which actually flew out of nine built, ended their days as research vehicles for the National Aeronautics and Space Administration. Because of their performance capabilities, with demonstrated speeds of Mach 2.2 and a zoom climb altitude of nearly 90,000 feet, with sustained levels of 60–65,000 feet, the Crusader III was an ideal space research aircraft for the embryo period of 1959–61.

As far as performance is concerned, the aircraft was never flown to its limits, due, primarily, to the limitations of such a small matter as windscreen construction. The acrylic could not take the high temperatures of the aircraft's upper performance envelope. Although the XF8U-3 was flown up to Mach 2.39 (1601 mph), it is thought that it could have attained Mach 2.6 (1750 mph) or 2.9 (1950 mph) at 35,000 feet. Commander Engen commented on the Crusader III's impressive performance:

It was immediately apparent we had an airplane that was not thrust limited. The airplane had so much power that it was still accelerating as fast at 2.0 Mach as it had been at 1.6 Mach. I reported at the time, and still firmly believe, that the plane could have accelerated out to 3.0 Mach—then an incredible feat—except for the acrylic windscreen which could not withstand the heat generated at speeds above 2.2 Mach. We were told that the canopy would become opaque 20 seconds before the windscreen failed. I spent as much time at high Mach numbers trying to analyze what 'opaque' looked like, as I did looking at the instruments.

But there were problems with the highly advanced F8U-3:

Early on, it was obvious that one could not always get to those very high speeds because there was an aerodynamic anomaly that developed in the duct depending on rate of acceleration, altitude and attitude. As you accelerated, you could feel the duct go 'critical' at 1.35 Mach. The indication was a duct rumble which started somewhere behind and under the pilot, and as you accelerated, it moved forward. You could feel the rumble in the whole airplane until it reached just under your feet, where the duct would 'unload' with the sound and fury of a 40 mm cannon going off right between your legs. It was an awesome sound and dust would fly all around the cockpit. It was repetitive and when it began, while accelerating, you never knew which to let go

1958, much to the lament of two generations of fighter pilots. While the Phantom, of course, went on to become one of the greatest aircraft in military aviation history, the XF8U-3 offered a tremendous potential and performance which only a few realized at the time.

In the spring of 1958, the Navy Preliminary Evaluation (NPE) Teams were established by the Commander, Naval Air Test Center, with one team of first, the stick or the throttle. I guarantee that each pilot resolved never to do it again.

After the end of the first phase of the NPE tests, this duct criticality was designed out of the airplane in less than six weeks—I consider that effort one of the greatest aerodynamic design fixes in the shortest time in the history of jet aircraft—and when we returned to test it at the end of November 1958, the F8U-3 was the most delightful airplane to fly I have ever seen. It had the flying qualities of a very nimble fighter. I likened it to the FJ-3 Fury which had control harmony and forces that made it one of the best airplanes in the Navy inventory.

At that time, we test pilots had not experienced automatic down-linking of flight data. This capability was incorporated in the F8U-3 by Vought and the installation did away with some very laborious data collection procedures which had always been the bane of test pilots and flight test engineers. There was a trailer near the Vought hangar at Edwards in which this data was received, recorded, and analyzed.

On one flight, I had been doing some less than thrilling performance flying, and I had completed all the points I had been asked to get. It was a beautiful day and as I dropped down over the Antelope Valley to return to Edwards, I had time to enjoy the Dash 3. I levelled off at about 3000 feet above the ground and did a loop, the first ever done in the Crusader III.

The airplane went around beautifully. I didn't say anything to anyone and landed. But, I had not turned off my data transmission switch and my manoeuvre was seen by everyone. As I taxied into the chocks, shut down, and opened the canopy, John Konrad, Chief Test Pilot for Vought, came up with a twinkle in his eye and slowly shook his finger at me. I had been found out.

The F8U-3 was amazingly free of problems and a delight to fly. In retrospect, had we been able to afford two airplanes in the Navy fighter inventory then, we would have had two very fine aircraft.

The limiting windscreen was being redesigned when the development contract was cancelled by President Dwight Eisenhower, who picked the F4H based on the relative findings of the NPE teams. There is no doubt that had the Crusader III gone into production, it would have been the world's fastest jet aircraft for some time. It is interesting to speculate on an F8U-3/F-4 partnership in the fleet, for had the Vought airplane been produced in numbers, it would have been the fleet's primary interceptor and dogfighter during the Vietnam War. All reports told of the aircraft's acceleration, manoeuvrability and high speed stability, prime requisites in air-to-air combat.

That the Crusader III lost out to the Phantom II is no indictment of either airplane or their respective manufacturers. They were designed to different requirements. The XF8U-3 was a fighter-interceptor,

ABOVE
Afterburner cooling airscoop installed on the first F8U-3 Crusader III can be seen on the fairing to the vertical stabilizer. F8U-2s and subsequent Crusaders were equipped with two airscoops on their tailcones for cooling the titanium aftersection (Art Schoeni)

LEFT
An in-flight view of the Crusader III shows the huge ventral fins in the flight position, and the large Sparrow missiles, three of which were carried

A Crusader III takes off from the NAS Dallas runway for a flight to Edwards Air Force Base in California. This is the second prototype, and it was joining the first which had been undergoing flight tests for several months

pure and simple. The F-4, however, had been designed around a newer, more encompassing set of requirements which reflected current thinking at the time. The Phantom met these new demands; the Crusader III did not. Every pilot on the evaluation teams wanted both airplanes, but economics dictated otherwise.

Donald Engen is over 6 feet tall, yet he appears lost in the capacious cockpit of the Crusader III. Everything about the -3 was huge, including its potential, which, sadly, was stillborn. Note Engen's European-style flight helmet, with external sun visor, resting on the windscreen bow (Donald Engen)

The Critical Wing Crusader

Aerodynamic research was another area in which the F-8 was involved. In 1969, NASA issued a development requirement for design and construction of a new wing. Called the Supercritical Wing, the new aerofoil reversed the shape of a conventional wing by having the top surface flat and the bottom surface curved. During wind tunnel tests, it was found that the new wing allowed aircraft to cruise at speeds closer to Mach 1 without the disconcerting and troublesome buffeting which accompanied sustained flight at that high speed. It was also hoped

that the Supercritical Wing would reduce take-off and landing distances as well as contribute to low speed handling characteristics.

Initial tests were conducted with a T-2 trainer, but by June 1971, an F-8A had been fitted with the new wing. Compared with the normal F-8 wingspan of over 35 feet, the Supercritical Winged F-8 had a span of 43 feet. The F-8 was painted with a cerulean blue fuselage and white wings and horizontal tail surfaces. The slender, long-span wings imparted a birdlike quality to the plane's appearance. This Crusader completed its part in the test programme and the General Dynamics F-111 was the next aircraft to pick up the Supercritical Wing programme in 1973.

ABOVE
By the time this photo was taken in 1960, the F8U-3 programme had been cancelled, and the three prototypes found work at NASA. Standing by a Regulus II submarine-launched missile, this -3 is garishly painted in orange dayglo for easier tracking (via Jim Sullivan)

BELOW
The Supercritical Wing F-8 at the Edwards Air Force Base NASA Test Facility in November 1974 (Peter Mancus, via Jim Sullivan)

ABOVE
With a straight F-8C as a wingman, the F-8 Supercritical Wing Crusader shows its unique wingshape

ABOVE RIGHT
Using an F-8K fuselage and a Lima wing, this hybrid Crusader is the only civilian-owned and operated F-8 still flying regularly. Owned by Phoenix-based Thunderbird Aviation, the beautifully restored and simply painted Crusader uses a Pratt & Whitney J57-P-55 engine and several internal custom avionics

BELOW RIGHT
Retired reserve Captain Dudley Moore leans proudly against the result of many hours of perseverance and restoration: the Thunderbird Aviation F-8K/L hybrid. Although its cannon ports are clearly visible, the heavily instrumented Crusader carries on more peaceful work in south-western skies. Note the large refuelling probe bulge directly above and behind Moore

A Civilian Crusader

Perhaps a fitting note on which to end this narrative of the career of the F-8 series is to tell of one Crusader which still flies, albeit with civilian registration numbers. While other retired military aircraft can be found still serving in various capacities, or thrilling weekend airshow crowds, the F-8 is a *rara avis* in the common man's world. Expense, the scarcity of flyable examples and the Crusader's demanding attributes are all probable reasons for the lack of a privately owned F-8.

But, on 12 March 1987, F-8 N19TB made its first flight, with F-8 veteran Dudley Moore proudly at the controls. Owned and operated by Thunderbird Aviation of Phoenix, Arizona, the Crusader was a hybrid, with an F-8K fuselage and tail, and a Lima's wing. Parts were obtained from LTV Products Group and salvage yards. The engine is a Pratt & Whitney J57-P-55.

The modifications are in the hundreds as the plane has been modernized for the 1980s. Nonessential military equipment was stripped, including armour, radar, gunsight, and gun chutes. Basic weight is 19,500 pounds.

The F-8 contains state of the art UHF/VHF radios, NAVSTAR Loran C, and VOR/DME (Switched). Navigational information is fed into a modern horizontal situation indicator (HSI). Everything, including the APC—approach power compensator—works like the original.

The ejection seat is vintage Martin-Baker, modified with a custom 28-foot chute. The face curtain and canopy interruptor are gone. Ejection is through the canopy, and the seat pack contains only the emergency oxygen bottle.

A custom video pod facing aft as well as custom high speed camera installations in the gun compartments are used for flight test procedures.

Moore did all the flight test and development work, involving 20 flights. The one-of-a-kind Crusader is parked on the flight test ramp at Hollomon Air Force Base, New Mexico, involved in supersonic flight test work at White Sands Missile Range. Moore, an airline pilot and retired Naval Air Reserve captain, has flown it to Mach 1.5—1000 mph—and reports it performs beautifully.

One of two RF-8Gs retained by Rockwell International, N110NR, is BuNo 144617, which saw service with VFP-306 before being brought from the huge storage depot at Davis-Monthan in January 1986. It was flown in May 1987, but, after 10 flights, it has remained on the ground. The programme it was serving has run out of funds, and although a second RF-8, BuNo 145607 from VFP-206, has arrived, both aircraft are grounded. They are maintained in flight status, however, and their engines and systems checked periodically (Rockwell, via Joe Davies)

A second F-8 is under reconstruction to be ready for flight in 1988. A third is also planned. The first F-8 rebuild took two and a half years and 19,000 man-hours, and $2,000,000 to complete, which is about the original cost in 1960 dollars.

Ironically, Moore received an FAA licence to fly the F-8 on 25 March 1987, the 32nd anniversary of the Crusader's first flight in 1955.

Rockwell International in Palmdale, California, also had obtained two RF-8Gs from VFP-206 and 306, after those reserve squadrons decommissioned. BuNos 144617 and 145607 were refurbished, although only 617 made any flights—in May 1987—in support of Rockwell's Advanced Technology Wing (ATW) programme.

The ATW uses a superplastic flexible wing that controls the shape of the upper surface to fit flight profiles, resulting in greatly enhanced manoeuvrability. Lack of money has put the ATW research on hold, but the company maintains the RF-8s in flight status, ready for an infusion of funds.

The Crusader series was probably built in too limited a number to expect it to find its way into many museums or private air forces. But Vought's last production fighter can be arguably considered to be one of the two most important naval aircraft of the post-Korea period. The other being, of course, McDonnell's masterpiece, the F-4. But, for many of the naval aviators of the 1960–70 decade, there was really only one choice.

I leave you with a mild bit of 1962 F-8 frivolity by an apparently jealous A-1 pilot of VA-145:

A Crusader Pilot's Creed

I am a United States Navy *Crusader* Pilot. My life is dedicated to protecting the skies of America between sunrise and sunset. Nothing shall deter me from my unwavering dedication to my duty except clouds, darkness or inoperative TACAN. My country has invested in me the faith of its people by training me to fly faster while doing less than any other pilot in the world. I shall always do my utmost, provided the weather is CAVU, to insure that this sacred trust shall not have been placed in vain. I shall never for a single moment forget, nor allow anyone in my general area to forget, that:
*I can fly 1000 miles per hour.
*I can carry a Sidewinder.
*My wing goes up and down.

I do hereby solemnly proclaim to observe faithfully the ensuing code of professional ethics, commensurate with my current elevated status:
1. Whenever Naval Aviators congregate in drinking establishments, I shall endeavour to conduct myself in a loud and obnoxious manner, especially if less fortunate, low performance-type pilots are present.
2. While deployed (and not yet off-loaded) I shall strive to maintain the long cherished tradition of day fighter pilots by attending every nightly movie, regardless of whether or not I am capable of following the plot.
3. I shall not permit the infrequent interruptions introduced by occasional annoying flights to prevent me from maintaining my proficiency in acey-ducey on a par with commonly accepted fighter pilot standards.
4. I will never go ashore without my F8U lapel pin and my baseball cap.
5. I will not bolter.
6. If, however, I should bolter, I will ascertain that an assorted variety of colourful alibis and excuses are readily available for explanation.
7. I will wear my space suit and helmet for all airshows, dependents' day cruise, PIO pictures, and those operational flights which do not require any movement in the cockpit. (Providing someone helps me in and out)

This is my creed and these are my ideals. With the aid of my afterburner, I shall do my utmost to justify the faith and confidence that has been placed upon my shoulders, even to the extent of flying during lunch-time.

Glossary

AAA — Anti-aircraft Artillery

Alpha Strike — A large offensive air strike, involving all the carrier air wing's assets, fighters, attack, refuelling, etc.

BARCAP — Barrier Combat Air Patrol. A fighter patrol between the carrier task force and enemy threat.

CAG — Air group commander. A somewhat archaic term, as wing designation was changed to CVW, and the commander was subsequently referred to as CAW; but CAG remained part of the vocabulary.

CAP — Combat Air Patrol

CV — Aircraft carrier. During Vietnam, normal acronym was CVA, designating an *attack* carrier, where CVS indicated an *anti-submarine* carrier.

CVW — Carrier air wing

LSO — Landing Signal Officer

MIGCAP — Standing patrol over the fleet or strike force to protect against any threat from enemy aircraft.

OINC — Officer-in-Charge

POL — Petroleum, Oil and Lubricants

SAM — Surface-to-air missile. A generic term but usually referring to the Soviet-built SA-2 Guideline.

SAR — Search and rescue

TARCAP — Target Combat Air Patrol. Fighters tasked with providing escort protection for the strike force.

Trap — An arrested landing aboard a carrier.

VA — Navy Light Attack Squadron

VF — Navy Fighter Squadron

VFP — Navy Light Photographic Squadron

VMCJ — Marine Composite Reconnaissance Squadron

VMF — Marine Fighter Squadron. (AW) was added in 1967 to denote all-weather capability but was a short-lived designation, and was overtaken by VMFA, for fighter and attack.

Specifications

Dimensions:
Span: 35 feet 8 in (10.87 m)
Length: 54 feet 6 in (16.61 m)
Height: 15 feet 9 in (4.80 m)

Remained the same for the entire F-8 series

Model Remarks	Power Plant	Armament	Empty Weight	Number built/remanufactured
F-8A (F8U-1)	Pratt & Whitney J57-P-4; 10,000 lb in mil/16,000 lb a/b	4 20 mm cannon and two AIM-9s	16,500	318
F-8B (F8U-1E, F-8L)	same	same	same	130B/61L
F-8C (F8U-2, F-8K)	J57-P-16; 10,500/16,000	4 20 mm cannon and 4 AIM-9s	same	186C/87K
F-8D (F8U-2N, F-8H)	J57-P-20; 10,700/18,000	same	same	152D/89H
F-8E (F8U-2NE, F-8J)	same	same, plus underwing stores, 4000 lbs	same	286E/136J
F-8E(FN)	J57-P-20A; 11,400/18,000			42
TF-8A (F8U-1T, NTF-8A)	J57-P-20			1
RF-8A (F8U-1P, RF-8G)	J57-P-4; 10,700/16,000 J57-P-420; 18,000 a/b (RF-8G)	none		144/73 RF-8G
F8U-3	J75; 25,000 lb in a/b	3 AIM-7s or AIM-9s	20,244 lbs	9 blt/ 3 flown

Span: 38 feet 8 in
Length: 58 feet 8.5 in
Height: 16 feet 4.5 in

Appendices

Appendix 1: Serial number allocations for the F-8

XF8U-1	138899–901 (901 cancelled)	F8U-2NE (F-8E)	149134–227, 150285–355, 150654–683, 150843–932
F8U-1 (F-8A)	140444–448 (140447–8, XF8U-2) 141336–363, 142408–415 143677–143821 145318–415		
		F-8E (FN)	151732–773
F8U-1E (F-8B)	145416–545	F8U-1P (RF-8A)	141363, 144607–625, 145604–647, 146822–905
F8U-2 (F-8C)	145546–603, 146906–147034	F8U-1T (TF-8A)	143710
F8U-2N (F-8D)	147035–147077, 147896–925, 148627–710		

F-8H (remanufactured F-8D)	F-8J (remanufactured F-8E)		
147042–4	149136–7	150317–8	150903–6
147046–51	149139	150320	150911
147054–8	149143	150323–6	150913
147060	149145	150328–30	150915
147062–3	149149–51	150333	150918
147065	149154–5	150336	150920–1
147067–72	149159	150339–41	150923
147897	149163–4	150343	150926–7
147901–2	149170	150346–7	150932
147904–6	149172	150349	
147908–9	149174–5	150351	
147914	149177	150353–4	
147916	149180	150654	
147918–9	149182	150656	
147922–5	119185–7	150658	
148628	149190	150660–4	
148630–2	149195–7	150669–70	
148634	149199	150672	
148636	149201–5	15004	
148638–40	149207	150677–8	
148643	149210–2	150680	
148647–52	149214–6	150682–3	
148655–62	149220–2	150844–5	
148664–6	149226–7	150849–52	
148677–8	150284	150855	
148680–2	150289	150859	
148684	150294–5	150861–4	
148686–9	150297	150868	
148691–5	150299	150871–2	
148697–700	150302	150877–9	
148703	150305	150882–3	
148705	150307	150885	
148707	150311	150887–90	
148710	150315	150898	
		150900	

F-8K (remanufactured F-8C)	F-8L (remanufactured F-8B)	RF-8G (remanufactured RF-8A)	
145548–50	145416	141363	
145553–4	145419–21	144607–8	
145557–60	145423	144613–20	
145562	145425	144623–5	
145565–6	145431	145607–9	
145568	145441–2	145611	
145572	145444–6	145613–5	
145574–5	145449–51	145616	
145579–80	145453–5	145622–5	
145583–4	145457–60	145627	
145587	145462–3	145629	
145590	145466	145631–3	
145592–6	145470–4	145635–7	
145598	145476–7	145639	
145603	145479	145641–3	
146908–11	145481	145645–7	
146916–8	145483	146827	
146931	145486	146835	
146933	145488–92	146838	
146936–7	145497–7	146844–6	
146939	145502–3	146848	
146941	145509	146855–6	
146944	145512	146858	
146947–7	145514	146860–1	
146951–3	145520–1	146863–5	
146955–6	145525	146866	
146960–1	145527–8	146870–1	
146963	145531–4	146873–4	F8U-3 146340–342 built and flown
146965–6	145542–3	146876	
146968		146882–3	Number of F-8s built
146970		146886	XF8U-1 2
146973–4		146889–90	F-8A 318
146979		146892	F-8B 130
146981		146895	F-8C 187
146983		146897–9	F-8D 152
146985–6		146901	F-8E 286
146990–2			F-8(FN) 42
146994–7			RF-8A 144
146999			
147000			Total 1261
147004–5			
147007			F-8s Remanufactured
147009–10			F-8H (F-8D) 89
147015–6			F-8J (F-8E) 136
147022–3			F-8K (F-8C) 87
147025			F-8L (F-8B) 61
147028–30			RF-8G (RF-8A) 73
147034			
			Total 446

Appendix 2: Crusader Losses Through Ejections, 1956–85*

*This table includes only losses incurred by ejection, not crashes. A few aircraft were ditched, only one of the four or five pilots surviving the exit of the aircraft after a crashlanding at sea. Due to varying levels of classification, these non-ejection incidents cannot be presented. Therefore this table is limited to actual ejections and subsequent loss of the aircraft. Due to inadequate record-keeping requirements, this information is incomplete, but the table does give a good idea of problem periods experienced during the F-8's career.

Date	Model	BuNo	Sqdn	Ship	Area	Rmks
4 May 56	F-8A	141337	Vought	—	US	
30 Jan 57	F-8A	141350	VX-3	—	US	
6 Jun 57	F-8A	141361	VF-32	—	US	
24 Jun 57	F-8A	143690	VF-32	—	US	
24 Jul 57	F-8A	141357	VX-3	—	US	
30 Jul 57	F-8A	142414	VF-32	—	US	
15 Aug 57	F-8A	143702	VF-154	—	US	
5 Sep 57	F-8A	143733	VX-3	—	US	
12 Sep 57	F-8A	141356	VF-32	—	US	
20 Sep 57	F-8A	143700	VF-32	—	US	
23 Sep 57	F-8A	143704	VF-24	—	US	
17 Oct 57	F-8A	142413	VF-32	—	US	
1 Nov 57	F-8A	143736	VF-103	—	US	
6 Nov 57	F-8A	143721	VF-32	—	US	
6 Jan 58	YF-8A	141343	NATC PAX	—	US	
7 Jan 58	F-8A	142415	?	—	US	
5 Mar 58	F-8A	143801	VF-154	CVA-19	—	
12 Mar 58	F-8A	143744	VF-96	CVA-41	—	
3 Apr 58	F-8A	144433	VF-24	—	US	
10 Apr 58	F-8A	143757	VF-32	CVA-60	—	
30 Apr 58	F-8A	143779	VF-154	CVA-19	—	
9 May 58	F-8A	143706	NAF China Lake	—	US	
11 May 58	F-8A	144455	VF-24	—	US	
10 Jul 58	F-8A	143765	VMF-334	—	US	First USMC
16 Jul 58	F-8A	143712	VF-11	—	US	
24 Jul 58	RF-8A	145605	VFP-63	CVA-41	—	First RF-8
13 Aug 58	F-8A	145332	VF-103	—	US	
18 Aug 58	F-8A	143717	VF-124	—	US	
4 Sep 58	F-8A	145407	VF-194	—	US	
25 Sep 58	F-8A	143747	VF-32	CVA-60	US	
26 Sep 58	F-8A	143805	VF-24	CVA-41	—	
6 Nov 58	F-8A	143687	NARF Norfolk	—	US	
17 Nov 58	F-8A	143763	VF-32	—	US	
19 Nov 58	F-8A	146364	VF-194	—	US	
20 Nov 58	F-8A	145340	VF-174	—	US	
9 Dec 58	F-8A	145341	VMF-334	—	US	Note BuNo sequence previous incident
9 Jan 59	F-8A	144460	VF-103	CVA-59	—	
22 Jan 59	F-8A	145376	VMF-334	—	US	
31 Jan 59	F-8A	145338	VMF-334	—	US	
20 Feb 59	F-8A	143781	VF-174	—	US	
23 Mar 59	F-8A	144451	VF-211	—	US	
3 Apr 59	F-8A	143761	VMF-334	—	US	
24 Apr 59	F-8A	143796	VF-211	—	US	
29 Apr 59	F-8A	144459	VF-96	CVA-61	—	
9 Jun 59	RF-8A	145619	VMCJ-1	—	US	
18 Jun 59	F-8A	143820	NATC PAX	—	US	
30 Jun 59	F-8A	145393	VF-194	—	US	
26 Jul 59	F-8A	143696	H&MS-32	—	US	
11 Aug 59	F-8A	144440	VMF-122	—	US	
24 Aug 59	F-8A	145465	NATC PAX	CVA-62	—	
10 Sep 59	F-8A	145414	VF-124	—	US	
23 Sep 59	F-8C	145556	VX-3	—	US	
7 Oct 59	RF-8A	145638	VAP-61	CVA-19	—	
30 Oct 59	RF-8A	146853	VFP-63	—	US	
12 Nov 59	F-8A	145373	VF-174	—	US	
13 Nov 59	RF-8A	146840	VFP-62	CVA-42	—	
17 Nov 59	F-8C	145573	VF-84	—	US	
21 Dec 59	F-8A	143798	VF-124	—	US	

Date	Type	Serial	Squadron	Carrier	Location	Notes
7 Jan 60	F-8C	145571	VF-84	CVA-62	US	
8 Jan 60	F-8A	143745	VMF-334	—	US	
5 Feb 60	F-8C	146954	VMF-451	—	US	
17 Feb 60	F-8A	144441	VF-124	—	US	
17 Mar 60	F-8B	145500	VMF-232	—	US	
25 Mar 60	RF-8A	146841	VFP-63	CVA-19	—	
29 Mar 60	F-8C	145552	VF-84	CVA-62	—	
15 Apr 60	F-8C	146978	VF-84	—	US	
17 May 60	F-8A	142411	VMF-312	—	US	
2 Jun 60	F-8B	145508	VMF-232	—	US	
7 Jun 60	F-8C	147039	NATC PAX	—	US	
7 Jun 60	F-8B	145418	VF-154	CVA-43	—	
13 Jun 60	F-8B	145484	VMF-235	—	US	
6 Jul 60	F-8C	147014	?	—	US	
16 Jul 60	RF-8A	146842	VFP-62	CVA-42	—	
3 Aug 60	F-8A	145405	VMF-334	—	US	
4 Aug 60	RF-8A	146868	VFP-62	CVA-42	—	
17 Aug 60	F-8A	143741	VF-124	—	US	
26 Aug 60	F-8A	145355	VMF-334	—	US	
6 Oct 60	RF-8A	146872	VFP-62	CVA-60	—	
10 Oct 60	F-8C	147019	VF-194	—	US	
11 Oct 60	F-8A	143740	VF-174	—	US	
17 Nov 60	F-8A	145374	VF-211	CVA-16	US	
21 Nov 60	RF-8A	146900	VFP-63	—	US	
26 Nov 60	F-8B	145496	VF-32	CVA-60	—	
1 Dec 60	RF-8A	145630	VFP-62	CVA-60	—	
2 Dec 60	F-8C	146958	VMF-333	—	US	
3 Jan 61	YF-8C	147040	NATC PAX	—	US	
11 Jan 61	F-8B	145447	VMF-312	—	Japan	
11 Jan 61	F-8C	147017	VF-103	CVA-59	—	
1 Feb 61	F-8A	145366	VF-51	US		
23 Feb 61	F-8C	146988	VF-124	—	US	
4 Mar 61	F-8A	143808	VF-51	—	US	
27 Mar 61	F-8B	145428	VMF-312	CVA-41	—	
28 Apr 61	F-8A	145377	VMF-333	—	US	
1 May 61	F-8B	145452	VF-154	—	Phil Is	
1 May 61	F-8B	145427	VMF-312	CVA-43	—	
6 May 61	F-8B	145424	VF-124	—	US	
22 May 61	RF-8A	146839	VFP-62	CVA-42	—	
12 Jun 61	F-8C	147003	VF-124	—	US	
22 Jun 61	F-8C	146923	VF-103	CVA-59	—	
17 Aug 61	F-8C	145570	VF-194	—	Hawaii	
26 Aug 61	F-8A	143708	VF-211	—	US	
30 Aug 61	RF-8A	145618	VFP-62	—	US	
9 Sep 61	F-8C	146982	VF-124	—	US	
19 Sep 61	F-8C	145578	VF-194	CVA-61	—	
20 Sep 61	F-8C	146912	VMF-323	—	US	
6 Oct 61	RF-8A	145634	VFP-62	—	US	After pilot's ejection, aircraft continued in flight for over one hour and had to be brought down over the water by a Sidewinder missile fired by another fighter.
16 Oct 61	F-8A	144452	VF-211	—	US	
16 Oct 61	F-8C	147033	VMF-333	—	US	
17 Oct 61	F-8C	146949	VMF-334	—	US	
21 Oct 61	F-8A	145357	VF-11	CVA-42	—	Well-photographed sequence showing aircraft landing gear igniting and F-8 going into catwalk as pilot ejects.
23 Oct 61	F-8A	143794	VF-191	—	Japan	
2 Nov 61	F-8C	146926	VF-194	—	Japan	
2 Nov 61	F-8C	147024	VMF-333	—	US	
12 Nov 61	F-8D	148653	VF-154	CVA-43	—	

15 Nov 61	F-8C	146922	VMF-333	—	Hawaii	
30 Nov 61	RF-8A	146850	VFP-63	—	US	
4 Dec 61	F-8B	145448	VMF-312	—	Japan	
10 Dec 61	F-8D	147915	VF-32	CVA-60	—	
15 Dec 61	F-8D	147900	VF-174	—	US	
25 Jan 62	F-8A	144442	VF-124	—	US	
8 Feb 62	F-8B	145493	VMF-232	CVA-19	—	
16 Feb 62	RF-8A	146887	VFP-62	CVAN-65	—	
27 Feb 62	F-8A(2)	145396	VF-124	—	US	2 aircraft collided during join-up; both pilots ejected. Only one BuNo recorded.
5 Mar 62	F-8A	145388	VC-4	—	US	
8 Mar 62	F-8C	146906	VF-103	—	US	
9 Mar 62	F-8A	145403	VF-191	—	US	
26 Mar 62	F-8C	146962	VMF-334	CVA-34	US	
28 Mar 62	RF-8A	146822	VMCJ-2	—	US	
2 Apr 62	RF-8A	146857	VFP-63	—	US	
13 Apr 62	RF-8A	146875	VMCJ-3	—	US	
21 Apr 62	F-8B	145485	VMF-122	—	US	
24 Apr 62	F-8A	143709	VF-174	—	US	
30 Apr 62	F-8D	148683	?	CVA-64	—	
7 May 62	F-8C	145567	VF-194	—	US	
8 May 62	F-8C	147013	VF-24	CVA-41	—	
22 May 62	F-8A	145375	VF-62	—	US	
22 Jun 62	F-8B	145541	VMF-312	—	US	
26 Jun 62	F-8A	143705	VC-4	—	US	
1 Jul 62	F-8D	149188	VF-33	CVAN-65	—	
4 Ju 62	F-8C	146967	VF-174	—	US	
6 Jul 62	RF-8A	145644	VFP-62	—	US	
10 Jul 62	F-8C	146946	VF-174	—	US	
11 Jul 62	F-8C	146964	VMF-334	—	US	
11 Jul 62	F-8B	145522	VMF-232	—	Phil Is	
14 Aug 62	F-8C	146934	VF-84	CVA-62	—	
25 Aug 62	F-8B	145517	VF-62	—	US	
14 Sep 62	F-8D	148685	VMF-235	—	US	
15 Oct 62	F-8C	145591	VMF-333	—	Puerto Rico	
16 Oct 62	RF-8A	145604	VFP-62	—	US	
17 Oct 62	F-8C	145586	VF-174	—	US	
17 Oct 62	F-8D	149156	VF-11	CVA-42	—	
7 Nov 62	RF-8A	146829	VFP-62	—	U	
15 Nov 62	F-8A	143728	VF-124	—	US	
4 Dec 62	F-8C	146914	VMF-334	—	US	
11 Dec 62	F-8D	149144	VF-11	CVA-42	—	
5 Jan 63	F-8B	145434	VMF-312	—	US	
24 Jan 63	F-8B	145480	VMF-251	—	—	
25 Jan 63	F-8D	147066	VF-124	CVA-19	—	
15 Feb 63	RF-8A	145640	VFP-63	CVA-43	—	
25 Mar 63	F-8D	148655	VMF-451	—	US	
26 Mar 63	RF-8A	146862	VFP-62	—	US	
16 Apr 63	RF-8A	146894	VFP-62	CVAN-65	—	
14 May 63	F-8C	145563	VF-194	CVA-61	—	
16 May 63	F-8B	145537	VF-62	CVA-38	—	
11 Jun 63	F-8C	146930	VF-124	—	US	
13 Jun 63	RF-8A	146832	VFP-63	—	US	
15 Jun 63	F-8E	149183	VF-124	—	US	
18 Jun 63	F-8E	149200	VMF-323	—	US	
20 Jun 63	F-8A	143692	VF-174	—	US	
30 Jul 63	F-8C	146977	VF-124	—	US	
2 Aug 63	F-8C	145597	VF-103	—	US	
5 Aug 63	F-8E	150312	VF-174	—	US	
26 Aug 63	F-8A	143729	VC-10	—	US	
28 Aug 63	RF-8A	144610	VFP-62	—	US	

Date	Type	BuNo	Squadron	Carrier	Location	Notes
20 Sep 63	F-8C	147008	VF-194	—	US	
9 Oct 63	F-8D	148674	VF-32	CVA-60	—	
10 Oct 63	F-8E	150338	VF-62	CVA-38	—	
17 Oct 63	F-8A	143787	VF-162	CVA-34	—	
22 Oct 63	RF-8A	144621	NARF NO ISL	—	US	
29 Oct 63	RF-8A	144622	VFP-63	VA-14		Note BuNo sequence from previous incident.
6 Nov 63	F-8D	148676	VF-154	CVA-43	—	
7 Nov 63	F-8C	145547	VF-124	—	US	
13 Nov 63	RF-8A	146834	VFP-62	—	US	
26 Nov 63	F-8B	145461	VMF-251	—	US	
13 Dec 63	F-8C	145577	VF-124	—	US	
19 Feb 64	RF-8A	146869	VFP-62	CVA-60	—	
25 Feb 64	F-8B	145501	VMF-232	—	Hawaii	
15 Mar 64	DF-8A	144439	VC-1	—	Hawaii	
1 Apr 64	F-8A	143725	VC-2	—	US	
17 Apr 64	F-8C	146959	VMF-333	—	—	
23 Apr 64	F-8E	149160	VF-124	—	US	
21 May 64	F-8B	145506	VMF-232	—	Hawaii	
6 Jun 64	RF-8A	Unknown	VAW-111	CVA-63	Vietnam (Vn)	This was first combat loss for the Crusader. This particular RF-8A was probably assigned to VFP-63, although the record assigns it to an airborne early warning squadron. Pilot ejected over Laos, was captured and later escaped.
8 Jun 64	F-8E	150314	VF-174	—	US	
10 Jun 64	F-8D	148669	VF-32	—	US	
19 Jun 64	F-8C	145581	VF-194	—	Japan	
22 Jun 64	F-8E	150847	VF-53	CVA-14	—	
14 Jul 64	F-8E	149206	VF-174	—	US	
24 Jul 64	F-8A	145334	VC-4	—	US	
5 Aug 64	F-8E	150319	VF-191	CVA-31	—	
13 Aug 64	F-8B	145504	VMF-232	—	Hawaii	
24 Aug 64	F-8C	145585	VC-4	—	US	
31 Aug 64	F-8E	150285	VMF-235	—	US	
8 Sep 64	F-8C	146935	VF-194	—	Japan	
17 Sep 64	F-8D	148641	VF-174	—	US	
21 Sep 64	F-8E	149135	VF-162	CVA-34	—	
24 Sep 64	RF-8A	143749	NATC PAX	—	US	
26 Sep 64	F-8E	150886	VMF-312	—	US	
9 Oct 64	F-8D	148629	VF-32	—	US	
14 Oct 64	F-8E	150856	VF-124	CVA-34	—	
16 Oct 64	F-8E	150929	VF-62	CVA-62	—	
12 Nov 64	F-8E	149224	VMF-122	—	Phil Is	
8 Dec 64	F-8A	145333	VC-5	—	Japan	
11 Dec 64	RF-8A	146888	VMCJ-1	—	US	
30 Dec 64	F-8B	145440	VMF-232	—	Hawaii	
7 Jan 65	F-8E	149166	VF-13	CVA-38	—	
9 Jan 65	F-8A	143748	NAS Dallas	—	US	First incident involving Naval Air Reserve Crusader.
13 Jan 65	F-8B	145467	VMF-251	—	US	
18 Jan 65	DF-8E	145346	VC-8	—	Puerto Rico	
11 Feb 65	F-8D	148633	VF-154	CVA-43	Vn	AAA-hit, pilot POW
18 Feb 65	F-8B	145538	NAF Washington	(VF-661)	—	
21 Feb 65	F-8E	150897	VF-211	CVA-19	—	
23 Feb 65	F-8E	150290	VMF-235	—	US	
1 Mar 65	F-8E	150928	VF-162	CVA-34	—	
8 Mar 65	RF-8A	145612	VMCJ-2	—	US	
8 Mar 65	F-8D	148690	VMF(AW)-451	—	US	
26 Mar 65	F-8D	148644	VF-154	CVA-43	Vn	AAA
29 Mar 65	F-8D	148642	VF-154	CVA-43	Vn	AAA

29 Mar 65	F-8D	148668	VF-154	CVA-43	Vn	AAA
7 Apr 65	F-8C	146925	VMF(AW)-334	—	US	
3 May 65	RF-8A	146833	VMCJ-2	—	US	
8 May 65	RF-8A	145620	VFP-63	CVA-41	Vn	AAA
8 May 65	F-8D	148637	VF-111	CVA-43	Vn	AAA
10 May 65	F-8D	147913	VC-10	—	US	
17 May 65	F-8E	150922	VF-174	—	US	
27 May 65	F-8D	148706	VF-111	CVA-41	Vn	AAA
28 May 65	F-8C	146976	VF-24	—	US	
1 Jun 65	RF-8A	146881	VFP-63	CVA-41	Vn	AAA
1 Jun 65	RF-8A	146852	VMCJ-1	—	Vn	AAA
22 Jun 65	RF-8A	146878	VFP-63	—	US	
30 Jun 65	F-8E	150657	VF-194	CVA-31	Vn	AAA
1 Jul 65	F-8E	150288	VMF(AW)-235	—	US	
16 Jul 65	F-8C	145600	VC-4	—	US	
29 Jul 65	F-8E	150337	VF-191	CVA-31	Vn	AAA
2 Aug 65	F-8A	145328	NAS Dallas Marine Air Reserve			
13 Aug 65	F-8D	147911	VF-111	—	Vn	AAA
13 Aug 65	RF-8A	146849	VFP-63	CVA-43	Vn	AAA
17 Aug 65	F-8D	148671	VMF(AW)-451	CVA-59	—	
22 Aug 65	RF-8A	146884	VMCJ-1	—	Vn	Non-combat
29 Aug 65	RF-8A	146828	VFP-63	CVA-34	Vn	AAA
8 Sep 65	RF-8A	146825	VFP-63	CVA-34	Vn	AAA
8 Sep 65	RF-8A	146826	VFP-63	CVA-43	Vn	AAA(?)
19 Sep 65	F-8E	150309	VF-13	CVA-38	—	
25 Sep 65	F-8E	149168	VF-194	CVA-31	Vn	Non-combat
5 Oct 65	F-8E	150848	VF-162	CVA-34	Vn	AAA
8 Oct 65	RF-8A	145617	VFP-63	CVA-43	Vn	Non-combat
14 Oct 65	F-8D	147899	VF-154	CVA-43	Vn	AAA
17 Oct 65	F-8E	149198	VMF(AW)-212	CVA-34	Vn	Non-combat
27 Oct 65	F-8E	150655	VF-191	CVA-31	Vn	SAM
3 Nov 65	F-8E	150893	VF-124	—	US	
5 Nov 65	F-8E	150665	VMF(AW)-212	CVA-34	Vn	AAA-POW
7 Nov 65	F-8E	149191	VMF(AW)-235	—	US	
17 Nov 65	F-8E	150308	VF-194	CVA-31	Vn	AAA
17 Nov 65	F-8E	150675	VMF(AW)-212	CVA-34	Vn	AAA
18 Nov 65	F-8E	150332	VF-191	CVA-31	Vn	AAA
18 Nov 65	F-8E	150875	VMF(AW)-212	CVA-34	Vn	Non-combat
28 Nov 65	F-8E	150327	VF-191	CVA-31	Vn	AAA-POW
28 Nov 65	F-8E	150854	VF-194	CVA-31	Vn	AAA
21 Dec 65	F-8E	150313	VF-174	—	US	
24 Dec 65	F-8E	150891	VF-211	CVA-19	—	
26 Dec 65	F-8E	150843	VF-53	CVA-14	—	
20 Jan 66	F-8E	150884	VF-124	CVA-41	—	
2 Feb 66	F-8E	149142	VMF(AW)-235	—	Vn	AAA?
9 Feb 66	F-8C	146932	VC-2	—	US	
11 Mar 66	F-8E	150846	VF-13	—	Puerto Rico	
25 Mar 66	F-8E	150673	VMF(AW)-235	—	Vn	AAA
30 Mar 66	F-8C	145561	NATC PAX	—	US	
3 Apr 66	F-8C	146919	VF-24	CVA-19	Vn	AAA
4 Apr 66	F-8E	149208	VF-124	—	US	
5 Apr 66	F-8C	146957	VC-2	—	US	
6 Apr 66	F-8E	150296	VF-111	CVA-34	—	
9 Apr 66	RF-8A	144611	VFP-63	CVA-19	Vn	AAA
14 Apr 66	F-8E	149179	VF-51	CVA-14	Vn	Non-combat
19 Apr 66	F-8E	150853	VF-53	CVA-14	Vn	AAA
19 Apr 66	RF-8A	146843	VFP-63	?	Vn	AAA
28 Apr 66	F-8E	149161	VF-124	—	US	
29 Apr 66	F-8E	150867	VF-211	CVA-19	Vn	Collision with ground.
2 May 66	F-8E	149169	VF-211	CVA-19	Vn	AAA
5 May 66	RF-8A	146831	VFP-63	CVA-19	Vn	AAA-POW
20 May 66	F-8B	145495	NAF Washington, DC Reserves	—		

Date	Type	BuNo	Unit	Ship	Loc	Cause
23 May 66	F-8E	150901	VF-211	CVA-19	Vn	AAA
27 May 66	F-8E	149181	VMF(AW)-232	—	Hawaii	
20 Jun 66	F-8C	145569	NAS Atlanta Reserves	—		
20 Jun 66	F-8E	150334	VF-124	—	US	
21 Jun 66	RF-8A	146830	VFP-63	CVA-19	Vn	AAA-POW
21 Jun 66	F-8E	149152	VF-211	CVA-19	Vn	Shot down by MiG; POW
29 Jun 66	F-8E	150892	VX-4	—	US	
11 Jul 66	F-8E	150902	VF-162	CVA-34	Vn	AAA
13 Jul 66	F-8D	147910	VF-174	—	US	
14 Jul 66	F-8E	150908	VF-162	CVA-34	Vn	Hit by MiG, pilot attempted to divert to Da Nang but exhausted fuel.
19 Jul 66	F-8E	150919	VF-162	CVA-34	Vn	SAM-POW
2 Aug 66	F-8E	150894	VF-124	—	US	
3 Aug 66	RF-8G	146870	VFP-63	CVA-43	Hawaii	
6 Aug 66	F-8E	150300	VF-162	CVA-34	Vn	AAA
11 Aug 66	F-8E	150880	VF-111	CVA-34	Vn	AAA?
13 Aug 6	F-8E	150866	VF-111	CVA-34	Vn	AAA
14 Aug 66	F-8E	150322	VMF(AW)-235	—	Vn	Non-combat
16 Aug 66	F-8E	150287	VMF(AW)-232	—	Hawaii	
17 Aug 66	F-8E	150321	VMF(AW)-235	—	Vn	Non-combat
23 Aug 66	F-8E	150907	VF-111	CVA-34	Vn	Non-combat
31 Aug 66	RF-8G	146874	VFP-63	CVA-34	Vn	AAA
4 Sep 66	F-8D	148646	VMF(AW)-451	—	US	
5 Sep 66	F-8E	150896	VF-111	CVA-34	Vn	AAA
24 Sep 66	F-8A	143767	NAS Dallas Reserves			
6 Oct 66	F-8E	150924	VF-162	CVA-34	Vn	AAA
8 Oct 66	RF-8G	146899	VFP-63	CVA-43	Vn	AAA?
9 Nov 66	F-8E	149153	VF-53	—	US	
11 Nov 66	F-8E	150858	VMF(AW)-235	—	Vn	AAA-POW
21 Nov 66	F-8E	150860	VF-124	—	US	
14 Dec 66	F-8E	149148	VF-194	?	Vn	AAA
6 Jan 67	F-8E	149184	VF-191	?	Vn	AAA-POW
11 Feb 67	F-8E	149192	VF-51	CVA-19		
24 Feb 67	F-8E	150659	VF-194	—	Japan	
28 Feb 67	F-8D	148670	VMF(AW)-212	—	Hawaii	
3 Mar 67	F-8D	148679	VF-13	CVA-38		
15 Mar 67	F-8C	147027	VF-24	CVA-31	Vn	AAA?
17 Mar 67	F-8D	147059	VF-62	CVA-38	—	
17 Mar 67	F-8E	149171	VMF(AW)-232	—	Vn	Non-combat
18 Mar 67	F-8D	148654	VF-13	CVA-38	—	
25 Mar 67	F-8E	149147	VF-53	CVA-19	—	
26 Mar 67	F-8C	145588	VC-4	—	US	
12 Apr 67	DF-8A	145411	VC-1	—	Hawaii	
12 Apr 67	F-8E	150876	VF-124	—	US	
24 Apr 67	F-8C	146915	VF-24	CVA-31	Vn	AAA
1 May 67	F-8E	150301	VF-51	CVA-19	Vn	Non-combat
4 May 67	F-8E	150316	VMF(AW)-232	—	Vn	AAA?
17 May 67	F-8A	143821	NAS Dallas Reserves			
17 May 67	F-8E	149189	VF-51	CVA-19	Vn	AAA?
19 May 67	F-8E	149213	VMF(AW)-232	—	Vn	AAA
19 May 67	F-8E	150930	VF-211	CVA-31	Vn	SAM?-POW
19 May 67	F-8E	?	VF-51/53	CVA-31	Vn	SAM-POW
1 Jun 67	F-8B	145475	NAS Willow Grove Reserves			
2 Jun 67	F-8E	149217	VF-124	CVA-43	—	
4 Jun 67	F-8E	149194	VMF(AW)-235	—	Vn	Non-combat
5 Jun 67	RF-8G	?	VFP-63	CVA-31	Vn	AAA-POW
16 Jun 67	F-8C	146969	VMF(AW)-334	—	US	
20 Jun 67	F-8E	149209	VMF(AW)-232	—	Vn	Non-combat
25 Jun 67	F-8A	143815	NAS Willow Grove Reserves			
26 Jun 67	F-8E	149219	VF-124	—	US	

2 Jul 67	F-8E	150286	VMF(AW)-232	—	Vn	AAA
16 Jul 67	F-8E	150925	VF-162	CVA-34	Vn	SAM
19 Jul 67	F-8E	150899	VF-162	CVA-34	Vn	AAA
20 July 67	F-8E	150916	VF-162	CVA-34	Vn	Non-combat
31 Jul 67	F-8C	146984	VF-111	CVA-34	Vn	SAM-POW
12 Aug 67	F-8C	146993	VF-111	CVA-11	Vn	AAA
8 Sep 67	F-8A	143764	NAF Washington, DC Reserves			
8 Sep 67	F-8C	146929	VF-111	CVA-34	Vn	AAA
11 Sep 67	F-8E	150910	VF-162	CVA-34	Vn	Non-combat
21 Sep 67	RF-8G	144623	VFP-63	CVA-43	Vn	AAA
2 Oct 67	F-8E	150912	VMFA-235	—	Vn	Non-combat
5 Oct 67	F-8A	143819	NAS Willow Grove Reserves			
5 Oct 67	F-8C	146938	VF-111	CVA-34	Vn	AAA-POW
26 Oct 67	F-8E	150310	VF-162	CVA-34	Vn	SAM-POW
11 Nov 67	F-8E	150292	VF-124	—	US	
17 Nov 67	F-8E	150869	VF-124	—	US	
21 Nov 67	RF-8G	145643	VFP-62	CVA-38	—	
5 Dec 67	F-8C	146907	VF-111	CVA-34	Vn	AAA?
2 Jan 68	F-8C	146989	VF-111	CVA-34	Vn	AAA?
4 Jan 68	F-8E	150865	VF-162	CVA-34	Vn	AAA
9 Jan 68	F-8E	150917	VMFA-235	—	Vn	AAA
2 Feb 68	F-8E	150667	VF-191	CVA-14	—	
14 Feb 68	F-8E	150909	VF-194	CVA-14	Vn	SAM
15 Feb 68	F-8E	150293	VRF-32	—	US	
25 Feb 68	F-8E	150335	VF-191	CVA-41	—	
12 Mar 68	F-8E	150306	VF-53	CVA-31	Vn	Bingo divert to Da Nang. GCA approach ended in trees.
16 Mar 68	F-8E	149225	VMFA-235	—	Vn	AAA
28 Mar 68	RF-8G	144616	VFP-63	?	Vn	AAA?
8 Apr 68	F-8B	145544	VC-5	—	Japan	
12 Apr 68	F-8A	142410	NAS Dallas Reserves	—	US	
19 Apr 68	F-8B	145526	?	—	US	
3 May 68	F-8E	149173	VMFA-235	—	Vn	AAA
6 May 68	F-8C	147026	VF-111	CVS-11	—	
22 May 68	RF-8G	146886	VFP-63	CVA-31	Vn	AAA-POW
15 Jun 68	F-8H	148656	VF-24	CVA-19	—	
25 Jun 68	F-8E	149158	VF-53	CVA-31	Vn	Non-combat
4 Jul 68	F-8E	149165	VF-194	CVA-14	—	
6 Jul 68	F-8A	143684	NAS Dallas Reserves			
21 Jul 68	RF-8G	145642	VFP-63	CVA-11	—	
25 Jul 68	F-8H	148658	VF-124	—	US	
4 Aug 68	F-8C	146920	VF-124	—	US	
19 Aug 68	F-8H	147924	VF-24	CVA-19	—	
24 Aug 68	F-8H	148694	VF-211	CVA-19	—	
10 Sep 68	F-8H	148680	VF-51	CVA-31	—	
17 Sep 68	F-8C	146942	VF-13	—	US	
24 Sep 68	F-8C	146945	VF-124	—	US	
3 Oct 68	F-8H	148631	VF-111	—	US	
20 Oct 68	F-8A	143795	NAS Atlanta Reserves			
7 Nov 68	F-8H	148707	VF-13	CVA-38	—	
15 Nov 68	F-8H	147923	VF-211	CVA-19	Vn	Non-combat
1 Dec 68	F-8J	149227	VF-51	—	US	
14 Jan 69	F-8B	145478	VC-5	—	Japan	
5 Feb 69	F-8H	147919	VF-24	CVA-19	—	
8 Apr 69	F-8J	150669	VF-194	—	US	
19 Apr 69	F-8A	145400	NAS Olathe Marine Reserves			
27 Apr 69	F-8J	150341	VF-51	CVA-31	—	
28 Apr 69	F-8J	150320	VF-53	CVA-31	—	

Date	Type	BuNo	Squadron	Carrier	Location	Notes
3 May 69	F-8A	143683	NAF Washington, DC Reserves			
9 May 69	F-8J	149226	VF-51	CVA-31	—	
17 May 69	F-8A	143715	NAS Willow Grove Reserves			
21 May 69	F-8J	150926	VF-194	CVA-34	Vn	Non-combat
24 May 69	RF-8G	146844	VFP-63	CVA-34	Vn	Non-combat
18 Jun 69	F-8A	143768	NAS Dallas Reserves			
23 Jun 69	F-8A	143775	VC-2	—	US	
3 Jul 69	F-8J	150656	VF-162	CVA-14	—	
6 Jul 69	F-8H	148636	VF-111	CVA-14	Vn	Non-combat
11 Jul 69	F-8H	148640	VF-24	CVA-19	—	
18 Jul 69	F-8K	146974	VC-4	—	US	
19 Jul 69	F-8A	145363	NAF Washington, DC Reserves			
2 Aug 69	F-8J	149214	VF-53	CVA-31	—	
2 Aug 69	F-8A	145365	NAF Washington, DC Marine Reserves			
5 Aug 69	F-8A	143680	NAF Washington, DC Marine Reserves			
12 Aug 69	F-8J	150330	VF-53	CVA-31	—	
13 Aug 69	F-8J	150349	VF-211	CVA-19	—	
12 Sep 69	F-8J	150861	VF-194	CVA-34	—	
27 Sep 69	F-8J	149172	VF-53	CVA-31	—	
9 Oct 69	F-8K	145596	VC-7	—	US	
26 Oct 69	F-8J	150284	VF-191	CVA-34	—	
22 Nov 69	F-8J	149212	VF-124	—	US	
28 Nov 69	F-8J	149211	VF-211	CVA-19	—	
1 Dec 69	RF-8G	145632	VFP-63	—	Phil Is	
15 Dec 69	F-8H	148695	VF-124	—	US	
17 Dec 69	F-8J	150921	VF-124	—	US	
22 Dec 69	F-8J	150879	VF-194	—	US	
6 Jan 70	F-8L	145425	NAS Atlanta Reserves		US	
9 Jan 70	DF-8A	143730	VC-5	—	Japan	
2 Feb 70	F-8J	150852	VF-194	—	US	
5 Feb 70	F-8K	145593	NAS Dallas Marine Reserves			
19 Feb 70	F-8J	150682	VF-124	—	US	
9 Mar 70	F-8L	145497	NAF Washington, DC Marine Reserves			
11 Mar 70	RF-8G	144619	VFP-63	CVA-34	—	
18 Mar 70	F-8H	148638	VF-124	—	US	
11 Apr 70	F-8K	146956	VC-5	—	Japan	
20 Apr 70	F-8H	148639	VX-4	—	US	
30 Apr 70	F-8H	148650	VF-162	CVS-38	—	
10 Jun 70	F-8K	146996	NAS Dallas Reserves			
31 Jul 70	RF-8G	146866	VFP-63	—	US	
12 Aug 70	F-8H	148660	VF-162	CVS-38	—	
4 Sep 70	F-8H	148699	VF-124	—	US	
9 Sep 70	F-8K	146951	VF-202	—	US	This was the first ejection after the reorganization of the naval air reserve 1 Sep 70, establishing squadrons in two designated carrier wings. Reorganization came as a result of the poor showing during 1968 Pueblo Crisis call-up.
21 Oct 70	F-8H	148643	VF-162	CVS-38	—	
28 Oct 70	F-8J	149202	VF-211	CVA-19	—	
14 Nov 70	RF-8G	145624	VFP-63	CVA-34	—	
22 Jan 71	F-8K	146937	NAS Dallas Marine Reserves (VMFA-112?)			
5 Feb 71	F-8J	149197	VF-211	CVA-19	—	

Date	Type	BuNo	Unit	Carrier	Loc	Notes
26 Feb 71	F-8J	149150	VF-124	—	US	
16 Mar 71	F-8J	150294	VF-211	CVA-19	—	
23 Mar 71	RF-8G	144613	VFP-63	—	Vn	Non-combat
4 Apr 71	F-8J	149196	VF-194	CVA-34	—	
23 Apr 71	F-8J	150878	VF-191	—	US	
21 Jun 71	F-8J	150868	VF-194	CVA-34	—	
24 Aug 71	F-8J	150315	VF-191	—	Japan	
3 Jan 72	F-8K	146953	NAF Washington, DC Marine Reserves (VMFA-321?)			
3 Mar 72	F-8K	146933	NAS Atlanta Marine Reserves			
18 Apr 72	F-8J	150883	VF-191	—	US	
24 May 72	F-8J	150311	VF-24	CVA-19	Vn	SAM-POW
16 Jun 72	RF-8G	145613	VFP-63	CVA-41	Vn	AAA
20 Jun 72	F-8J	150923	VF-211	CVA-19	Vn	AAA
12 Jul 72	F-8J	150927	VF-124	—	US	
22 Jul 72	RF-8G	146873	VFP-63	CVA-41	Vn	AAA-POW
1 Aug 72	RF-8G	145636	VFP-63	—	US	
5 Sep 72	RF-8G	146861	VFP-63	CVA-19	Vn	Non-combat
5 Sep 72	F-8J	?	VF-24/211?	CVA-19	Vn	Non-combat
27 Sep 72	F-8J	150325	VF-194	CVA-34	Vn	Non-combat
29 Sep 72	F-8H	147902	VF-201	—	US	
26 Nov 72	F-8J	150887	VF-191	CVA-34	Vn	Non-combat
13 Dec 72	RF-8G	144608	VFP-63	CVA-34	Vn	Non-combat. This aircraft was the RF-8A(F8U-1P) used by then-Major John H Glenn to set a transcontinental west-to-east speed record in 1957.
19 Apr 73	F-8K	145560	VMFA-321	—	US	
8 May 73	F-8H	147048	VMFA-112	—	US	
31 May 73	F-8J	150677	VF-211	CV-19	—	
9 Jun 73	F-8J	150340	VF-24	CV-19	Vn?	Non-combat
3 Jul 73	F-8K	145574	NAS Atlanta Marine Reserves (VMFA-?)			
10 Jul 73	F-8J	149159	VFP-63	—	US	VFP-63 acquired F-8Js in order to keep aviators current in Crusader. As the F-14 programme advanced, VF-124 gave the duties of the F-8 RAG to VFP-63.
14 Jul 73	RF-8G	145615	VFP-306	—	US	
26 Jul 73	F-8J	149186	VF-211	CV-19	—	
1 Aug 73	F-8H	147062	VMFA-112	—	US	
18 Aug 73	RF-8G	144625	VFP-206	—	US	
23 Sep 73	F-8J	149190	VF-191	CV-34	—	
10 Oct 73	F-8J	150872	VF-191	—	US	
18 Oct 73	F-8H	147904	VX-4	—	US	
18 Oct 73	F-8H	147908	VMFA-112	—	US	
24 Oct 73	F-8J	149137	VFP-63	CVT-16	—	
9 Nov 74	F-8J	149195	VF-211	—	US	
24 Mar 75	F-8J	150353	VFP-63	—	US	
8 Apr 75	F-8J	149139	VF-194	—	US	
11 Jun 75	F-8J	149221	VFP-63	—	US	
28 Jul 75	F-8J	149163	VF-194	CV-34	—	
29 Jul 75	F-8J	149187	VF-194	CV-34	—	
24 Sep 75	F-8J	150318	VFP-63	—	US	
1 Jun 76	RF-8G	146876	VFP-63	—	US	
15 Jul 76	RF-8G	146892	VFP-63	—	US	
12 Aug 76	RF-8G	146848	VFP-63	—	US	

2 Dec 76	RF-8G	146871	VFP-63	—	US
11 May 77	RF-8G	145629	VFP-63	CV-67	—
18 May 77	RF-8G	146895	VFP-63	—	US
18 Jul 77	RF-8G	141363	VFP-63	—	US
30 Aug 77	RF-8G	145616	VFP-63	—	US
13 Oct 79	RF-8G	145646	VFP-63	CV-43	—
28 Aug 80	RF-8G	144615	VFP-306	CV-63	—
9 Jun 81	RF-8G	146897	VFP-63	CV-62	—
19 Jul 81	RF-8G	145641	VFP-63	CV-43	—
11 Mar 85	RF-8G	146855	VFP-206	—	US

Appendix 3: Squadrons Which Flew the Crusader
(from a list compiled by Thomas C Irwin)

VF(AW)-3	Blue Nemesis	VF-214	Red Checkertails	VMF-321	Black Barons
VF-11	Red Rippers	VF-661	Firefighters	VMF-323	Death Rattlers
VF-13	Fighting Thirteen	VF-703	Stallions	VMF-333	Shamrocks
VF-24	Fighting Renegades	VF-931	unknown	VMF-334	Falcons
VF-32	Swordsmen	VF-201	Hunters	VMF-451	Warlords
VF-33	Tarsiers	VF-202	Superheats	VMCJ-1	
VF-51	Screaming Eagles	VF-301	Devil's Disciples	VMCJ-2	Playboys
VF-53	Iron Angels	VF-302	Stallions	VMCJ-3	Eyes and Ears
VF-62	Yellow Tails	VFP-62	Fighting Photo	VMF-351	unknown
VF-84	Jolly Rogers	VFP-63	Eyes of the Fleet	VMF-511	unknown
VF-91	Red Lightnings	VFP-206	Hawks	VMJ-4	unknown
VF-103	Sluggers	VFP-306	Peeping Toms	VU/VC-1	Blue Allii's
VF-111	Sundowners	VSF-76	unknown	VU/VC-2	Blue Tails
VF-124	Crusader College	VSF-86	unknown	VU/VC-4	unknown
VF-132	Swordsmen	VC-13	Saints	VU/VC-5	unknown
VF-141	Iron Angels	VCP-61	unknown	VU/VC-7	Tallyhoers
VF-142	Ghost Riders	VMF-112	Wolfpack	VU/VC-8	Red Tails
VF-143	Pukin' Dogs	VMF-122	Crusaders	VU/VC-10	Challengers
VF-154	Black Knights	VMF(AW)-212	Lancers	VC-3	Drone Rangers
VF-162	Hunters	VMF-215	Fighting Corsairs	VX-3	unknown
VF-174	Hell Razors	VMF(AW)-232	Red Devils	VX-4	unknown
VF-191	Satan's Kittens	VMF(AW)-235	Death Angels	H&MS-13	unknown
VF-194	Red Lightnings	VMF-251	Thunderbolts		
VF-211	Checkmates	VMF-312	Checkerboards		

Appendix 4: F-8 and RF-8 Crusader Deployments During Vietnam
(From a list compiled by René J. Francillon)

Squadron/Air Wing	Model	Carrier	Tail Code & Modex	Deployment Dates
VF-24 *Checkertails*				
VF-24/CVW-21	F-8C	USS *Hancock* (CVA-19)	NP 4xx	21 Oct 64–29 May 65
VF-24/CVW-21	F-8C	USS *Hancock* (CVA-19)	NP 4xx	10 Nov 65–1 Aug 66
VF-24/CVW-21	F-8C	USS *Bon Homme Richard* (CVA-31)	NP 4xx	26 Jan 67–25 Aug 67
VF-24/CVW-21	F-8H	USS *Hancock* (CVA-19)	NP 2xx	18 Jul 68–3 Mar 69
VF-24/CVW-21	F-8H	USS *Hancock* (CVA-19)	NP 2xx	2 Aug 69–15 Apr 70
VF-24/CVW-21	F-8J	USS *Hancock* (CVA-19)	NP 2xx	22 Oct 70–2 Jun 71
VF-24/CVW-21	F-8J	USS *Hancock* (CVA-19)	NP 2xx	7 Jan 72–3 Oct 72
VF-24/CVW-21	F-8J	USS *Hancock* (CVA-19)	NP 2xx	8 May 73–8 Jan 74

VF-51 *Screaming Eagles*

VF-51/CVW-5	F-8E	USS *Ticonderoga* (CVA-14)	NF 1xx	
VF-51/CVW-5	F-8E	USS *Ticonderoga* (CVA-14)	NF 1xx	28 Sep 65–13 May 66
VF-51/CVW-5	F-8E	USS *Hancock* (CVA-19)	NF 1xx	5 Jan 67–22 Jul 67
VF-51/CVW-5	F-8H	USS *Bon Homme Richard* (CVA-31)	NF 1xx	27 Jan 68–10 Oct 68
VF-51/CVW-5	F-8J	USS *Bon Homme Richard* (CVA-31)	NF 1xx	18 Mar 69–29 Oct 69
VF-51/CVW-5	F-8J	USS *Bon Homme Richard* (CVA-31)	NF 1xx	2 Apr 70–12 Nov 70

VF-53 *Iron Angels*

VF-53/CVW-5	F-8E	USS *Ticonderoga* (CVA-14)	NF 2xx	14 Apr 64–15 Dec 64
VF-53/CVW-5	F-8E	USS *Ticonderoga* (CVA-14)	NF 2xx	28 Sep 65–13 May 66
VF-53/CVW-5	F-8E	USS *Hancock* (CVA-19)	NF 2xx	5 Jan 67–22 Jul 67
VF-53/CVW-5	F-8E	USS *Bon Homme Richard* (CVA-31)	NF 2xx	27 Jan 68–10 Oct 68
VF-53/CVW-5	F-8J	USS *Bon Homme Richard* (CVA-31)	NF 2xx	18 Mar 69–29 Oct 69
VF-53/CVW-5	F-8J	USS *Bon Homme Richard* (CVA-31)	NF 2xx	2 Apr 70–12 Nov 70

VF-111 *Sundowners*

VF-111/CVW-2	F-8D	USS *Midway* (CVA-41)	NE 4xx	6 Mar 65–23 Nov 65
VF-111/CVW-16	F-8E	USS *Oriskany* (CVA-34)	AH 1xx	26 May 66–16 Nov 66
VF-111 Det 11/CVW-10	F-8C	USS *Intrepid* (CVS-11)	AH 1x	11 May 67–30 Dec 67
VF-111/CVW-16	F-8C	USS *Oriskany* (CVA-34)	AH 1xx	16 Jun 67–31 Jan 68
VF-111 Det 11/CVW-10	F-8C	USS *Intrepid* (CVS-11)	AK 1xx	4 Jun 68–8 Feb 69
VF-111/CVW-16	F-8H	USS *Ticonderoga* (CVA-14)	AH 1xx	1 Feb 69–18 Sep 69
VF-101/CVW-8	F-8H	USS *Shangri-La* (CVS-38)	AJ 1xx	5 Mar 70–17 Dec 70

VF-154 *Black Knights*

VF-154/CVW-15	F-8D	USS *Coral Sea* (CVA-43)	NL 4xx	7 Dec 64–1 Nov 65

VF-162 *Hunters*

VF-162/CVW-16	F-8E	USS *Oriskany* (CVA-34)	AH 2x	5 Apr 65–16 Dec 65
VF-162/CVW-16	F-8E	USS *Oriskany* (CVA-34)	AH 2xx	26 May 66–16 Nov 6
VF162/CVW-16	F-8E	USS *Oriskany* (CVA-34)	AH 2xx	16 Jun 67–31 Jan 68
VF-162/CVW-16	F-8J	USS *Ticonderoga* (CVA-14)	AH 2xx	1 Feb 69–18 Sep 69
VF-162/CVW-8	F-8H	USS *Shangri-La*(CVS-38)	AJ 2xx	5 Mar 70–17 Dec

VF-191 *Satan's Kittens*

VF-191/CVW-19	F-8E	USS *Bon Homme Richard* (CVA-31)	NM 1xx	28 Jan 64–21 Nov 64
VF-191/CVW-19	F-8E	USS *Bon Homme Richard* (CVA-31)	NM 1xx	21 Apr 65–13 Jan 66
VF-191/CVW-19	F-8E	USS *Ticonderoga* (CVA-114)	NM 1xx	15 Oct 66–29 May 67
VF-191/CVW-19	F-8E	USS *Ticonderoga* (CVA-14)	NM 1xx	27 Dec 67–17 Aug 68
VF-191/CVW-19	F-8J	USS *Oriskany* (CVA-34)	NM 1xx	16 Apr 69–17 Nov 69
VF-191/CVW-19	F-8J	USS *Oriskany* (CVA-34)	NM 1xx	14 May 70–10 Dec 70
VF-191/CVW-19	F-8J	USS *Oriskany* (CVA-34)	NM 1xx	14 May 71–18 Dec 71
VF-191/CVW-19	F-8J	USS *Oriskany* (CVA-34))	NM 1xx	5 Jun 72–30 Mar 73

VF-194 *Red Lightnings*

VF-194/CVW-19	F-8C	USS *Bon Homme Richard* (CVA-31)	NM 4xx	28 Jan 64–21 Nov 64
VF-194/CVW-19	F-8E	USS *Bon Homme Richard* (CVA-31)	NM 4xx	21 Apr 65–13 Jan 66
VF-194/CVW-19	F-8E	USS *Ticonderoga* (CVA-14)	NM 4xx	15 Oct 66–29 May 67
VF-194/CVW-19	F-8E	USS *Ticonderoga* (CVA-14)	NM 4xx	27 Dec 67–17 Aug 68
VF-194/CVW-19	F-8J	USS *Oriskany* (CVA-34)	NM 2xx	16 Apr 69–17 Nov 69
VF-194/CVW-19	F-8J	USS *Oriskany* (CVA-34)	NM 2xx	14 May 70–10 Dec 70
VF-194/CVW-19	F-8J	USS *Oriskany* (CVA-34)	NM 2xx	14 May 71–18 Dec 71
VF-194/CVW-19	F-8J	USS *Oriskany* (CVA-34)	NM 2xx	5 Jun 72–30 Mar 73

VF-211 *Checkmates*

VF-211/CVW-21	F-8E	USS *Hancock* (CVA-19)	NP 1xx	21 Oct 64–29 May 65
VF-211/CVW-21	F-8E	USS *Hancock* (CVA-19)	NP 1xx	10 Nov 65–1 Aug 66
VF-211/CVW-21	F-8E	USS *Bon Homme Richard* (CVA-31)	NP 1xx	26 Jan 67–25 Aug 67
VF-211/CVW-21	F-8H	USS *Hancock* (CVA-19)	NP 1xx	18 Jul 68–3 Mar 69
VF-211/CVW-21	F-8J	USS *Hancock* (CVA-19)	NP 1xx	2 Aug 69–15 Apr 70
VF-211/CVW-21	F-8J	USS *Hancock* (VA-19)	NP 1xx	22 Oct 70–2 Jun 71
VF-211/CVW-21	F-8J	USS *Hancock* (CVA-19)	NP 1xx	7 Jan 72–3 Oct 72
VF-211/CVW-21	F-8H	USS *Hancock* (CVA-19)	NP 1xx	8 May 73–8 Jan 74

VMF(AW)-212 *Lancers*

VMF(AW)-212/CVW-16	F-8E	USS *Oriskany* (CVA-34)	WD 1xx	5 Apr 65–16 Dec 65

VFP-62 *Fighting Photos*

VFP-62 Det 42/CVW-1	RF-8G	USS *Franklin D Roosevelt* (CVA-42)	AB 9xx	21 Jun 66–21 Feb 67

VFP-63 *Eyes of the Fleet*

VFP-63 Det E/CVW-19	RF-8A	USS *Bon Homme Richard* (CVA-31)	PP 9xx	28 Jan 64–21 Nov 64
VFP-63 Det B/CVW-5	RF-8A	USS *Ticonderoga* (CVA-14)	PP 93x	14 Apr 64–15 Dec 64
VFP-63 Det F/CVW-14	RF-8A	USS *Constellation* (CVA-64)	PP 93x	5 May 64–1 Feb 65
VFP-63 Det M/CVW-9	RF-8A	USS *Ranger* (CVA-61)	PP 9xx	5 Aug 64–6 May 65
VFP-63 Det L/CVW-21	RF-8A	USS *Hancock* (CVA-19)	PP 9xx	21 Oct 64–29 May 65
VFP-63 Det D/CVW-15	RF-8A	USS *Coral Sea* (CVA-43	PP 9xx	7 Dec 64–1 Nov 65
VFP-63 Det A/CVW-2	RF-8A	USS *Midway* (CVA-41)	PP 9xx	6 Mar 65–23 Nov 65
VFP-63 Det G/CVW-16	RF-8A	USS *Oriskany* (CVA-34)	PP 9xx	5 Apr 65–16 Dec 65
VFP-63 Det E/CVW-19	RF-8A	USS *Bon Homme Richard* (CVA-31)	PP 9xx	21 Apr 65–13 Jan 66
VFP-63 Det B/CVW,55	RD-8A	USS *Ticonderoga* (CVA-14)	PP 93x	28 Sep 65–13 May 66
VFP-63 Det L/CVW-21	RF-8A	USS *Hancock* (CVA-19)	PP 90x	10 Nov 65–1 Aug 66
VFP-63 Det G/CVW-16	RF-8A	USS *Oriskany* (CVA-34)	AH 6xx	26 May 66–16 Nov 66
VFP-63 Det A/CVW-2	RF-8G	USS *Coral Sea* (CVA-43)	PP 89x	29 Jul 66–23 Feb 67
VFP-43 Det E/CVW-19	RF-8G	USS *Ticonderoga* (CVA-14)	PP 91x	15 Oct 66–29 May 67
VFP-63 Det B/CVW-5	RF-8G	USS *Hancock* (CVA-19)	PP 91x	5 Jan 67–22 Jul 67
VFP-63 Det L/CVW-21	RF-8G	USS *Bon Homme Richard* (CVA-31)	PP 9xx	26 Jan 67–25 Aug 67
VFP-63 Det 11/CVW-10	RF-8G	USS *Intrepid* (CVS-11)	AK 4xx	11 May 67–30 Dec 67
VFP-63 Det 34/CVW-16	RF-8G	USS *Oriskany* (CVA-34	AH 6xx	16 Jun 67–31 Jan 68
VFP-63 Det 43/CVW-15	RF-8G	USS *Coral Sea* (CVA-43)	NL 771x	26 Jul 67–6 Apr 68
VFP-63 Det 14/CVW-19	RF-8G	USS *Ticonderoga* (CVA-14)	NM 6xx	27 Dec 67–17 Aug 68
FP-63 Det 31/CVW-5	RF-8G	USS *Bon Homme Richard* (CVA-31)	NF 60x	27 Jan 68–10 Oct 68
VFP-63 Det 11/CVW-10	RF-8G	USS *Intrepid* (CVS-11)	AK 4xx	4 Jun 68–8 Feb 69
VFP-63 Det 19/CVW-21	RF-8G	USS *Hancock* (CVA-19)	NP 6xx	18 Jul 68–3 Mar 69
VFP-63 Det 43/CVW-15	RF-8G	USS *Coral Sea* (CVA-43)	NL 5xx	7 Sep 68–18 Apr 69
VFP-63 Det 14/CVW-16	RF-8G	USS *Ticonderoga* (CVA-14)	AH 60x	1 Feb 69–18 Sep 69
VFP-63 Det 31/CVW-5	RF-8G	USS *Bon Homme Richard* (CVA-31)	NFF 60x	18 Mar 69–29 Oct 69
VFP-43 Det 34/CVW-19	RF-8G	USS *Oriskany* (CVA-34)	NM 6xx	16 Apr 69–17 Nov 69
VFP-63 Det 19/CVW-21	RF-8G	USS *Hancock* (CVA-19)	NP 60x	2 Aug 69–15 Apr 70
VFP-63 Det 43/CVW-15	RF-8G	USS *Coral Sea* (CVA-43)	NL 60x	23 Sep 69–1 Jul 70
VFP-63 Det 38/CVW-0	RF-8G	USS *Shangri-La* (CVS-38)	AJ 6xx	5 Mar 70–17 Dec 70
VFP-63 Det 31/CVW-5	RF-8G	USS *Bon Homme Richard* (CVA-31)	NF 60x	2 Apr 70–12 Nov 70
VFP-63 Det 34/CVW-19	RF-8G	USS *Oriskany* (CVA-34)	NM 6xx	14 May 70–10 Dec 70
VFP-63 Det 1/CVW-21	RF-8G	USS *Hancock* (CVA-19)	NP 60x	22 Oct 70–2 Jun 71
VFP-63 Det 3/CVW-5	RF-8G	USS *Midway* (CVA-41)	NF 60x	16 Apr 71–6 Nov 71
VFP-63 Det 4/CVW-19	RF-8G	USS *Oriskany* (CVA-34)	NM 60x	14 May 71–18 Dec 71
VFP-63 Det 5/CVW-15	RF-8G	USS *Coral Sea* (CVA-43)	NL 60x	12 Nov 71–17 Jul 72
VFP-63 Det 1/CVW-21	RF-8G	USS *Hancock* (CVA-19)	NP 60x	7 Jan 72–3 Oct 72
VFP-63 Det 3/CVW-5	RF-8G	USS *Midway* (CVA-41)	NF 60x	10 Apr 72–3 Mar 73
VFP-63 Det 4/CVW-19	RF-8G	USS *Oriskany* (CVA-34)	NM 60x	5 Jun 72–30 Mar 73
VFP-63 Det 5/CVW-15	RF-8G	USS *Coral Sea* (CVA-43)	NL 60x	9 Mar 73–8 Nov 73
VFP-63 Det 1/CVW-21	RF-8G	USS *Hancock* (CVA-19)	NP 6xx	8 May 73–8 Jan 74

Index